Down to Earth

Down to Earth

Applying Business Principles to Environmental Management

Forest L. Reinhardt

Harvard Business School Press
Boston, Massachusetts

A version of the material in chapter 2 was published in the *California Management Review* 40, no. 4 (Summer 1998), under the title "Environmental Product Differentiation: Implications for Corporate Strategy." ©1998 by The Regents of the University of California.

LIBRARY OF CONGRESS CATALOGING-IN-PUBLICATION DATA
Reinhardt, Forest L., 1958–
    Down to earth : applying business principles to environmental
management / Forest L. Reinhardt.
        p.   cm.
    Includes index.
    ISBN 1-57851-192-5 (alk. paper)
    1. Environmental economics—United States.   2. Environmental
management—Economic aspects—United States.   I. Title.
HC110.E5R415 1999
333.7'0973—dc21   99-30610
                                                                CIP

The paper used in this publication meets the requirements of the
American National Standard for Permanence of Paper for Publications and
Documents in Libraries and Archives Z39.48-1992.

For Susie, with love

Contents

Preface

THIS BOOK is intended to help managers think rigorously and imaginatively about how they can respond to social demands for environmental performance while delivering superior returns to their shareholders.

The debate on business and the environment has been framed in all-or-nothing terms. People ask whether firms ought to be "green," as though there were a categorical answer. This kind of rigid thinking would immediately be seen as inappropriate if applied to most other aspects of business management. Does it pay to build your next plant in Singapore? Increase your debt-to-equity ratio? Sue your competitors for patent infringement? Of course the answer is, "It depends." And so with the environment. The appropriate environmental policies for a firm depend on the firm's circumstances: the basic economics of its industry, its position within the industry, its internal capabilities, and the strategy it has chosen. *There is no one-size-fits-all environmental policy*, just as there is no strategy in marketing or finance that will yield universal success if applied indiscriminately to all firms.

Much recent writing about business and the environment ignores this basic fact. On one hand, some academics have argued that companies in general will benefit if they actively promote environmental and social causes like recycling, small-scale agriculture, and solar energy. The basic idea seems to be that the earth is in trouble and so it ought to be profitable to devise solutions to the problem. There are two problems with this line of thought. First, it is not certain that these

fashionable causes really contribute much to overall well-being. Second, social problems, however distressing, do not by themselves create opportunities to make money. We need to look at industry structure, competitive position, managerial competence, and the other factors that influence profitability, rather than relying solely on a list of social or environmental concerns.

To justify the view that companies should devote more effort and money to environmental improvements, some observers of management assert that the environment is best approached as a problem involving the social responsibility of business. The evidence in this book does not fully support that view. Companies that manage the environment successfully—satisfying environmental demands while delivering superior value to their shareholders—do not see the environment exclusively as a problem of social responsibility, but rather as a fact of life to be incorporated into business plans like any other. This is not to say that ethics are unimportant or that managers' personal values should not affect how they behave with respect to the environment. But to think about the environment primarily as a problem of social responsibility or ethics is to miss opportunities to incorporate it into basic business decision making in ways that increase profits, reduce risk, or both.

Taking the social responsibility perspective still further, some people have concluded that environmental pressures are so great as to require some kind of "paradigm shift," or a new conceptualization of the corporation's role in society. For example, Vice President Al Gore wrote that "we must make the rescue of the environment the central organizing principle for civilization."[1] For better or worse, though, this sort of change is highly unlikely. In this book I take as a premise that companies are in business to make money for their owners, and that they can pursue the satisfaction of other stakeholders only insofar as it serves this basic purpose. An alternative paradigm, more prevalent in Europe, holds that shareholders are just one constituency among many that the firm must satisfy. I adhere to the first view not necessarily because of any normative judgment but because it seems a better empirical description of American economic life, and because it provides a stiffer test for the business policies discussed here.

Another common view of the environment is that it represents a burden for managers. Certainly concern about the environment, especially when translated into government regulation, has added to the

costs of doing business, curtailed managers' ability to make decisions, and diverted resources and management attention from other pressing problems and opportunities. But the evidence in this book does not fully support the gloomy position that the environment is only a burden for business. Like the idea that it always pays to be "green," the idea that it never pays for a firm to invest in superior environmental performance is incorrect. For some businesses, the environment can be more than a cost burden, and investments in superior environmental performance can deliver a financial return.

For these reasons, business managers will benefit if they see the environment *as a business problem,* amenable to solutions involving traditional business tools. They can improve their management of environmental problems by applying principles that are already known to work in strategy, finance, marketing, and organizational design. Societal concern about the environment can alter any of the basic conditions facing a business, including customer attitudes, prices, regulations, technological options, scale economies, competitors' relative cost positions, business risk, and the value of reputation. Luckily, managers already know a great deal about these phenomena. Of course the successful management of environmental issues may require some alterations of traditional business analysis and strategy design. To devise responsible and realistic solutions to environmental problems, however, it is neither necessary nor even desirable to reinvent business management.

THIS BOOK presents five basic approaches to reconciling shareholder value and environmental performance, with a chapter devoted to each. Drawing on both analytical reasoning and studies of individual businesses, the chapters shed light on the circumstances under which these approaches may be feasible. Not all of the approaches will be open to all businesses. On the other hand, the approaches are not mutually exclusive: some firms will be in a position to use two or more of them.

First, suppose that a firm's managers want to increase their expected profits while improving their environmental performance, but they recognize that these improvements will entail additional cost to the firm. In this case, one approach is to improve environmental performance and then capture the extra costs from consumers. This is a

strategy of *environmental product differentiation*. Conceptually it is quite straightforward. As a practical matter, though, one might wonder how it can work: will consumers pay more for environmental quality? It turns out that in some cases they will. Although not every firm can succeed with this sort of strategy, the prospects are not as unequivocally gloomy as one might fear. Chapter 2 of this book discusses the circumstances under which companies can succeed with product differentiation strategies.

A second way that a firm might be able to reconcile shareholder value and environmental performance is by *managing competitors*. Incurring additional costs to improve environmental performance can be consistent with increasing profits if competitors' costs rise even further. A firm wishing to raise rivals' costs has two principal options. One is to try to influence government regulation so that its rivals are disadvantaged. Here, the idea is that a firm works to bring about government regulation under which its rivals suffer larger cost increases than the initiating firm. Alternatively, or in addition, the firm can attempt to create private regulatory institutions that develop explicit or tacit agreements not to compete along environmental lines, thus binding its rivals' hands in much the same way as government regulation. As with product differentiation, not every firm is in a position to pursue a strategy of this kind, but the potential rewards are large enough that managers should consider whether their firms could succeed with such a strategy. Chapter 3 explores the factors that contribute to the success or failure of such initiatives.

These first two approaches presume that improvements in environmental performance cost money. But it is possible to imagine circumstances under which this might not be true. In other words, it may be that managers, by scrutinizing their operations in the light of environmental concern, can find private cost savings that more than offset the cost of public good provision. This approach could be called *reducing costs within the firm*. The circumstances under which this might be possible are the topic of chapter 4.

The question of the environmental "free lunch" has been hotly debated.[2] Some commentators have argued that opportunities of this sort are pervasive; others, emphasizing that managers already spend considerable effort on reducing costs, express skepticism that environmental pressure can result in additional savings. One reason the debate has been so heated is that from a public policy standpoint, it is quite

significant whether such opportunities are widespread or rare. If they are widespread, the economy can actually benefit from tougher environmental regulation, a fact that regulators have been quick to notice. If they are rare, the net costs of tighter regulation will be higher, and the desirable level of regulation will be less stringent. This is all of primary importance to government officials and their advisers. But it is of secondary importance to managers in firms. An executive in company A may be interested in whether two or twenty-two of the firms B through Z have "free lunch" opportunities. But his or her principal concern is to evaluate the likelihood that they exist in firm A. Fortunately, this is a far more tractable task than answering the larger social question.

Differentiating products, managing competitors, and identifying cost savings within the firm need not occur independently. Some of the most intriguing attempts to turn environmental pressure into competitive advantage involve combining these approaches. Typically such a hybrid approach is aimed at *redefining markets;* the firm is trying substantially to change the way firms in its industry compete, so that both the firm and the environment benefit. For example, agricultural biotechnology firms are trying to deliver crop protection to farmers in an entirely new way. Instead of manufacturing and selling pesticides, they are embedding genetic information in the seeds of the crop plants so that the plants themselves are inedible to the pests. Chapter 5 analyzes environmental approaches that are based on the redefinition of markets, using the basic building blocks discussed in the earlier chapters.

Chapter 6 explicitly introduces business risk. Because no future cash flow is ever absolutely guaranteed, risk considerations will inevitably arise in the approaches just discussed. Further, *managing risk and uncertainty* more effectively than rival firms can itself be a source of competitive advantage. Despite its broad relevance, risk management is somewhat different from the other approaches discussed in this book. First, although not every firm tries to differentiate products along environmental lines or to initiate private regulatory regimes, every firm must manage environmental risk. Second, risk management is inherently more complex than any of the other approaches. It requires managers not only to assess the risk and to determine the right mix of policies for reducing and shifting it but also to design incentives for other decision makers so that all levels of the company will manage risk appropriately.

Chapter 6 analyzes these complexities and discusses some possible avenues for the improvement of risk management. Executives need

to make sure they have considered all the tools available to manage environmental risk. In particular, firms often use different techniques to reduce environmental risk from those they use to reduce other types of business risk. While this arrangement is common, it may not be optimal, and it may never have been subjected to extended scrutiny. Failing to think systematically about these questions leaves potential opportunities for improvement unexploited.

Following these chapters on the five approaches, chapter 7 consolidates the book's managerial lessons. Chapters 2 through 6 focus on the economic logic of environmental management, emphasizing the factors that influence sensible policy choices. But the success of any of the approaches in a particular firm will depend as well on administrative and managerial factors, including the firm's information and incentive systems, its culture, and its relationships with regulators, environmentalists, and the public. The longer histories in chapter 7 integrate these administrative concerns with the economic and strategic material of the earlier chapters.

In particular, chapter 7 focuses on the evolution of environmental policy in three firms for which environmental issues are critically important: Chevron Corporation in the oil and gas business, Georgia-Pacific Corporation in forest products, and Monsanto Company in chemicals and agricultural biotechnology. The three case histories raise questions about the uses of information for strategy formulation and for managing relations with regulators and other groups. They explore the variety of incentive mechanisms available for implementing environmental policies in decentralized firms. And they analyze firms' efforts to shape the institutions that affect their problems, opportunities, and overall environmental performance.

Chapter 8 reviews the lessons from the earlier chapters and points out some mistakes that managers should try to avoid in environmental decision making. The chapter also sets out some questions that managers ought to ask themselves about the environmental policies of their own firms. Although the book raises these questions in an environmental context, they are applicable to management decisions in any situation in which imperfect markets, government intervention, and changing social expectations complicate business decision making. Because environmental problems are business problems, it makes sense that the questions to ask would be the same as those managers would ask about their strategies more generally.

Because the approaches discussed here will not be equally useful at all firms, the book's chapters are relatively self-contained. The book is neither a math textbook nor a mystery novel, and it is not absolutely necessary to read it front to back.

To EXPLORE the relationships between the environment and share-holder value, I draw both on analytical reasoning and on case studies of particular businesses. While the use of case studies in business education is well established, they can also be extremely useful in research.[3] Combining analytical reasoning and case studies is an especially promising approach to studying business and the environment because many of the important variables do not lend themselves well to quantitative measurement. Further, since the profitable approach to environmental management depends on the economic circumstances confronting the firm, a simple analysis of profitability as a function of some variable related to environmental "pro-activity" is likely not to be very enlightening.

Many economists and students of management prefer formal statistical tests involving large samples of firms to case studies, in part because they may fear that cases can be selected in some consciously or unconsciously biased way. To counteract these scholars' skepticism of the case method, writers of books and articles that are based on cases sometimes assert that they chose their examples, if not completely at random, at least in accordance with some putatively unbiased procedure. But I did not select my cases at random. Nor, when I set out to write the book, did I systematically identify the largest, the most profitable, or the most environmentally aggressive firms as objects of study. Instead, I have chosen case histories that allow exploration of the several approaches to environmental management that are most important and potentially most useful to managers.

I have already introduced the main purpose of this book: to examine systematically the relationships between the environment and business practice. But thinking systematically about environmental management pays dividends in the form of enhanced insights into business management more generally. One cannot think clearly about business and the environment without also thinking about strategy in imperfectly competitive markets, the trade-offs between centralization and decentralization, the tension between short-term and long-term

objectives, the value of information, the need for flexibility, and the management of risk. Over the course of the book, I will touch on all of these larger questions.

The managers discussed here face problems of astonishing variety. To devise sensible business plans, they must understand concepts from scientific arenas as diverse as marine biology, atmospheric chemistry, and the physics of groundwater movement. They also need to take into account a political landscape in which at least some of the rules remain to be written, and where strict retroactive liability for predecessors' actions, alliances with traditional enemies, and other unusual institutional arrangements are all possible. At the same time, they need to sell their products, perhaps to textile producers in China, perhaps to yuppies in Seattle. And they must effect change in firms that range from new business ventures to venerable—even stodgy—industrial giants. Flaubert is supposed to have said that anything is interesting if you look at it long enough. I hope that the questions of science, politics, business, and leadership that arise in this book will provoke readers' curiosity even on first inspection.

Acknowledgments

I could not have written this book without the generous support of the Harvard Business School's Division of Research. Nor would it have been possible for me to write it without the help of managers in a large number of firms. Some of those firms and individuals are named in the text, but many are not. Whether or not they are named, I owe a great deal to them.

A number of my colleagues at Harvard have commented on earlier drafts of part or all of this book, or have helped me clarify my thinking about the issues it discusses. I am especially grateful to Tom McCraw, Cynthia Montgomery, Dick Vietor, and Steve Wheelwright, who in a series of meetings in 1997 and 1998 helped me to define the appropriate scope, organization, and tone for the book. I also learned a great deal from Jim Austin, Joe Badaracco, Kent Bowen, Bill Bruns, Bob Dolan, Alexander Dyck, Pankaj Ghemawat, George Lodge, David Moss, Lynn Paine, Tom Piper, Howard Raiffa, Kash Rangan, Hank Reiling, Julio Rotemberg, Bruce Scott, Deb Spar, Robert Stavins, Howard Stevenson, Richard Tedlow, Peter Tufano, and Lou Wells. I am grateful to each of them.

I am indebted to the students in my Harvard MBA classes who have helped me think through the questions discussed in the book.

I am also grateful, for stimulating conversations and helpful advice, to Alan Beckenstein, Sarah Cliffe, Ralph Earle, Susie Ertman, Robert E. Grady, Stuart Hart, Bob Hellman, Jake Jacoby, Leena

Lankoski, Daniel B. Luten, Susan McCraw, Kimberly O'Neill Packard, Elizabeth Reinhardt, Howard Reinhardt, Jackie Prince Roberts, Chris Rosen, Jonathan Rouner, John Sawhill, Elizabeth Teisberg, David Vogel, and referees at the *California Management Review, Interfaces,* the *Journal of Industrial Ecology,* Harvard Business School Press, and the Massachusetts Institute of Technology Press.

I am thankful to acquisitions editor Nikki Sabin and her colleagues at HBS Press for their logistical help and intellectual insights. I am indebted to Monica Mandelli for help with research, to Max R. Hall for his editorial assistance, and to Jennifer Burns, J. P. Gownder, Emily Richman, and David Zug for outstanding help with both research and editing. And I am grateful to Elizabeth Sampson for all kinds of administrative support.

Any remaining errors are mine.

The Environment as a Business Problem

IN CONSIDERING contemporary problems of environmental management, it is important to remember that over the past thirty years or so, the citizens, companies, and governments of the industrialized world have made significant progress in improving the condition of the natural environment. In the United States, emissions of carbon monoxide have fallen by 23 percent since 1970, despite a doubling in real economic activity and a near doubling of the car and truck fleet. During the same period, annual American emissions of lead have fallen from 219,000 tons to 5,000 tons.[1] Similar progress has occurred in reducing water pollution: to take the most spectacular example, there is no danger today of the Cuyahoga River in Cleveland catching on fire, as it did in the late 1960s.[2] Also since the late 1960s, average concentrations of sulfur oxides in the ambient air above Japan have fallen by over 80 percent.[3] And cadmium levels in the Rhine have fallen by a factor of ten since 1975.[4] Diplomats have concluded a series of international treaties that first capped, and then phased out, the use in industrial countries of chemical compounds that deplete stratospheric ozone.[5] Three decades ago, even optimists would have considered progress of this magnitude implausible.

In spite of these successes, the subject of the environment still triggers frustration and bitterness among large and disparate groups of people. Many business people are enormously frustrated both with the current regulatory apparatus and with new pressures for increased

1

environmental expenditure expressed in the media, the regulatory agencies, and the courts. At the same time, many employees and customers of these companies, in their roles as taxpayers and citizens, continue to press for improved environmental quality, arguing that important problems remain unaddressed and that business attention to environmental matters has been insufficient or even misguided.

If we are so healthy, why don't we feel better? Four related reasons suggest themselves.

First, although the rich countries of the world bought an enormous amount of environmental quality over the past thirty years, that progress was expensive. The twenty-nine members of the rich countries' club, the Organization for Economic Cooperation and Development (OECD), devote about 2 percent of their incomes to environmental expenditures. This equals the nations' spending on higher education or research and development, and exceeds the amount devoted to criminal justice systems. Most of this environmental money is spent by firms, which gives some clues to the business community's frustration about the environment. Worse yet, the progress has cost more money than was really necessary, partly because of badly designed government regulation, and partly because the companies did not manage every aspect of the problem in the most efficient way.[6]

Second, it is now clear that environmental pressure is not going to abate. After the 1994 elections, some American business managers entertained hopes of a regulatory rollback, but these hopes quickly proved unrealistic. Incomes are rising, and richer people demand more environmental quality. Scientific advances enable us to detect substances in the environment at ever lower levels. Formal and informal expectations about protection from environmental insults rise in tandem with the expected compensation for any damages.

On top of these trends, we now confront a new generation of environmental problems, some of them global, including the loss of biodiversity and the possibility of climate change. Many scientists are convinced that these new problems are at least as significant as the ones we have been so expensively solving. Back-of-the-envelope calculations suggest that the price tag for addressing this new batch of problems might equal the cost of all our previous environmental efforts, unless we can address them with considerably more attention to economic efficiency.

Third, this new set of challenges arises in an era when global competition is increasingly important in markets for products and for

capital investment, compared with conditions in the 1960s and 1970s, when industrial nations first began seriously to address environmental concerns. On the first Earth Day in 1970, imports amounted to 5.4 percent of American gross domestic product. On the twenty-fifth anniversary of that celebration, the ratio was 13.2 percent. Global competition for capital has intensified even more rapidly: foreign direct investment has increased at twice the rate of international trade. This globalization of competition complicates the search for solutions to environmental problems, like climate change and biodiversity loss, whose effects spill across international boundaries. Globalization also means that increasing numbers of managers, even if their own firms do business in only one country, confront competitors based elsewhere who may face fewer environmental pressures.

Fourth, significant numbers of people still see the environment exclusively in moral terms, and insist that the right amount of pollution is zero. But to make this assertion is equivalent to saying that the right amount of leisure time for each person is 168 hours per week. These objectives may be desirable in some abstract sense, but their relevance for decision making is limited because they assume that pollution control or leisure time is free. Most of the time environmental quality has an opportunity cost: that is, it ordinarily costs money, and whoever is called upon to pay this money will have other desirable things on which to spend it. Pretending that environmental quality has no opportunity cost does not make it true, but greatly complicates the search for workable solutions.

Reasonable people may disagree about the severity of our current problems from a scientific standpoint, but there is no doubt about the significance of the economic stakes for business. The environment as an issue is not going away. And no one should have to muddle through future environmental challenges as we did through the earlier ones.

Fortunately, this is not necessary.

As discussed in the preface, fundamental business principles of strategy, finance, marketing, and organizational design can contribute to the solution of firms' environmental problems. For example, differentiating a product along environmental lines is similar to other types of product differentiation. The search for strategic ways to tie competitors' hands is similar whether or not the environment is involved. And so on. Naturally, some alterations of traditional business analysis and strategy design are required to apply these tools to environmental management problems. But if the goal is to devise responsible, realis-

tic solutions to environmental problems, it is neither necessary nor desirable to stray far from basic management principles.[7]

Most successful managers owe a large part of their success to their optimism and opportunism. In other aspects of business life, they search relentlessly for opportunity in adversity and are proud of their ability to find it. The initiative and opportunism that managers routinely bring to other aspects of their work, if applied to the management of environmental problems, can contribute meaningfully to the performance of their businesses.

THE BASIC ECONOMICS OF ENVIRONMENTAL MANAGEMENT

To understand the logic of environmental management in firms, we will use some basic principles from economics. These ideas are introduced in the next few pages and are elaborated in later chapters.

THE CREATION AND CAPTURE OF VALUE

The creation and capture of value are the central purposes of any business enterprise.[8] A business creates value when it produces goods or services worth more than the total costs of all the resources needed to make them, including not just materials and labor but also capital equipment and managerial skill. If a company is creating value, it is generating enough revenue to pay workers, suppliers of inputs, and managers, and also to pay its shareholders the opportunity costs of their capital (i.e., the "normal" return shareholders could have earned if they had invested their capital elsewhere).[9] Unless its operations are somehow subsidized, a firm that fails to create value cannot survive.

In order to remain in business, a firm must not only create economic value but also capture it. In a textbook world of perfectly competitive markets, value creation and value capture are the same.[10] But, in practice, market imperfections and the intervention of government make the capture of economic value by its creators far from automatic.

EXTERNALITIES AND OTHER MARKET IMPERFECTIONS

In particular, the idea that a business could ever "do well by doing good"—or voluntarily providing environmental benefits beyond what is

required by law—seems to violate economic logic. The costs that pollution and environmental degradation impose on society (in the form of increased illness, damage to plant and animal life, and so on) are classic examples of externalities; that is, their effects are not reflected in market prices. Because of this, it might seem that any business that tried to provide or preserve more environmental quality than is lawfully required would incur higher costs than its competitors, and that its customers would abandon it in search of lower prices.

Another way of expressing the same thought is to say that when externalities exist, the private cost and the social cost of economic activity are not the same. The private cost of an activity is just the total cost of all the resources used, valued at market prices. The social cost of the activity is the aggregate value to society of all the resources used, whether or not those values are reflected in market prices. Fish killed by pollution from a steel mill are part of the social cost of producing the steel, but they may not be part of the private cost.

Firms interested in maximizing profits are supposed to minimize private costs. Therefore, if private and social costs are equal, firms trying to earn a profit will unintentionally minimize social costs, making business a vehicle for overall efficiency. But this is not the case if private costs and social costs diverge, as they will if firms can treat clean air or water as a free good. Logically, if environmental externalities create differences between private costs and social costs, companies that try voluntarily to take social costs into account will lose more money than those that look exclusively at private costs.[11]

For better or worse, though, the world is not so simple. *Market failures do not crop up one at a time. The markets in which externalities are important generally depart from the perfectly competitive markets of economic textbooks in other ways as well.* In those real-world markets, firms and their customers may not have complete information about economic conditions, including the costs and benefits of various practices and the values of particular commodities.[12] This leads to the possibility of using environmental performance as a signaling device to communicate with customers or other interested parties about the firm and its products; it also leads to the possibility that environmental scrutiny can help firms reduce their total costs. In addition, firms in real-world markets often have some control over the prices they charge, which raises the possibility that the company can recover cost increases from its customers. Finally, markets in which the environment is

important are also very likely to be distorted by government intervention, further complicating managers' decisions.

Given the simultaneous existence of more than one market failure and the presence of government, some companies can both respond to social environmental pressure and deliver increased value to shareholders. Because this will be possible for some firms and not others—depending on the particular market imperfections and types of government behavior that each confronts—managers need to think creatively and carefully about their own circumstances and the resultant opportunities.

PUBLIC GOODS

A good is called "public" if my consumption does not reduce the amount available for you to consume (i.e., consumption is "nonrival"), and if it is not feasible for me to exclude you from consuming it, whether or not you have helped to pay for it (i.e., the good is "nonexcludable," a word that appears in dictionaries of economics but not dictionaries of English).[13] If a public good is produced at all, then everyone consumes the same amount. National defense and street lighting are classic examples of public goods; not accidentally, both are usually provided by governments.

Environmental quality, in some of its aspects, is a public good. Consider, for example, the enjoyment we derive from knowing of the continued existence of lions. Suppose we never intend to go to Africa to see them; we just like to know that they are there. This "existence value" is a pure public good: it is nonexcludable, and its consumption is nonrival. You and I may place very different values on it; the value that I attach to it could be zero, or even negative, but this is a different issue, and one that applies to streetlights and national defense as well. Again, simple economic logic suggests that if it is not possible to exclude people from consuming a good for which they have not paid, then companies will not find the good profitable to make. And again, this would be strictly true if the existence of public goods were the only way in which the world departed from perfect competition.

But government intervention in markets, incomplete information, and other peculiarities make public goods interesting from a business standpoint. The fact that national defense is a public good certainly does not prevent companies from profitably supplying defense-related

goods to governments. Similarly, clean air is a public good, but businesses make money selling pollution control equipment to governments and to other firms. Further, many private goods are substitutes or complements for public goods: the cleanliness of the local river is important to producers of bottled water and sellers of fishing equipment. Finally, although we think of environmental quality as a public good, most environmental benefits are really bundles of different goods that are public to a greater or lesser degree. The existence value of the lions is a pure public good, but the privilege of seeing them is both excludable and, to some extent, rival, and companies make money from selling this privilege.

ECONOMIC INSTITUTIONS, GOVERNMENT INTERVENTION, AND NONGOVERNMENTAL ORGANIZATIONS

Whether a good is public depends not only on its innate characteristics but also on the institutions and laws that govern economic behavior, and these vary from time to time and from place to place. Access to trout streams in the American West is usually a public good; access to similar streams in Scotland is almost always private. Similarly, a factory's release of an air pollutant can be an externality in one country and a private cost in another, depending on the government programs in place to control the air pollution.

These are particular examples of the more general point that government policies and economic institutions affect any firm's ability to create and capture value. Economic institutions are the "rules of the game" that govern how individuals and organizations interact. They include formal rules, like the U.S. Constitution, the Clean Air Act, and the rules of the Financial Accounting Standards Board (FASB). They also include informal rules and codes of behavior, like the traditions and conventions that influence the workings of the U.S. Congress.[14] Economic institutions influence the development of technology and the exercise of market forces. They also affect firms' opportunities to create and capture value directly, since they define and constrain property rights and sanction or prohibit certain types of behavior.[15] In this context, then, government can be either an ally or an adversary for a firm attempting to capture value.

Any government intervention in markets, like any change in economic institutions, has two kinds of effects: it increases or decreases over-

all social costs and benefits, and it changes the distribution of the benefits and costs. Governments often seek actively to redistribute income.
The progressiveness of the tax code is an especially striking example, but
other examples abound. When the American government imposes a tariff
on sugar imports, it benefits American sugar producers at the expense of
American sugar consumers and of sugar producers abroad. But government policies that seek to redistribute income affect overall costs and
benefits as well. In the tariff case, consumers and foreign producers collectively lose more than domestic producers gain. More generally, it is virtually impossible for government to affect the distribution of income
without having some effect on overall social well-being.

At the same time, it is certainly true that many government policies do result in increased aggregate well-being. Well-designed pollution control laws are a good example: if the costs that an air pollutant
imposes on society are greater than the costs incurred to clean it up,
then regulation can increase the overall efficiency of the economy and
therefore increase aggregate well-being. The government in this case is
actually bringing about the creation of value just as firms do: the good
that it is producing (pollutant-free air) is worth more than the total
costs of producing it. Firms that ally themselves with the government
in such value-creating initiatives may benefit.

Government agencies are not the only organizations that try to
affect companies' environmental performance. A large number of environmental groups seeks to affect company behavior indirectly (changing the regulatory framework through activities in legislatures and
courts) and directly (using a variety of other tactics to put pressure on
corporate executives). Environmental groups are wildly heterogeneous.
Some use multimillion-dollar budgets to hire Ivy League lawyers, scientists, and economists who work on a broad range of environmental
issues worldwide; others are focused on a single issue in a particular
community. Community-based groups on the other side of environmental issues, advocating less government intervention and increased
tolerance for environmental externalities, have also appeared, although
so far they are not nearly as powerful as the traditional environmental
organizations and their grassroots counterparts.

For firms in environmentally sensitive businesses, these groups,
along with governments, are among the most important actors in what
Stanford business professor David Baron calls the "nonmarket environment."[16] Implicitly or explicitly, they are asserting that because of

public goods and externalities, they have some legitimate decision rights over the company's assets. Company managers must take them seriously, not only because the regulators and the courts do so, but also because the managers may find opportunities to learn from some environmentalists, or even form alliances with them in ways that further both the environmentalists' agenda and the interests of the firm.

Where externalities and public goods coexist with other departures from the competitive paradigm (such as market power and incomplete information), a firm may be able to increase its expected value through the voluntary provision of environmental goods. In addition, government intervention itself, whatever its motivations, results in more departures from the assumptions of perfect competition and hence further complicates the firm's decision. In fact, a number of firms, especially in Europe and North America, assert that they are pursuing "beyond-compliance" environmental policies, or providing environmental public goods to a greater degree than required by law. The question remains: under what circumstances will policies of this sort make sense from a business perspective? To provide an answer, we need to consider the objectives that corporate environmental management can serve.

MOTIVES OF CORPORATE ENVIRONMENTAL MANAGEMENT

Corporate environmental policies, like corporate activities more generally, serve several objectives. They can be aimed at increasing the value of the firm, either in readily measurable ways like a reduction in ongoing out-of-pocket costs, or in intangible ways that involve corporate culture, reputation, and employee commitment. They can be aimed at reducing business risk, again either in readily measurable or in intangible ways. They can be motivated by a desire to adhere to personal or organizational codes of ethics. In practice, these various motives are difficult to disentangle, and any important business decision is likely to involve all three. Finally, much of what firms do in the environmental arena is intended to promote organizational learning, which ultimately can be aimed at increasing value, improving risk management, or defining and maintaining appropriate ethical commitments.

The simplest assumption one can make about the objectives of a firm's managers is that they are trying to maximize the firm's value,

which is to say the present value of its future profits. To understand the ability of a firm to capture the value it creates, it is helpful to think of a linked set of firms that together deliver a set of goods or services to ultimate consumers. The activities of these firms make up the value system of any firm within that set. The firm's own portion of the links is called its value chain.

A firm's success or failure depends on its entire value system as well as its own value chain. Any market power that the firm or any other entity in the system may possess, whether it arises from preferential access to resources, proprietary technology, government favoritism, or some other factor, will influence the firm's ability to create and capture value and thus its ability to deliver superior returns to shareholders.[17]

When a company earns "supernormal profits" or "superior returns," it is delivering to its shareholders returns that exceed the opportunity cost of the capital provided. It could be doing so in one or more ways. It could be using market power to capture value created by other firms in its value system. Or it could be operating more efficiently than its competitors and capturing those efficiency gains. For example, it could be earning returns on earlier investments in proprietary technologies. Alternatively, it could be earning returns on earlier investments in product design that have given it market power, protected from competitive entry by patents or brands. A firm with access to natural resources that can be extracted more cheaply than those of its competitors will also tend to earn supernormal profits.

This logic extends to the environment in straightforward ways. A company that is able to improve its customers' ability to add value may be able to capture some, or even all, of the value of this improvement. In the next chapter, for example, we will examine dye makers whose product innovations lower the environmental costs of their customers. The dye manufacturers are able to capture some of this value through increased prices. In other industries, by contrast, firms that have created environmental value have been unable to capture it for their own shareholders.

At the same time, some of the value that a firm might create through investments in the environment may be very difficult to measure. The goodwill of regulators or the residents of a community in which the firm has a factory is surely valuable, but this value is difficult to quantify. Perhaps even more important, and even more difficult

to measure, are the effects of a company's environmental policy on its employees' morale and commitment to the organization. In several of the case studies in this book, managers' ideas about these intangibles had significant effects on their decisions.

Managers care about risk as well as value creation. In particular, they care about the possibility that their business's profits will be far below the expected value, especially, as with environmental issues, if the arena is complicated by scientific and regulatory uncertainty. This is true as an empirical matter but also from a normative point of view: in general, shareholders should want their managers to concern themselves not just with the expected value of profits but also with risk.[18] Firms invest in environmental quality as a way of reducing the probability or the cost of uncertain but adverse outcomes (e.g., accidents or other environmental insults) that could lead to business interruptions, liability, punitive regulation, or damage to corporate reputations.

Risk considerations are difficult to disentangle from value considerations, both conceptually and practically. The conceptual difficulty arises because in fact no payoff to any investment is ever absolutely certain; it doesn't make sense to talk about maximizing the present value of a firm's cash flows without taking into account the possibility that the cash flows might be different from those anticipated. At a practical level, value and risk are entangled because the two objectives are rarely independent. Risk management objectives often conflict with the maximization of expected value: that is, it frequently costs money to reduce business risk. Under other circumstances, though, the two objectives might be congruent: if a business can manage risk more effectively than its competitors, this superior management can be a source of competitive advantage and thus of increased expected value. This is most obviously true for businesses like insurance companies, whose fundamental competency is the analysis and management of risk, but it can be true for firms in other service businesses or manufacturing as well.

In addition to value and risk, managers care about adherence to personal or social codes of ethics. Ethical considerations may play a significant role in shaping managers' responses to particular decisions. Just as value and risk are difficult to disentangle, ethics are difficult to disentangle either from value or from risk. To say that managers ought to worry either about expected value or about risk is itself to make a statement about ethics. Conversely, much of what we call ethical

behavior is perfectly consistent with, perhaps the consequence of, the utilitarian philosophy that leads us to seek to create value and reduce risk.

Behavior that adheres to individual and social codes of ethics can yield significant, if intangible, benefits. It is not uncommon for managers to assert that they had to follow a particular course of action with respect to the environment in order to be consistent with the company's values. If company managers communicate even implicitly that a responsible attitude toward environmental questions is an important part of the company culture, and then take actions inconsistent with those claims, the costs in terms of lost credibility can be considerable. Companies, like other organizations, are cultural as well as economic entities. If they are to maintain the respect of customers and employees, their actions need to be consistent with the values they espouse.

More broadly, it is easy to see that managers sometimes pursue particular courses of action for reasons of conscience. Nevertheless, this book contains fewer explicit discussions of ethics than of value creation and risk management. The reason is not that ethics are unimportant. Rather, actions taken for ethical reasons commonly need to be justified to interested parties both within and outside the firm on the basis of increases in expected value or of reductions in risk. Managers have to be able to make a persuasive link between their strategies and their shareholders' well-being, regardless of the original (and indiscernible) impulse behind those strategies. We would not applaud corporate managers who donated their company's research and development funds to their church, no matter how worthwhile the church's activities, unless the managers could persuasively argue that the company would benefit more from this donation than from the R&D. Environmental policies may be motivated by considerations beyond economics, but their implications for expected value and risk need to be considered systematically.[19]

Put another way, it is possible that companies' environmental investments represent a diversion of shareholder wealth to serve the managers' own well-being. The same market imperfections that can create opportunities for increased value and reduced risk may also be exploited by managers to their own ends. Managers who make investments that improve the environmental performance of their businesses may reap personal benefits in the form of reduced psychological stress or enhanced status within the community. For example, the

shareholders of a company may want a manager to oppose tooth and nail some proposed new local environmental rule, but the manager's job will be less stressful, and his relationships with his neighbors easier, if he acquiesces to the regulation. It is for this reason that environmental investments, even if motivated by ethical considerations on the part of managers, ordinarily have to be justified within the firm in terms of value creation or risk reduction.

Whatever the motive or motives of a firm's environmental policies, the ability to locate and assimilate information about environmental problems is critically important. Given the uncertainties that firms confront, it is not surprising that successful firms strive to improve their ability to learn about the particular problems that are relevant to their own decisions. Uncertainties are pervasive in the scientific arena; in legislatures, regulatory agencies, and the courts; and also in the marketplace. Hence many environmental management initiatives have as one of their objectives the promotion of organizational learning: obtaining more factual information about the environmental impacts of a particular process, developing a deeper understanding of customers' or regulators' attitudes toward the environment, or figuring out how to put management systems in place that will enable the organization to continue to learn. Management teams that successfully promote this kind of learning can create a long-term edge in identifying and exploiting opportunities to increase profits, to manage business risk more effectively than competitors, and even to define and ensure adherence to codes of ethics or company values.

ECONOMICS, MANAGEMENT, AND LEADERSHIP

Squeezed between ongoing demands for responsible environmental stewardship and unrelenting competitive pressure, companies today face stiff managerial challenges. But these challenges turn out to be special cases of familiar problems. In other words, the environmental challenges involve changes in customer tastes, in the regulatory arena, or in competitive dynamics. And, like other changes external to the business, they can impel modification both to the firm's strategy and to the internal management processes.

The environment can be approached as a business problem like other business problems. Selling "green" products is a special case of

product differentiation. Investments in environmentally friendly production technologies can be analyzed as questions of decision making under uncertainty in which the trade-off between flexibility and commitment is critical. A firm that is contemplating a radical alteration in the way it serves its customers must consider buyers' switching costs, competitors' responses, and internal change requirements, regardless of whether the alteration is driven by environmental considerations. In each of these cases, the analysis is more complicated if a public good is at issue, but the presence of public goods does not invalidate the use of the basic analytical tools that a good manager would instinctively bring to bear on the problem.

Business responses to environmental problems have to make sense in terms of accounting, finance, marketing, and operations. Again, a company's ability to succeed in the face of increasing environmental pressure will depend on the same factors that determine corporate success more generally, such as the structure of the firm's industry, its competitive position, and its ability to manage technological and human resources.

At the same time, the environmental questions confronting firms involve not only economics and management but also leadership. Although much of the progress that firms have made in the environmental arena has been accomplished through incremental improvements to existing strategies, some spectacular accomplishments—and some promising prospects for further achievement—entail leaps of faith, discontinuous thinking, and commitment to a vision that is defined with reference to a desirable objective rather than to the status quo. Analysis, while necessary, should not serve as an excuse for inaction or as a screen for a failure of imagination.[20]

But vision is not preferable to analysis. Each is the necessary complement to the other. In the absence of leadership and vision, executives relying on analysis and management cannot seize all available opportunities; on the other hand, careful analytic thinking is clearly necessary to determine which of the many possible leaps of faith might lead to desirable results. This book concentrates on analysis and management, examining the ways in which various business approaches to the environment play out in different industrial and organizational settings. It is beyond the scope of any book to apply the analysis to every situation that readers may confront, much less to provide categorical advice about far more personal matters involving vision and ethics. But

an enhanced sense of the possibilities in environmental management, as they emerge from the analytical reasoning and case histories that follow, will help readers develop their own visions of how their firms can simultaneously deliver environmental quality and shareholder value.

Environmental Product Differentiation

CERTAIN PRODUCERS of toilet tissue, outdoor wear, tuna, beef, investment services, trash bags, and herbicides have positioned their products as environmentally preferable, with the idea of capturing a price premium, winning new customers, or both. Of the possible ways to reconcile their need to deliver shareholder value with intensifying demands for improved environmental performance, perhaps the most straightforward is to provide environmentally preferable products and then capture the extra costs from consumers. That approach is the topic of this chapter.

The idea behind environmental product differentiation is as follows. A business creates products that provide greater environmental benefits, or that impose smaller environmental costs, than similar products. Alternatively, or in addition, it produces goods and services in ways that are less environmentally burdensome than the production processes of its competitors.[1] These changes in the products or the production process raise the business's costs, but they also enable it to command a price premium in the marketplace or to capture additional market share, leaving it at least as well off as before.[2]

More broadly, the changes undertaken by the firm to improve environmental performance might compromise some product attribute, other than low price, about which customers care: quality or convenience, for example. Again, the basic idea is that customers may be willing to trade off these other attributes in order to purchase the

environmentally preferable product, in the same way as they are tolerant of some increase in price.

The objection to the basic idea behind environmental product differentiation seems straightforward as well. Environmental quality is a public good. Firms are generally uninterested in providing public goods because they find it hard to recover the costs they incur in doing so. But why should this same logic not apply to the firms' customers? Would we not expect people in retail stores buying final consumption goods, or companies buying intermediate goods, to approach the problem of public goods in the same way? And would this not doom strategies of product differentiation?

It turns out that no categorical answer is possible. Whether a business can succeed in differentiating products along environmental lines will depend on the characteristics of industry structure, business-government relations, and organizational capability that determine corporate success more generally. Some firms have a profitable option to differentiate products or processes along environmental lines; for others, any time spent pursuing such strategies is squandered. Executives need to know into which category their businesses—and those of their competitors—fall.

To make environmental product differentiation succeed, a business must satisfy the following three requirements:

1. It must find, or create, a willingness among customers to pay for environmental quality.
2. It must establish credible information about the environmental and other attributes of its products.
3. Its innovation must be defensible against imitation by competitors.

These requirements pertain to product differentiation more generally, but each acquires special importance, and presents particular problems, in the context of environmental product differentiation.[3]

It is natural when thinking of environmental product differentiation to think of companies like Ben & Jerry's, the Body Shop, and Patagonia, or of mass-market product innovations like dolphin-safe tuna or biodegradable garbage bags. While these phenomena will be considered later, it is useful to begin by examining industrial markets, where the economic logic of willingness to pay is more straightforward. Industrial marketers, in firms that seem quite different economically

and ideologically from Ben & Jerry's or the Body Shop, are demonstrating ways of creating environmental value and then recovering it from customers. We will study two such initiatives, first examining some basic facts and then considering how those facts relate to willingness to pay, credible information, and barriers to imitation. Then we will turn to the ways in which these same requirements play out in consumer goods markets.

ENVIRONMENTAL DIFFERENTIATION IN INDUSTRIAL MARKETS

In industrial markets, willingness to pay is driven almost entirely by considerations of total cost. Brand identification and image tend to play smaller roles than in consumer marketing. This bottom-line customer focus in industrial markets can actually facilitate environmental product differentiation. In particular, an industrial product can be differentiated if it enables customers to reduce the environmental impacts of their own operations, thereby incurring fewer environmental costs. If the firm initiating the scheme can reduce the private environmental costs of its industrial customers, it may be able to capture some of that cost reduction.

A firm's ability to do so depends on the other two requirements for successful differentiation: information and barriers to imitation by competitors. Customers must be made aware of the total cost reduction that arises from the use of an environmentally preferable product, which implies the need for a credible way of delivering this information. And if the approach is to succeed, the firm differentiating its product needs a way of preventing rivals from introducing closely related products, so that it can capture some of the value that it is creating for its customers.

This chapter will consider two examples: the introduction of environmentally preferable textile dyes by Ciba Specialty Chemicals of Switzerland, and Monsanto Company's repositioning of Roundup herbicide.

CIBA SPECIALTY CHEMICALS: LOW-SALT TEXTILE DYES

Ciba Specialty Chemicals, headquartered in Basel, Switzerland, is one of the world's largest producers of textile dyes. The dye business

developed in Basel during the nineteenth century partly because of the town's proximity to French and German textile centers, partly because of the relative laxity of Swiss patent law, and partly because wastewaters from the dye factories could conveniently be discharged into the Rhine River.

Ciba is a successor company to Ciba-Geigy, itself the product of earlier mergers in the Swiss chemical and pharmaceutical industries. Ciba-Geigy merged with Basel rival Sandoz in 1996, and then spun off its specialty chemicals operations. The spin-off created Ciba Specialty Chemicals, a tightly focused firm whose units did 8.4 billion Swiss francs' worth of business in 1998 ($5.8 billion at 1998 average exchange rates) selling pigments, textile dyes, and other chemical products. Many of these compounds are used in relatively small quantities to enhance the performance or value of plastics, paints, lubricants, detergents, and other materials in common industrial and household use.[4]

In 1998, Ciba's colors division generated 2.3 billion Swiss francs in revenue selling pigments and textile dyes. In dyes, Ciba held a global market share of about 13 percent, putting it a close second in market share behind DyStar, a joint venture of German giants Hoechst and Bayer, and slightly ahead of another German giant, BASF. Competition, however, is product-line-specific, with markets segmented according to the type of fiber to be dyed and the process used for dyeing. The textile dye business is a difficult one, with numerous competitors and increasing cost competition from manufacturers in developing countries, where many of the industry's customers are located. As cost competition has intensified, Ciba and other European producers have invested heavily in scientific R&D to try to develop differentiated products.

Within the textile dye business, one of Ciba's most important product lines is its reactive dyestuffs, which are intended for use on cotton, rayon, and other cellulose fibers. The purchasers of reactive dyestuffs commonly use them in batch processes. First they dissolve the dyestuffs in water, along with other auxiliary chemicals designed to enhance the dyes' performance characteristics. Then they add the textiles that are to be dyed. Next they introduce salt (sometimes ordinary table salt, or sodium chloride; sometimes sodium sulfate) into the dye bath, which drives the reactive dyestuffs out of solution and onto the fibers. When this happens, the dyestuffs, as their name implies, react chemically with the fibers of the textiles, in a process called fixation.

Excess dye, salt, and auxiliaries are then rinsed from the textiles, often in a multistep process at temperatures approaching the boiling point. This rinsing process must be thorough, since any excess unfixed dye that remains on the fabric will bleed later from the finished garments. A by-product of the rinsing stage is a mixture of water, unfixed dye, salt, and auxiliaries, which ordinarily must be treated before it is released to streams or lakes.

Reactive dyes are large, complicated organic molecules whose chemical constituents include chromophores, which give the dyes their color, and reactive groups, which allow the fixation to take place. The first reactive dyes contained one reactive group per molecule, but more recently developed dyes contain two such groups: they are bi-reactive, not monoreactive. This bireactivity means that any given molecule has a better chance of reacting with the fiber, so the dye's fixation rate is higher.[5]

Bireactive dyes provide several advantages over monoreactive ones. First, less dye is required, since a higher fraction fixes to the cloth. Second, the lower quantity of unfixed dyestuff means that rinsing is simpler and hence less expensive. Third, for the same reasons, the textile firms' wastewater treatment costs are lower. Finally, bireactive dyes tend to have higher reproducibility: that is, the color of the fabric is more predictable across batches. If a batch is too light, it must be returned to a dyebath, which increases costs by at least 20 percent. If the color is too dark or unlevel, the dye must be stripped off before the fabric is put back in a dyebath; together, the stripping and new dyeing more than double the dyeing costs of the batch. A dye that helps textile makers avoid these problems saves them money. Introduced in the mid-1980s, bireactive dyes account for about half of all of the reactive dyes sold in North America and Europe as of 1998; their share is lower in developing countries.

In 1995, Ciba introduced a new line of bireactive dyestuffs called Cibacron LS.[6] A low-salt (LS) molecule consists of two reactive groups, two chromophores, and a patented molecular "bridge" that allows these four constituent groups to be combined in a single molecule. This chemical structure creates several further benefits for the textile manufacturer. Higher fixation rates than with traditional bireactive dyes mean that still less dye is required. Less salt is needed to push the dyestuff from the solution onto the textile; conventional bireactive dyes might require 800 grams of salt per kilogram of textile to be dyed,

whereas an LS dye might require a quarter of that amount. This savings in procurement costs for salt alone might represent a percentage point or two of a textile dyer's revenues, a significant fraction of potential profits in an industry with razor-thin margins. Finally, reproducibility is enhanced, increasing quality and further lowering costs of rework. Ciba looked actively for a low salt dye for exactly these reasons: to add value to customers through lower environmental costs and increased reproducibility. The LS dyes are protected by patents and by the unpatentable but relatively complicated chemistry required to make them.

Although LS dyes are gaining share at the expense of traditional reactive dyes, adoption by customers is by no means universal. One impediment is that of "optical price." In economic theory, what ought to matter to the textile producer is the total cost of using the LS dyes versus conventional reactive dyes; thus, although the LS dye itself may be more expensive per pound than conventional dyes, less dye and less salt are needed, wastewater treatment costs fall, and the costs of correcting mistakes are lower. Nevertheless, some customers apparently focus on the price of the dye per pound, that is, the optical price. Whether this attitude reflects a psychological tendency to concentrate on partial rather than total changes, or whether it is simply a negotiating tactic aimed at extracting some of the value created by innovative suppliers, the consequences for firms like Ciba can be significant.

MONSANTO: PROMOTING CONSERVATION TILLAGE

In the early 1990s, Monsanto Company repositioned its main herbicide product, Roundup, as a complement to environmentally friendly agricultural practices. Combined with other investments in production technology and marketing, these efforts have extended the scope and longevity of the Roundup market and positioned the company for a leap into agricultural biotechnology.

Monsanto, an $8.6 billion company based in St. Louis, has a long history of scientific and technological innovation. It developed glyphosate herbicide in 1970 and began selling the product under the trade name Roundup in 1974. The company makes over ninety other glyphosate-based herbicides besides Roundup and sells these products in over a hundred countries. Glyphosate herbicides kill any sprouted plants with which they come in contact, whether these are weeds or

crop plants. The herbicides work by inhibiting the production of a particular enzyme that is necessary for the plant's production of certain proteins, killing the whole plant "from the leaves to the roots."[7] Thereafter, the compound decomposes in the soil, with a half-life of about sixty days, into carbon dioxide, nitrogen, water, and phosphate. Prior to its decomposition, glyphosate binds to soil particles, so it tends not to move into groundwater; it has no residual effects on plants in the soil. According to company documents, "Since the protein that is targeted is found only in plants, Roundup can be used around humans and animal wildlife without significant adverse effects when it is used according to label directions."[8]

Roundup was initially positioned as a premium-priced product for high-value crops. Monsanto lowered the price gradually to increase penetration, and revenues rose each year. The success of glyphosate herbicides was critical to the company's overall strategic direction during this period. The agricultural group, whose product portfolio was dominated by Roundup and its relatives, contributed 21 or 22 percent of total company revenues, but over half of the company's total operating income, in each year from 1988 to 1992. Profitable and expanding Roundup sales were critical sources of internal funds for the company's expansion into biotechnological products for agriculture.

In the early 1990s, Monsanto repositioned Roundup as the logical complement to conservation tillage, a soil conservation measure encouraged both by government policy and by basic agricultural microeconomics. Farmers till their fields largely to control weeds. To do so, they may use sophisticated, special-purpose equipment costing tens of thousands of dollars, animal power, or even hand tools; in any case, the tillage represents a significant fraction of the variable cost of the crop. If farmers use Roundup on the fields before planting, they need to till less or not at all. Conservation tillage creates public goods in the form of reduced water pollution caused by soil runoff from fields. It provides private benefits to farmers by conserving soil and reducing labor and energy requirements. Nearly a third of all acres planted in the United States now use some form of conservation tillage, and Monsanto has reported that "more than 40 percent of the volume growth for Roundup in the last few years has come from expanded use of conservation tillage practices."[9] In all, volumes of glyphosate herbicides (measured in pounds, not dollars) rose by more than 50 percent between 1987 and 1990, and then increased by nearly 50 percent again between 1990 and 1992.[10]

Farmers can capture the benefits of conservation tillage and glyphosate use no matter whose glyphosate they apply. In the United States, glyphosate is still protected by Monsanto patents. In other countries, for Monsanto to capture the value of these practices, it must be able to sell glyphosate for less than its generic competitors or create some other mechanism for capturing this value. It is pursuing both of these strategies. Investments in patentable improvements in process technology defend Monsanto's low-cost position in the product category.

At the same time, the company is investing heavily in developing Roundup Ready crop varieties engineered to resist the effects of the herbicide. Fields planted with these crops can be treated with Roundup after the crops and weeds have sprouted, allowing weed control regimes that can lower both the grower's out-of-pocket costs and the total social cost of bringing the crops to market. Monsanto's intent with these innovations is to build on its Roundup franchise and facilitate a move into agricultural biotechnology.[11]

In 1997, Monsanto spun off its chemical operations into an independent company called Solutia. It has retained its nutritional and pharmaceutical businesses, which make such products as NutraSweet and Equal sweeteners, as well as treatments for ulcers, insomnia, and hypertension. It has also retained its agricultural product lines. The division between agricultural chemicals like Roundup and biotechnology-based products is increasingly blurry, and Monsanto looks to both as it tries to reposition itself as a contributor to more productive and environmentally sensible agricultural practices in the United States and abroad.

Monsanto's repositioning of Roundup, and especially the firm's applications of biotechnology to agricultural markets, have generated considerable controversy and drawn criticism from some environmental groups. The Union of Concerned Scientists, for example, argued that "the environmental benefit Monsanto claims for Roundup Ready soybeans is associated with the move away from popular pesticides like atrazine, whose active ingredients persist in the environment. Even granting that glyphosate is less toxic than atrazine and generally to be preferred to it, a switch from one herbicide to another does not result in environmentally sound agriculture. . . . US agriculture remains shackled to intensive chemical use."[12] The Union of Concerned Scientists and other organizations assert that the total social costs of bioengineered crops are both uncertain and likely to be large. Although criticism of

Monsanto has been directed primarily at its agricultural biotechnology rather than at the repositioning of Roundup, the company's overall strategy involves a greater risk of political unpopularity and regulatory backlash than would a marketing strategy not tied to the environment.

REQUIREMENTS FOR SUCCESS
AS THEY PERTAIN TO INDUSTRIAL MARKETING

Drawing on these case examples, we are in a position to analyze the requirements for successful environmental product differentiation—willingness to pay, information, and barriers to imitation—as they play out in industrial markets.

Requirement 1: Willingness to pay. Customers in industrial markets will be willing to pay premiums for environmentally differentiated products if, and only if, the products lower the customers' overall costs. This is a straightforward story, and one that applies very broadly to differentiation in industrial markets. In both of the case examples just discussed, the customers of the businesses are confronting new environmental costs. Monsanto and Ciba lower these costs by offering differentiated products, and they can capture some of the value they are thereby creating.

Environmental differentiation is possible in industrial markets even if the costs the customer is avoiding are uncertain. For example, the benefits to textile dyers of Ciba's LS products depend, in part, on the wastewater regulations that local governments impose on the dyeing factory. The dyers could find the LS dyes attractive in part because they provide a hedge against tighter regulations in the future. This is a particular example of a more general idea: products that help industrial customers manage risk more effectively can add value to those customers' operations, and the firm providing those products may be able to capture some of the value.

In the Monsanto case example, the benefits to the growers who buy Roundup are diverse. Some of these benefits are certain and readily quantifiable, like reductions in direct costs for tilling. Some are uncertain, in the form of insurance against future government regulations with respect to soil erosion. And some are certain but very difficult to quantify, like the effect of reduced erosion on the future agricultural productivity of the farm.

Environmental differentiation is possible even if all the benefits to the customer are difficult to quantify. For example, publishers of some mass-market magazines in North America and Europe have been under pressure from readers to switch to paper produced without chlorine, the by-products of which can be toxic to humans and other organisms. Although no regulatory requirements to do so were forthcoming, the publishers were sufficiently concerned about their goodwill with these customers to communicate these demands to their suppliers or pulp and paper. They were willing to pay a premium for paper made from pulp bleached without chlorine in order to protect their reputations as "responsible" publishers. (This story turned out, however, not to have a happy ending for the pulp manufacturers, as we will see later in this chapter.)

In the Monsanto and Ciba cases, government regulation or the threat of regulation is an important determinant of customers' costs and hence of their willingness to pay for environmentally differentiated products. This is a widespread phenomenon: environmental quality is a public good, and firms are often unwilling to invest in its provision unless they face some regulatory requirement. Firms differentiating products along environmental lines risk an erosion in willingness to pay if regulatory requirements later loosen.

For example, during the 1970s and 1980s, federal and state authorities in the United States created a niche for producers of electricity who used processes that were considered more environmentally benign. Governments required their electric utilities to buy power from windmills or trash-to-steam plants at prices that approximated "avoided costs," which made the construction of such facilities attractive in an era of rising interest rates and oil prices. To sweeten the pot further, some governments offered direct tax benefits to the builders of innovative sources of electricity. Others required their utilities to purchase the electricity for rates even higher than "avoided costs": this legislation had the effect of using electric utilities as tax collectors, with the new generators receiving the revenues. When fossil fuel prices fell in the late 1980s and 1990s, governments sought, in some cases successfully, to discontinue the subsidies to alternative energy sources, and the niche producers were unable to compete on the basis of cost.[13]

In general, the trend in environmental regulation, both in industrial countries and in the developing world, has been toward tighter rather than looser rules as per capita incomes increase and population

densities rise. It is not only the stringency of the regulations that affects willingness to pay, however, but also the specific, fine-print details of the rules themselves. In order to hedge the risks of regulatory change, companies can sometimes insist on contractual protections, but more generally they should look for other ways to tie governments' hands and make it difficult for them to revert to the older rules of the game. Alliances with other politically important groups, lock-in of policies through international agreements that cannot readily be revisited, and related tactics can all play roles here.

Requirement 2: Credible information. In any marketing situation, customers want credible information assuring them that the products possess the attributes that the seller claims. For repeat purchases, the seller only needs to demonstrate that the product is the same as the one purchased in the past: this is one of the functions of brands. But sellers of innovative products may find it costly and difficult to provide credible information about their offerings, and without such information their differentiation strategies cannot succeed. In this respect, Monsanto's environmental differentiation of Roundup was easier than Ciba's differentiation of dyestuffs along environmental lines. Monsanto was repositioning a famous product whose characteristics were already well known, whereas Ciba was introducing a new technology.

Products that affect public goods like the environment also must be marketed in a broader social arena involving regulators, nongovernmental organizations, and the public. Here Ciba's task was easier than Monsanto's. Ciba's new technology did not involve any obvious environmental costs, whereas the social cost argument in favor of using Roundup hinges on arguments about the relative social costs of soil erosion and herbicide use. The difficulty in assigning social costs to these phenomena has contributed to controversy over Monsanto's policies.

Beyond this distinction, the two firms had some common advantages in their attempts to provide credible information to customers. Both companies had long track records of successful product introductions and had invested heavily in technical support for customers. Further, the customers had enormous incentives to invest in information about the differentiated products: each product related to the core of its customers' production process and had the potential to affect a large fraction of the customers' total costs. Hence it made sense for the customers to spend considerable time and effort understanding how

the product would affect their costs. Had the companies been selling environmentally differentiated office supplies or some other product peripheral to their customers' core processes, the customers would have had little incentive to make these investments in information.

Requirement 3: Barriers to imitation. The third requirement for successful environmental product differentiation is that the innovation must not be readily replicable by competitors. In the Ciba example, the innovations are protected both by patents and by a considerable amount of scientific understanding that, although not formally patentable, is formidably difficult for competitors to replicate. In the Monsanto Roundup herbicide example, complementary investments are necessary to defend a low-cost position within the differentiated niche.

By contrast, recall the story of the magazine publishers and paper bleached without chlorine. Although the pulp and paper companies' customers were apparently willing to pay more for chlorine-free paper, the companies found it impossible to capture any of the value they were creating by bleaching their pulp without chlorine. This ocurred because the wide availability of technologies for nonchlorine bleaching prevented any single firm (or small group of firms) from sustaining a strategy of differentiation. The new bleaching technologies involved capital investments that, once sunk, could not be recovered. Having sunk these costs, the pulp and paper companies found it difficult to restrain themselves from price competition that passed the value they were creating to their customers.

There are, of course, cases in both industrial and consumer markets in which a first mover would want its competitors to have to match its behavior, for example, if the first mover's innovation made its own costs higher than those of its rivals, but lower than its rivals' costs would be if they had to match the innovation. In such a case, the first mover desires not differentiation but a collective shift to a new product or process. The first mover can try to engineer such a change through the government regulatory structure or by setting up private regulatory bodies or codes of conduct. Examples of such strategies include DuPont's exit from the chlorofluorocarbon (CFC) business, and the Responsible Care program of the Chemical Manufacturers Association. These collective action strategies are discussed in chapter 3.

ENVIRONMENTAL PRODUCT
DIFFERENTIATION IN CONSUMER MARKETS

Armed with an understanding of the basic requirements for successful environmental differentiation along environmental lines—willingness to pay, credible information, and protection from imitators—we can analyze the more complicated problems that arise when companies differentiate products in consumer markets. We begin with two case examples from markets with widely differing structural characteristics: high-end outdoor apparel, and canned tuna.

PATAGONIA: ENVIRONMENTALLY
DIFFERENTIATED CLOTHING

Patagonia, Inc., a privately held company based in Ventura, California, sells about $150 million worth of sportswear and outdoor clothing each year. In 1993, it began using fabric made from recycled polyethylene terephthalate (PET) bottles for most of its polyester fleece garments and advertised the change heavily in its catalogs. In quality and product performance, the material was thought to be equal but not superior to the virgin polyester that the company had previously used, and it was 7 to 10 percent more expensive.[14] Patagonia decided not to raise product prices to reflect this raw material cost increase, instead selling the recycled-PET garments at the same price as comparable garments made of virgin polyester.[15]

Patagonia sells its products largely to wealthy individuals who are not very price-sensitive. It employs several distribution channels: it sells directly to consumers through its catalogs, maintains a dozen or so stores that sell exclusively Patagonia clothing, and sells its goods to several hundred other outdoor retailers, some of which, like Recreational Equipment, Inc. (REI), are themselves producers of outdoor wear. Patagonia's products enjoy a reputation for extremely high quality, bolstered not only by unconditional guarantees but also by mesmerizing photographs in company catalogs of "Patagoniacs" skiing down near-vertical faces or shooting terrifying rapids in kayaks. At the same time, many of its customers, as a company executive put it in a magazine interview, "may not be pushing the product to the edge."[16] In other words, the company sells much of its clothing—designed for Himalayan blizzards or midocean typhoons—to people unlikely to stray

more than a few miles from their cars. Moving away from its initial focus on such high-performance clothing, Patagonia has sold more and more casual sportswear. The prices of its products, recycled or otherwise, exceed those charged by competitors like L. L. Bean and Eddie Bauer, often by 50 percent or more.

Patagonia is an unusual firm in several ways, deeply influenced by the environmentalist vision of its founder, mountaineer Yvon Chouinard. Its executives assert that environmental product differentiation is integral to its broader objective: to be a company in which making money is only one of several goals, with participatory decision-making, contributions of profit to environmental causes, and a corporate culture friendly to women seen as equally important.[17] In the early 1990s, after unrestrained growth and a proliferation of expenses and inventory costs had led to Patagonia's first layoffs, Chouinard even stated that the company would henceforth forswear growth altogether.[18]

This did not happen. Since 1993, when the recycled fiber garments were introduced, Patagonia sales have increased rapidly, averaging 11 percent growth per year. This is slower than the rate of the 1980s but considerably faster than the outdoor clothing market as a whole. The company does not disclose what fraction, if any, of the growth is attributable to the recycling of fiber for jackets, either directly or through a halo effect on the company's other products.

In 1996, Patagonia switched to 100 percent organic cotton for its cotton sportswear. At the time, according to company executives, "prices for organic cotton ran 50 percent to 100 percent higher than commodity cotton," leading to total production cost increases that ranged, for different products, between 15 and 40 percent. Drawing on customer interviews and focus group results, the company concluded that its customers would be willing to pay higher prices for organic cotton, but it decided to "reduce our margins on most products to moderate retail price increases to a maximum of 20 percent."[19] The company asserted that it was absorbing about half of the cost increase, but the retail prices of the garments rose four to five dollars on average. An executive said, "It's a significant increase in cost, which initially reduced our profit margin. We hoped the customers would see the value in a product made with organic cotton. Fortunately, they did."[20]

Patagonia's market research prior to the switch to organic cotton convinced company executives that "the most significant reason for purchasing Patagonia is quality. . . . environmental concerns, either in

terms of the company's performance or characteristics of the product, were less important to customers." In response to this research, Patagonia's marketing strategy explicitly linked the environment and product quality: "We expanded our definition of quality to include the environment."[21]

Meanwhile, Patagonia executives continue to worry in public about the environmental consequences of their company's operations. In one of their catalogs, they wrote, "Patagonia has an emerald green reputation. Is it deserved? . . . The fact remains: the clothing industry is dirty, and the production of our clothing takes a significant toll on the earth. No Patagonia products are genuinely sustainable."[22]

STARKIST: DOLPHIN-SAFE TUNA

In April 1990, StarKist Foods, Inc. decided to purchase and sell exclusively dolphin-safe tuna. StarKist is the canned tuna subsidiary of H. J. Heinz, a $9 billion Pittsburgh-based firm whose other products include Weight Watchers diet aids, pet foods, and branded condiments like ketchup. Prior to its decision to adopt a dolphin-safe policy, Star-Kist bought most of its tuna from firms with fishing operations in the eastern tropical Pacific Ocean, off the coast of Latin America. In that region, for reasons still not understood, yellowfin tuna tend to swim beneath schools of dolphins. In the typical tuna harvesting procedure of the 1960s and early 1970s, a boat's crew would locate and chase a school of dolphins, drop a basketlike net called a purse seine under the school when the chase was over, and haul in both the dolphins and the tuna underneath. Each such chase was called a "dolphin set," and during the course of a fishing trip a boat might make dozens of sets. In this process, several hundred thousand dolphins were killed each year through the mid-1970s.[23]

These dolphins did not belong to species that were considered endangered. On the other hand, biologists thought that dolphin populations were lower than they would be in the absence of tuna fishing. American regulations issued in 1975 under the 1972 Marine Mammal Protection Act set quotas of dolphin fatalities for U.S. boats; the quotas ratcheted down over time so that by the early 1980s American boats were killing fewer than 20,000 dolphins annually. By modifying equipment so that the dolphins could escape when the nets were hauled in, it turned out to be possible to continue to "fish on dolphins"—that is,

to use dolphins to locate the tuna—while greatly reducing the number of dolphins killed. The fleets of other nations also adopted these technologies to some extent, so that the total annual dolphin fatalities throughout the 1980s were lower than they had been in the 1960s and early 1970s.[24]

Dolphin deaths did not cease entirely, however. In 1989 an activist named Sam LaBudde, working for the small environmental group Earth Island Institute, took along a video camera while working as a cook on a Panamanian tuna boat. He later released a videotape, shot surreptitiously during his trip, that showed dolphins dying during tuna fishing operations. The video showed dolphins struggling against the nets in futile attempts to reach the surface to breathe, or crushed in the heavy winches used to haul in the nets. This gruesome footage galvanized the public relations campaign that Earth Island Institute had been waging against the tuna canners, and the organization was able to enlist movie stars and other celebrities to put pressure on the government and companies to end any killing of dolphins.

This pressure created a dilemma for StarKist executives. If they stopped buying eastern tropical Pacific tuna altogether and instead purchased exclusively in the western tropical Pacific, StarKist's costs per ton of tuna would increase in absolute terms. The costs would also increase relative to those of StarKist's main competitors, Bumble Bee Seafoods (owned by a Thai agribusiness company) and Van Camp Seafood (which owned the Chicken of the Sea brand, and in turn was owned by an Indonesian firm).[25] A move from the eastern to the western Pacific would also entail a switch from yellowfin tuna to a variety called skipjack, which was considered inferior in taste.

On the other hand, StarKist executives felt that consumers might be willing to pay a premium for dolphin-safe tuna; one survey conducted for the company suggested that half of consumers might pay twenty-one cents extra per can.[26] In a product category where brand loyalty was weak and price competition fierce, this number was naturally of great interest to Heinz executives: at the time of the controversy, the StarKist subsidiary accounted for about $560 million in annual sales and $40 million in operating income (before interest and taxes), a return on sales substantially below corporate averages.

Heinz chief executive Anthony O'Reilly and StarKist president Keith Hauge announced the company's switch to dolphin-safe tuna on April 12, 1990. Dolphin-safe tuna, for Heinz, meant tuna caught on a

fishing voyage during which no dolphin sets were undertaken. If a boat made even one dolphin set during a fishing trip, StarKist pledged not to buy any of that trip's cargo. This was called a "no encirclement" policy because it precluded boat captains who wanted to sell to Heinz from fishing on or encircling any dolphins. Earlier, Heinz had considered a looser "no mortality" policy that would allow it to purchase any tuna caught during a set in which no dolphins were killed. But this policy might not have satisfied environmentalists, who wanted a complete cessation of fishing on dolphins. It also might have been vulnerable to "overcalling" from competitors, who could have responded by announcing a "no encirclement" policy of their own.

StarKist's two main competitors announced dolphin-safe procurement policies (also specifying the tougher "no encirclement" standard) within a few hours of StarKist's announcement.[27] United States legislation prevented Mexican tuna, caught on dolphin sets in the eastern tropical Pacific, from entering U.S. markets, buffering the three firms from competition from the sources they had abandoned. Although the tuna embargo was held to be illegal under the General Agreement on Tariffs and Trade, it remained in place through the late 1990s. Meanwhile, other U.S. legislation provided criteria for tuna labeled "dolphin-safe" that were essentially the same as those adopted by StarKist. Despite the insulation from Mexican competition, StarKist was unable to capture any price premium after its two main competitors matched its strategy.

Customers' actual behavior belied their answers in marketing surveys. J. W. Connolly, president of Heinz U.S.A., later recalled that "consumers wanted a dolphin-safe product, but they were not willing to pay more for it. If there was a dolphin-safe can of tuna next to a regular can, people chose the cheaper product. Even if the difference was one penny. It was disappointing that the environmentalists were not able to come through for us at the cash register."[28] Although Heinz increased its market share over the following years, it did so at the cost of intensified price competition, and the value of the StarKist operation as a going concern has reportedly declined.[29]

Fishing practices in the western tropical Pacific also turned out to be environmentally problematic. Instead of fishing on dolphin, boats' crews looked for rafts of logs and other naturally occurring flotsam, below which the skipjack tuna tended to congregate. But large numbers of immature and hence unusable skipjack, as well as other crea-

tures (some of them endangered), also perished as they were pulled in with the nets. For each dolphin saved in the eastern Pacific, thousands of immature tuna and dozens of sharks, mahimahi, yellowtail, sea turtles, and other marine animals died in the western part of the ocean.[30] At the same time, however, Earth Island Institute continued to maintain that any dolphin deaths were morally unacceptable.[31]

In August 1997, President Bill Clinton signed legislation that changed the definition of "dolphin-safe" to include "no mortality" tuna and not just "no encirclement" tuna.[32] This legislative change, not widely noted in the mainstream press, enabled StarKist (and its competitors) to return to the eastern tropical Pacific and purchase tuna from suppliers who fish on dolphin as long as none of the mammals were killed in the particular set in which the tuna was caught.

THE THREE REQUIREMENTS REVISITED

The framework already developed suggests why Patagonia's differentiation efforts have been successful and clearly shows why StarKist's failed. Despite their responses to marketing surveys, tuna consumers demonstrated no willingness to pay for environmental product attributes, and StarKist had no protection from imitation in any case. It may seem difficult to generalize from the experience of Patagonia, since the company sells to an unusually price-insensitive segment of the market; and it may seem discouraging to try to generalize from the experience of StarKist, since that experiment in differentiation was not successful. It turns out, though, that these examples, in combination with the analysis already presented, shed considerable light on the ways in which willingness to pay, information, and imitation problems matter in consumer markets.

Requirement 1: Willingness to pay. Patagonia and StarKist both faced the problem of trying to get consumers—that is, households—to pay for public goods. We need to understand the circumstances under which this is possible.

First, note that some environmental benefits turn out to be private goods. For example, many consumers are willing to pay a premium for pesticide-free vegetables and fruits. But the absence of pesticides is a private health-related consumption good, like the presence of vitamins. One would expect that willingness to pay would be

high, as for other goods that consumers believe directly benefit their health. This suggests that environmental differentiation can succeed if the environmental characteristics of the product or process are inextricably bundled with conventional private goods. A good example is "designer beef," which comes from cattle raised without hormones and free from exposure to herbicides. Such meat may be preferable to ordinary beef for both health and environmental reasons, allowing its producers to deliver tandem benefits to their consumers.[33]

This line of attack may seem to be of little use at Patagonia or StarKist. The presence of living dolphins on the high seas is a pure public good. Similarly, organic cotton and recycled polyethylene are indistinguishable in performance from their conventionally produced counterparts. At first glance, the bundling of private and public goods does not appear possible for either firm.

More generally, however, under certain circumstances people do incur private expenses to provide public goods. They recycle cans, bottles, and newspapers even though doing so requires time and trouble. They donate funds to environmental groups and providers of other public goods. Individual behavior in a broad range of similar activities—charitable contributions to churches and other social welfare organizations, gifts by alumni to their schools, and so on—both supports the idea that voluntary public good provision is widespread and suggests some insights into the circumstances that induce it.

Individuals may contribute to public good provision because the general knowledge that they have done so confers prestige within a community. College buildings are often named after large donors, suggesting that the endowment of a building at one's old college campus is not always a fully disinterested event. A related possibility is that people may contribute to public good provision in hopes of affecting others' behavior. Such motives may account for lapel pins advertising that the wearer just gave blood, or bumper stickers announcing "I give the United Way." Enlightened self-interest might also affect behavior: some organizations, like churches, perform services for the community that supports them, and people may contribute to them in part as an insurance policy. This last motive, however, does not seem particularly strong in the case of environmental goods, since the benefits of environmental quality are spread over very large numbers of people.

At the same time, it is overly reductionistic to try to boil down all charitable giving and voluntary public good provision to a search for

status, influence, or insurance: altruistic motives and ideas about personal responsibility play a role as well. The willingness to pay for public goods depends on difficult-to-define social expectations as well as on strictly economic criteria. For example, littering along American highways fell sharply in the 1960s, catalyzed by a government advertising campaign, although there was no dramatic change in the economic costs or benefits of this practice. The point here is not that businesses ought to try to engineer such changes, but that analyzing individuals' behavior from a narrow economic perspective will not always yield accurate predictions.[34] It is possible to try to bundle all of these impulses into an economic utility function that includes charitable contributions or adherence to ethical codes among its arguments. But a more intuitive line of approach would recognize that some motives are not "economic"—that is, that they do not follow from narrow self-interest—and then try to understand the economic implications of this noneconomic behavior.

Patagonia's customers may be willing to pay more for its environmentally differentiated products for altruistic reasons, or because the consumption of the products makes a statement to the consumers' friends and acquaintances: the company's products are meant to be worn in public and sport discreet but (to consumers in the target market) instantly recognizable logos. By contrast, StarKist's ability to induce customers to pay more for environmentally differentiated tuna was limited by the fundamental nature of the product: an unglamorous source of cheap protein that is consumed in the home.

This suggests that environmental differentiation opportunities are constrained by other product characteristics and by the past success or failure of other differentiation efforts. StarKist and its competitors had a long history of unsuccessful differentiation efforts, with weak brands, rampant price competition, and very little product innovation. By contrast, participants in Patagonia's market—outdoor wear—have long and successful histories of differentiation, and it is possible to build on previous differentiation successes to create willingness to pay for public goods.

Whatever its origins, willingness to pay for environmental attributes in goods and services is certain to differ across consumers, suggesting that market segmentation plays a critical role in product differentiation strategies. Following a survey of American consumers, some leading advertising executives asserted that it was useful to think

of five segments with respect to environmental behavior. "True-blue greens," who "practice what they preach" on environmental issues, accounted for 11 percent of the population; they contributed financially to environmental groups and were willing to undertake lifestyle changes for environmental reasons. "Greenback greens," another 11 percent of the population, with the same average income as the "true-blue greens," were also active in donating financially to environmental organizations but were thought less likely to make adjustments to their lifestyles. "Sprouts," at 26 percent of the population, were thought more likely to make lifestyle adjustments. The rest of the population was characterized as "cynics" or "basic browns," with lower income and educational levels and an indifferent or hostile attitude toward environmentalists' concerns.[35]

These data are consistent with the idea that education levels and income, which are positively correlated with each other, are also positively correlated with willingness to pay for public goods. Environmental quality seems to behave like a luxury good: more precisely, demand for environmental quality is elastic with respect to income. Several studies have shown that the congressional representatives of wealthier districts are more likely to favor environmental legislation.[36] Rich countries spend a higher proportion of their income on environmental goods, and casual observation suggests that this is true of individuals as well. Wealthier people may be more interested in status than less wealthy ones, or simply better able to fund their altruistic impulses, or both.[37]

Although these demographics create opportunities for firms like Patagonia to segment markets, they create problems for companies unable to target different customers with specific products. Businesses that are differentiating products along environmental lines need to decide what to do about similar, but less environmentally beneficial, products.

Marketers and strategists draw a useful distinction between horizontal and vertical differentiation.[38] Vertical differentiation makes the product more appealing to all consumers; horizontal differentiation makes the product more valuable to some consumers but less appealing to others. Using this vocabulary, environmental differentiation is bound to be horizontal because not all consumers will attach the same benefits to a product's environmental characteristics.

If a business can differentiate vertically, improving environmental performance while keeping its production costs and all other product

attributes constant, then obviously it should do so: the customers who care about the environment will be willing to pay more, and the others will, at worst, be indifferent. But such opportunities tend to be rare: more commonly, to imbue a product with new characteristics entails the sacrifice of other characteristics, an increase in costs, or both.[39] Then the differentiating firm risks defections from consumers who are not willing to pay more or to obtain fewer nonenvironmental benefits in order to support the environmental good. Recall that this was Star-Kist's situation: skipjack from the western Pacific is inferior in taste to eastern Pacific yellowfin, and it costs more to produce.

In general, a company's response under these circumstances would be to offer both kinds of products. But horizontal differentiation of this sort may be unusually difficult in the environmental arena because environmental benefits are public goods. If a business tries to differentiate products horizontally by offering different versions of the same product, some environmentalist consumers may see the firm's environmental efforts as insincere. Perceptions of sincerity seem to be important in defining customer attitudes toward environmental product differentiation, a problem discussed in more detail later.[40] Patagonia solves this problem by selling exclusively to a particular market segment. Among businesses like StarKist that sell to mass markets, however, the risk of alienating one or several segments may be significant.

There is, however, a broader interpretation of the Patagonia case example that implies an innovative solution to the problem of willingness to pay. One way of creating willingness to pay for public goods is to bundle them with private goods. Rather than just segmenting markets, Patagonia is using its environmental performance to communicate about itself and its values in such a way that private and public goods are intertwined for its consumers. Consumers may make positive inferences about Patagonia from the fact that it is trying to increase the use of organic cotton; the provision of public goods can enhance brand equity and give customers confidence in the company and its products.

Patagonia's highly public search for a new way of doing business implies a new kind of relationship with customers, reinforced by unconditional guarantees, extremely high product quality, and an explicit commitment to ethical codes of behavior. The value of the environmental component of this overall corporate differentiation strategy is impossible to quantify, but it seems to resonate strongly with customers (who are likely to be outdoors-loving people and hence like-

ly to be environmentalists anyway), and it also contributes to the highly differentiated position that Patagonia has been able to create for itself. In this context, Patagonia's recycled polyethylene and organic cotton products could create a significant halo effect for the company's other offerings, creating benefits for the company's entire portfolio of products.[41]

The lessons of this broader interpretation of the Patagonia case example are widely applicable to other firms. If corporate concern about the environment is consistent with the other signals the company is sending to customers, then the environmental goods the company is providing get bundled with the quality of the company's products, the company's statements about the importance of ethical behavior, the customer's own concern for the environment, and the customer's relationship with the company, in the same way that environmental benefits and private consumption benefits are intertwined for consumers of organic vegetables or "designer beef."

From this perspective, StarKist's marketing tactic failed from a value creation standpoint because it was an add-on characteristic not integrated with the overall positioning of the product, the overall positioning of the company, or the other aspects of the business's strategy. From the point of view of Heinz CEO O'Reilly, the central motive in the dolphin-safe initiative may have been risk management rather than value creation. One of the critical aspects of the tuna controversy was the possibility—never realized—that environmentalists' outrage over dolphins might lead to trouble for other Heinz products, like ketchup, that were far more lucrative than canned tuna. When viewed as a tactic of corporate risk management, protecting the reputation of other Heinz brands, StarKist's introduction of dolphin-safe tuna may have been successful. According to this argument, the switch to dolphin-safe tuna could have been motivated by corporate-level attempts to maximize the value of the company's entire portfolio of brands, taking into account a possible halo effect of the StarKist switch on the other products. But because the switch lacked any connection to a larger strategy that might have created some willingness to pay among customers, it could not succeed from the standpoint of value creation at the business unit level.

Requirement 2: Credible information. In the industrial market examples of Monsanto and Ciba, the differentiated product was central to the customer's core economic activities and accounted for a significant

fraction of the customer's total costs. These conditions created strong incentives for the customer to invest in information about the product. In consumer markets, especially if the product accounts for a very small fraction of the customer's total budget, it may be difficult for companies to attract enough attention to communicate credibly about the product's environmental attributes. Further, there are often considerable technical difficulties in identifying "environmentally preferable" products in an unambiguous way. Companies have adopted a variety of approaches to this problem of information, including the use of government-sponsored eco-labels, third-party certification, and self-certification initiatives.

Outside the United States, a number of business-government partnerships have arisen to create "eco-labels": certification schemes for products that meet environmental standards. The most deeply entrenched of these schemes is the "Blue Angel" program, begun by the German government in the late 1970s. The Angel has been imitated by national bodies in France, Japan, and elsewhere; by a consortium that draws its members from the Nordic countries; and more recently, in response to a proliferation of national labels, by the European Union.

Under each of these programs, teams of government officials and business executives develop lists of criteria by which particular products should be judged. The writers of the criteria try to examine all the environmental impacts of the products, not just in manufacture but also in raw material sourcing, use, and disposal. Paper products, for example, might be evaluated by the fraction of raw material that is recycled, and by the amount of air and water pollution generated per ton of product during manufacturing. The standards tend to be relative rather than absolute: that is, they are designed so that only a small fraction of all the products available will satisfy them. If environmental performance improves across the board, the criteria are tightened.

The architects of eco-labeling schemes assume that consumers are willing to pay more for environmentally preferable products but need help in identifying those products. Collecting and digesting information about the environmental performance of various products can be enormously time-consuming, especially given the proliferation of unilateral claims by companies.[42] A credible eco-labeling scheme allows customers to exploit economies of scale in processing this information by delegating the work to a central body.

Eco-labels have not fully solved the problem of credible information. Some of the difficulties are direct consequences of scientific

uncertainty. Others arise from uncertainty about the relative values of various unpriced environmental impacts; for example, it is difficult to determine the value of additional carbon dioxide versus additional landfills versus an incremental increase in the probability of the extinction of a species of animal or plant. Others are imposed by the structure of the eco-labeling schemes themselves. Because most standards are not absolute but relative, with products compared against others in the same product category, the definition of the "category" is absolutely critical. A lightweight, fuel-efficient gasoline-powered lawnmower may look environmentally friendly in comparison with heavier models, but it is quite burdensome environmentally when compared with non-motorized lawnmowers. The particular selection criteria matter as well. Manufacturers whose products are disadvantaged by an eco-labeling criterion are quick to charge that it is politically biased in favor of local producers, and that it serves as a form of eco-protectionism.[43]

In the United States, the "dolphin-safe" seal that adorns cans of tuna is a government-sponsored eco-label. Shortly after StarKist and its competitors announced their intention to buy only "no-encirclement" tuna, Congress passed the Dolphin Protection Conservation Act of 1990. The act established criteria for labeling "dolphin-safe" tuna that were basically the same as those adopted by the companies.[44] (This did not solve the companies' problems, of course, because they stemmed not just from consumer confusion about the environmental impacts of various fishing techniques but also from an absence of consumer willingness to pay and from cutthroat competition among the companies.) More generally, however, support in the United States for government eco-labeling schemes has been limited, and no private body has proven equal to the funding, logistical, and reputation-building tasks required to set up a widespread, credible eco-labeling scheme.

In any case, government eco-labels may not serve the interests of firms pursuing environmental differentiation strategies. By putting pressure on other firms in the industry to adopt environmentally preferable production or product characteristics, eco-labels may hasten imitation and erode the differentiating firm's market position. A firm seeking to differentiate products along environmental lines needs to consider carefully whether its competitive position will be improved or impaired by eco-labels.[45]

Responding to the absence of an established body for certification, some North American firms have obtained formal or informal certification

from outside groups that are thought to be more credible, or at least more environmentally oriented, than the firms themselves. Executives entering such relationships hope that their claims will acquire credibility from the certifying organization's reputation. The Canadian supermarket chain Loblaw, for example, when introducing environmentally differentiated private-label goods, arranged for two Canadian environmental groups to endorse some of the products in exchange for a contribution of 1 percent of revenues.[46] But such arrangements are very risky for the firm. An environmental advocacy group may not have the resources to draw up criteria and to monitor firm performance. Further, such a group may be very reluctant to tie its own brand equity to that of a firm, especially if (as is common) the criteria on which the certification is based can be attacked as arbitrary or environmentally inadequate. If the company tries to compensate the advocacy group for incurring out-of-pocket costs and bearing this reputational risk, the group's reputation may suffer when the financial aspects of the arrangement become public. This problem beset Loblaw's alliance with its Canadian environmental partners.

Alternatively, companies can make unilateral declarations of environmental friendliness. The early experience with such self-certification schemes was mixed, as some of the claims turned out to be debatable. To cite one famous example, in 1989 Mobil Corporation began billing some of its trash bags as degradable: they broke down in the presence of air, water, and light. Environmental groups, several state governments, and the Federal Trade Commission (FTC) then complained that the claims were misleading, since most trash bags end up in landfills where light, water, and air are absent. In 1992, Mobil agreed to stop making any such claims for the bags. At about the same time, the FTC issued nonbinding guidelines on the use of such terms as "biodegradable" and "ozone-safe."[47]

Ambiguity about the environmental benefits of the trash bags may have been especially problematic because the product's environmental impact can depend on how it is used as well as on how it is produced. Even if all the impacts occur in the production stage, however, ambiguity will still be a problem: in the tuna case, the net environmental benefits of the switch out of the eastern tropical Pacific depend, among other things, on the relative values of dolphins, immature tuna, and other marine animals. Social cost accounting for Monsanto's biotechnological crop protection products is even more difficult. It may seem clearer that Patagonia's recycling of plastic bot-

tles into pullovers results in positive net environmental benefits. Even in this case, however, some commentators, calling attention to the fuel and equipment used in the recycling process, have argued that the benefits are overstated and perhaps even negative.[48] Given problems of this sort, difficulties with "self-certification" schemes like Mobil's are predictable. Customers often have no way to assess companies' environmental claims directly, and may not see firms as completely credible sources of information about the environmental impacts of their own products.

Here again, the fit between environmental product differentiation and the overall positioning of the firm is critical. A firm that has previously acquired a reputation for providing credible information about other aspects of its business is far more likely to succeed with a self-certification scheme than one without such a reputation. Narrowly, one can think of a company's brand as making it easier for a customer to process information about the product and enhancing the customer's confidence in a purchase decision; more broadly, it represents perceived quality and the reputation of the firm that stands behind it.[49] If this reputation encompasses a concern for environmental quality, consumers are far more likely to trust unilateral declarations about the environmental attributes of products.

Requirement 3: Barriers to imitation. As a differentiation strategy, the StarKist dolphin-safe initiative would have failed even if consumers had been willing to pay more for dolphin-safe tuna because StarKist's procurement policy could easily be imitated by other firms. Under some circumstances, a firm may want to force its rivals to imitate its own behavior; DuPont's CFC business, discussed in the next chapter, provides one example. But StarKist faced a cost disadvantage in dolphin-safe tuna, so it could not have been pursuing a strategy of forcing imitation. As in industrial markets, if rivals can match the product innovation at equal or lower cost, product differentiation will not be successful. The firms will give up, in the form of lower prices to their customers, the value they are creating.

From the imitators' perspective, the tuna story is not much happier. Chicken of the Sea and Bumble Bee clearly anticipated StarKist's move to no-encirclement tuna, or they would not have been able to respond on the day it was announced. At the same time, they apparently would have preferred to see StarKist maintain its purchasing policies,

rather than moving collectively to dolphin-safe tuna. None of the firms had a plan in place to avoid price wars or the quality problems that would arise with a move to western Pacific skipjack. One general implication of the StarKist case is that companies need to anticipate their rivals' differentiation moves and to have contingency plans in place that will exploit the situation or at least contain the damage. The introduction of environmentally differentiated products by a rival, even if it is ultimately unsuccessful, can harm other firms in the industry by eroding margins, creating political and public relations difficulties, or both.

From the perspective of the innovator, barriers to imitation in consumer markets can include the ones discussed previously in the context of industrial markets: patent protection, unpatentable but proprietary know-how, and so on. The relationships that firms have already developed with their customers may be an equally important mechanism for blocking imitators.

It is in this context that the integration of Patagonia's environmental strategy with its overall corporate image and manner of doing business is so important: potential imitators find it much more difficult to replicate than a simple product repositioning. Patagonia's attempts to increase the use of organic cotton, like its contributions of profits to environmental activists, its vivid catalog photography, and its public soul-searching about the role of the corporation in society, help to create an unusually strong bond with customers. In this relationship, the company's concerns about the environment, product quality, and relationships with suppliers and customers are all bundled together. Environmental product differentiation is an organic outgrowth of an entire company culture. Other firms can replicate it only to the extent that they too have invested in a similar culture and similar relationships with customers. Again, the environmental positioning should be not an afterthought but an integral part of the business strategy.[50]

Managing Competitors

THE FIRMS discussed in the previous chapter are trying to differentiate their products along environmental lines and to prevent competitors from following in their footsteps. By contrast, the firms discussed in this chapter want to force their competitors to follow the examples they set. The approach of the firms in this chapter is to compel changes in competitors' behavior in ways that create advantage for the first movers.

In most Western countries, the provision of public goods is viewed as the natural function of government, not of private enterprise. Street lighting, national defense, and clean air are most commonly provided through government action. Either the government levies taxes and uses the proceeds to provide the public good itself, as is the case with national defense, or it writes regulations requiring private parties to provide the good, as is the case with clean air. A government role is considered necessary because usually only governments enjoy the powers to impose taxes or to coerce certain kinds of behavior. Without these powers, private entities find it difficult to solve the problem of collective action: how to penalize private entities that don't contribute to the provision of the public good.

Similarly, regulation—explicitly dictating certain kinds of behavior on the part of companies—has also been seen as a governmental function in most Western countries. It is largely to overcome problems of collective action that governments write regulations. So, for example, governments require all companies to clean their wastewater because

otherwise competitive pressures would discourage any firm from doing so. It is commonly assumed that voluntary programs will not accomplish the same end because companies ordinarily cannot exert the kind of coercive power that enables governments to punish noncompliance.

There are, however, two ways in which companies may be able to pursue solutions to these problems of collective action. Some companies have confronted their collective action problems head-on by organizing themselves into bodies that act like government regulatory agencies. In this chapter, this option is represented by two initiatives: the Responsible Care program undertaken by the Chemical Manufacturers Association, and the American Forest & Paper Association's Sustainable Forestry Initiative. A second possibility for solving the collective action problem is to enlist the help of the government or other social groups to put pressure on competitors. Here this option is represented by DuPont's activity in the markets for chlorofluorocarbons and their substitutes, and by the behavior of gasoline marketers in California.

If they are successful in pursuing either of these options, companies can respond to social pressure for more environmental quality while also maintaining or bettering their financial performance. Put another way, successful collective action strategies enable companies to avoid the "race to the bottom" that otherwise can create trade-offs between shareholder value and the provision of environmental goods.

The chances of succeeding with this approach are affected by industry structure and by the political and social context in which the initiative is conducted. Clearly, the chances of success depend in part on the firm itself: a firm needs a cost advantage that it can exploit to gain an advantage over its rivals. But government bodies also play critical roles in the approaches discussed in this chapter, whether the firm enlists the help of the government directly or attempts a private regulatory solution. Thus, even if the industry's structure and the firm's capabilities favor such an approach, it can still fail in the political arena. Managers contemplating approaches of this sort need to take careful account of their economic and political circumstances, along the lines suggested in this chapter.

THE CREATION OF PRIVATE REGULATORY BODIES

One set of strategies for solving collective action problems involves creating new institutions that behave like government regulatory agencies.

In these collective self-regulatory schemes, all the firms in an industry agree to raise their costs so that each can add more environmental value without disadvantaging itself unduly in the private marketplace. Firms that find themselves under regulatory or social pressure to increase environmental spending, but fear the cost disadvantages that will result if their competitors don't follow suit, will be attracted to this approach.

It is easy to see why a self-regulatory scheme could be preferable to a government regulatory program from the perspectives of the companies in an industry. The managers in those companies might reasonably want to maintain their managerial discretion in responding to future problems. Self-regulatory schemes should be easier to alter if later circumstances call for change. More immediately, managers might think they are capable of writing more sensible standards than any government regulator because they have superior information about their own production processes. Finally, they may well dislike the uncertainty that a government regulatory program creates. Compared with traditional government programs, self-regulatory schemes offer companies greater flexibility, greater control, and hence less risk. In fact, one of the principal motives for self-regulatory programs seems to be to reduce the probability of government regulation, the likely stringency of that regulation, or both.

But the management of regulatory risk never seems to be the only motive of such schemes. Under some circumstances, large firms can use private regulatory bodies to gain advantage over their smaller counterparts. Ostensibly, the firms that participate in such an arrangement are agreeing not to compete on the basis of short-term environmental cost minimization. That is, while they will continue to compete to produce better products or to reduce their other production costs, they will not try to shave their environmental costs in pursuit of short-term competitive advantage because they fear that this sort of behavior will create even more undesirable long-term effects. One could draw an analogy to commercial airline safety. Airline companies tacitly agree not to compete with one another on the basis of their safety records, either by advertising accident rates or by trying aggressively to reduce safety-related costs.

At the same time, however, the costs of adhering to a given set of regulatory standards are bound to fall unequally across companies in an industry, whether those standards are set by a government agency or by

the firms themselves. In the environmental area, some of the costs of compliance are likely to be fixed rather than variable with the size of the firm, allowing larger firms to take advantage of economies of scale. Hence the programs may disadvantage smaller firms. Here an analogy could be made not to flying but to soft drinks. The largest producers of carbonated soft drinks impose fixed costs on their smaller competitors by advertising on national television: Coca-Cola and Pepsi raise their own costs but force smaller firms to raise their costs even further as a fraction of sales. Given these economics, it is not surprising that self-regulatory schemes tend to be initiated by the larger firms in an industry.

For other reasons, too, one might expect the larger firms in an industry to lead the initiative for self-regulation. They may already have more sophisticated environmental management systems, so that their costs of compliance with a given set of standards may be lower, even ignoring the effects of the scale economies. The bigger firms may also be more concerned with protecting their reputations as reliable social partners. This would imply that the benefits of improved reputation would be greater for larger firms.

But this same economic logic explains why private regulatory initiatives can be so difficult to implement. If some firms (often the smaller ones) must bear disproportionately high costs while receiving relatively smaller benefits, they will be tempted to defect from the regulatory system. And the smaller firms, by threatening to defect, may be able to force the bigger ones to bear a larger share of the costs of the regulation. The leaders of a regulatory initiative must be careful not to push the laggards too far or too fast lest they trigger widespread defections that cause the initiative to fail.[1]

In other words, industry self-regulatory programs are not value-neutral exercises in the collective management of environmental risk. They also change the nature of competition in the industry and hence benefit some firms at the expense of others. Firms that will benefit from such programs, however, face some predictable but very thorny problems. Not surprisingly, the problems are exactly the ones that confront governmental bodies trying to design regulatory programs. To be successful, a government program of command-and-control regulation must have measurable performance standards, access to information about compliance, and credible enforcement mechanisms; it also must be consistent with other laws. Moving the regulatory body from the public to the private sector does not eliminate the need for any of these conditions.

All of these considerations arise in the following case examples, which discuss the development of private regulatory bodies in chemicals and forest products.

CHEMICAL MANUFACTURERS
ASSOCIATION: RESPONSIBLE CARE

When a 1984 gas leak at a Union Carbide subsidiary's pesticide plant in Bhopal, India, killed more than 2,000 people, the American chemical industry was already reeling from a series of environmental catastrophes.[2] In the late 1970s and early 1980s, scientists, government officials, and environmental activists focused public attention on Hooker Chemical's Love Canal dump site near Niagara Falls, on the widespread presence of polychlorinated biphenyls (PCBs) in the Hudson River, and on other hazardous waste problems around the country. In a climate of widespread mistrust of the chemical industry, Congress passed a spate of laws that drastically affected the companies' operating flexibility and raised the specter of further government control.

In 1976, Congress enacted the Toxic Substances Control Act and the Resource Conservation and Recovery Act. These laws required companies to track all of their hazardous wastes through a complicated system of manifests and permits, and gave the federal Environmental Protection Agency (EPA) explicit authority to ban substances that posed unreasonable risks to health and the environment. In 1980, in the immediate aftermath of the Love Canal incident, Congress passed the Comprehensive Environmental Response, Compensation, and Liability Act, better known as the Superfund law, which imposed retroactive, strict, joint and several liability on generators and handlers of industrial wastes. Firms that generated wastes, even if they had been in compliance with all laws in the past, could be held liable for the entire costs of cleaning up any site to which they had contributed. Chemical industry executives were used to thinking of themselves as agents of progress and technological change, and to them this legislation seemed gratuitously punitive. Many of the industry's adversaries, however, considered the laws just desserts.

In the aftermath of the Bhopal disaster, executives at the large American chemical producers legitimately feared that further government regulation would seriously undermine their ability to manage their companies. To demonstrate their commitment to environmental

responsibility as a way of forestalling further regulation and resurrecting their image in the public eye, the largest companies proposed a regulatory program called Responsible Care. This program is intended to induce the firms in the chemical industry to provide public goods and respond to public concerns in a number of environmental fields.

The initiative encompasses ten "guiding principles" and six management codes, focusing on community awareness and emergency response, pollution prevention, process safety, the reduction of risk from distribution of chemicals, employee health and safety, and product stewardship. For example, the code on community awareness and emergency response, the first to be put in place, calls on members to provide information on health, safety, and environmental questions to residents of towns near their plants, and to spend time and money on preparedness for emergencies like accidental spills. The other five codes establish similar requirements in other aspects of environmental management. The program, begun in Canada and the United States, is now active in several dozen countries.[3]

Responsible Care is implemented by the companies' main trade group, the Chemical Manufacturers Association (CMA), which was founded in 1872. The CMA's 185 members include all of the largest chemical manufacturers and many of the smaller companies; together, they account for over 90 percent of chemical manufacturing capacity. CMA has traditionally performed the conventional functions of a trade association, including legislative lobbying, public relations, and technical support.

The Responsible Care program added regulatory functions to the CMA's portfolio. Staff members of the trade association, in consultation with executives from member companies, are supposed to evaluate each member firm's progress toward implementation of the various codes. The CMA has enforcement powers as well, since "good-faith efforts to attain the goals of each Code" are a condition for continued CMA membership.[4]

The implicit rationale for Responsible Care is that many environmental management activities will not pay for themselves through private cost savings or marketplace opportunities, and thus some sort of regulatory structure must be established to prevent free riding. The CMA created Responsible Care to provide that structure without requiring an active role by the government.

Environmental releases of substances regulated by the EPA have declined in the years since the program was initiated, and injury and

accident rates for CMA members have fallen from levels that were already well below those for American manufacturing as a whole.[5] The Responsible Care codes, however, do not contain numerical targets for pollution or waste generation of the sort one might expect to find in government regulations; their direct orientation is toward changing management processes and procedures rather than actual pollution levels. Hence, the principal direct measure of the initiative's performance is the extent to which member companies have instituted "action plans" to implement each of the six codes. Members report their progress to CMA staff; the association does not audit these reports. By 1995, managers at most of the sites operated by CMA members reported that they had put management practices in place to implement most of the six Responsible Care codes.

For CMA's "product stewardship" code, however, fewer than half of members' sites had an implementation plan in place. The CMA drafted that code "to make health, safety, and environmental protection an integral part of designing, manufacturing, marketing, distributing, using, recycling and disposing of chemical products."[6] According to one industry publication, "companies have come to realize that they no longer can afford to surrender responsibility for their products at the close of a sales transaction."[7] The companies want to maintain some control over the use and disposal of their products because of concerns about the adverse publicity and potential liability that could arise if these products later create an environmental insult. Product stewardship systems monitor the movements of products through use, possible resale, and ultimate disposal so that the manufacturers can manage these risks. Unlike the other five Responsible Care codes, however, product stewardship must be implemented at a company-wide level rather than facility by facility.[8] This requirement makes it more difficult for firms to implement and for CMA to monitor. While a variety of product stewardship initiatives might make practical sense, it is difficult for the CMA to define meaningful performance measures in light of the wide variety of practices encompassed by the code.[9]

The proportion of member plants with management practices in place for the other five codes is considerably higher than for product stewardship. Eighty-one percent of facilities reported that they maintain a quantitative inventory of wastes and releases, as required under the pollution prevention code; 83 percent reported that they "maintain a process for responding to distribution accidents or incidents" under

the distribution code.[10] But even these figures mask some underlying problems: they indicate that one in six facilities has no process for responding to distribution accidents, and one in five does not maintain an inventory of wastes.

Some industry observers think that the larger firms in the industry were already implementing policy changes along the lines of the Responsible Care codes prior to the initiative's establishment, and that the main operational effects of the program have occurred at small and medium-sized companies.[11]

As of 1998, no firms had left the CMA rather than conform to the codes. CMA executives publicly express nothing but satisfaction with the way their initiative is evolving, although they emphasize that their work is not complete. J. Lawrence Wilson, chairman of CMA's board and CEO of Philadelphia-based Rohm & Haas, wrote, "More must be done if we are to achieve our goal of earning the public trust. During the past eight years, we have come to understand what we must do to earn that trust—improve our performance. We know how we must do it—by instituting the Responsible Care Codes at each member company and working tirelessly to improve upon them."[12]

NECESSARY CONDITIONS
FOR SUCCESSFUL PRIVATE REGULATION

Persistent dissatisfaction with government regulation, the continued pressure for improved environmental performance, and the widespread favorable publicity accorded Responsible Care all contribute to the appeal of private regulatory programs more generally. It is instructive, therefore, to look at how the large chemical companies overcame the various barriers to the success of their program, as a way of understanding the degree to which private regulations might succeed in other industries.

First, a regulatory program, public or private, must have a way to fund its start-up costs. Before the program has any effect on behavior, staff must be hired, regulations drafted, and potential legal and technical problems resolved. For private regulatory undertakings this problem can be significant. In the chemical manufacturers' case, the solution arose naturally from the structure of the industry: with a few very large firms and a number of smaller ones, there were readily identifiable industry leaders who could bear the up-front costs of the initiative.

Second, no regulatory program can succeed if it is incompatible with other social rules. Government regulatory initiatives are often challenged in court because someone asserts that they conflict with some other existing law. Private regulatory programs face the same risk. The obvious danger for these programs is that they will run afoul of antitrust laws. So far at least, American antitrust authorities have condoned what might have been seen as a collusive initiative designed to reduce competition, increase the fixed costs of doing business in such a way as to disadvantage smaller firms, or both. Clearly this cannot guarantee that all self-regulatory programs will escape such scrutiny. One might expect, however, that reasonable antitrust authorities would tolerate self-regulatory programs if the competitive asymmetries are not too sharp and the social benefits of the program seem clear.

Third, any regulatory program must serve the interests of enough companies and other actors that opponents cannot assemble a coalition capable of blocking it. In the case of government programs, legislators, activists, or other "policy entrepreneurs" can sometimes force regulatory programs on industries even if all the firms in the industry oppose them. With private regulation, not only is the active support of some firms a necessity, but these firms must be able to overcome opposition from the others.

In the chemical industry, in the mid-1980s, opposition was almost nonexistent. When Responsible Care was established, the chemical industry faced the risk not just of some adverse publicity, but of punitive regulation that would have dramatically impaired the managerial flexibility of its firms. The crisis was industry-wide rather than firm-specific: an accident at a small chemical firm would have had the same kind of regulatory consequences for Dow or DuPont as an accident at one of their own plants. Thus the industry leaders were trying to address two problems at once. One problem was the real or perceived deterioration of environmental quality that arose from the companies' operations; clearly this environmental quality is a public good. The other was erosion of the industry's reputation and its ability to manage itself; reputation and managerial latitude are "club goods," or public goods for the firms within the industry. The intimate connection between the environmental public good and the managerial club goods enabled the initiative to succeed.

A fourth condition for success is the inclusion of all important competitors within an industry. This requirement is at the root of the

apparent tension between environmental protection and a liberal international trade regime. In a world of free trade, if producers in one nation agree to raise their costs to fund environmental measures, they risk collectively losing market share to competitors based in other countries not bound by this agreement. At the same time, supporters of liberal trade rules worry that environmental standards will be used as a veil for protectionism, buffering inefficient domestic producers from foreign competition. In fact, the North American Free Trade Agreement (NAFTA) was modified specifically to address fears that inappropriately lax or overly tight domestic environmental rules would skew trade patterns. The revision provided for the creation of a Commission on Environmental Cooperation and established mechanisms to settle disputes among the parties.[13] Private attempts at collective action will founder if they do not include all of the producers of the good in question and its close substitutes, no matter where these firms are based.

Here again, the CMA confronted a fortuitous set of circumstances. Many of the firms in the chemical industry have a truly global presence, with manufacturing facilities throughout the industrial world. The presence of firms with manufacturing operations in many countries facilitates the transfer of technology and managerial ideas. Equally important, global firms are significant actors in the chemical industries of developing countries, where governments otherwise might be tempted to allow firms to externalize environmental costs. The CMA's ability to export Responsible Care to developing countries has played an important role in the program's success.

Fifth, any regulatory program must have credible mechanisms for standard setting, monitoring, and enforcement. Responsible Care came by these fortuitously, as a consequence of the structure of the chemical industry. The manufacture of a particular commodity chemical does not differ significantly from place to place: technologies are well understood, and manufacturing equipment is traded freely. In consequence, a perchloroethylene plant in Singapore looks similar to one in Louisiana, and a single set of technical standards could be written that would logically apply to both. Further, firms in commodity chemical businesses routinely buy and sell intermediate products from one another, giving them both knowledge about each other's operations and a mechanism by which to enforce any agreements, although American antitrust authorities would not be expected to permit the CMA to

make compliance with responsible care an explicit requirement for doing business with its members.

Finally, if private regulation is to succeed as an approach to increased profits, the architects of the regulatory program must have some cost advantage that they can exploit under the new regulatory regime. In the case of Responsible Care, the large companies that were the driving force behind the program enjoyed advantages over smaller firms due to economies of scope in pollution control. Economies of scale may be significant as well—pollution control equipment for a plant that makes 50 million pounds of carbon tetrachloride a year may cost less than twice as much as the equivalent equipment for a 25-million-pound plant—but the more significant cost savings may occur at the firm level. A company with $10 billion in chemical revenues does not require a hundred times as many lawyers, auditors, environmental engineers, and so on as a firm with $100 million in revenues. Regulatory programs that impose fixed costs on all participants tend to favor the large at the expense of the small.

For further insight into how industry structure and economic fundamentals influence the success of self-regulatory programs, it is instructive to examine an industry whose basic structure makes self-regulation considerably more difficult than it has been for the chemical manufacturers.

THE WOOD PRODUCTS INDUSTRY'S
SUSTAINABLE FORESTRY INITIATIVE

In October 1994, the American Forest & Paper Association (AF&PA) launched a private regulatory program called the Sustainable Forestry Initiative (SFI). The AF&PA's members include all of the largest wood products companies in the United States, as well as numerous smaller companies; total membership at the time of the initiative's establishment was about 200 firms. Together these companies controlled over 50 million acres of American timberland and accounted for over $160 billion in revenue from basic forest products like lumber, plywood, pulp, paper, and paperboard.

Like the CMA's Responsible Care program, the SFI developed in response to serious public relations problems. In this case the difficulties arose from widespread clear-cutting, loss of wildlife habitat, and other aesthetic or ecological damages to the companies' timberlands. According to the SFI's autobiography, the initiative was "developed by

professional foresters, conservationists and scientists who recognized the public's demand for genuine change in the practice of forestry—action, not just words."[14]

Also like Responsible Care, the SFI includes overall statements of principle, as well as an "action plan" encompassing objectives for member companies, implementation guidelines, and performance measures. The central part of the association's statement of basic principles discusses "the AF&PA membership's belief that forest landowners have an important stewardship responsibility and commitment to society." The first of the principles commits AF&PA members "to practice sustainable forestry to meet the needs of the present without compromising the ability of future generations to meet their own needs by practicing a land stewardship ethic which integrates the reforestation, managing, growing, nurturing, and harvesting of trees for useful products with the conservation of soil, air and water quality, wildlife and fish habitat, and aesthetics." Other principles relate to the protection of "forest and lands of special significance (e.g., biologically, geologically, or historically significant)," the continuous improvement of forest practices, and the monitoring, measurement, and enforcement of companies' results.[15]

As its name implies, the initiative focuses on timberlands management. Environmental impacts that arise in the manufacture of pulp and paper, lumber, and other products are not included. For this reason, the initiative is of interest mostly to companies that own timberland. Nine of the twelve objectives in the SFI's action plan relate only to such companies (e.g., "promptly reforest harvested areas"; "minimize the visual impact" of harvests; "contribute to biodiversity by enhancing landscape diversity and providing an array of habitats"). Two of the remaining objectives relate to public reporting and opportunities for public comment on the initiative. The twelfth objective calls on member companies to inculcate the same kinds of sustainability practices in the entities from which they purchase timber. [16]

As in the case of Responsible Care, "good-faith progress in implementing the [SFI] Action Plan" is required for continued membership in the trade association.[17] In 1995 and 1996, according to the association, "a few companies decided not to commit to the SFI, and subsequently resigned their membership to protest the cost of complying with the action plan. And 15 company memberships were terminated after the companies failed to commit to the SFI."[18] By 1998, AF&PA membership was roughly 130 companies, down from about 200 a few years before.[19]

The association itself does not formally track reasons for resignations, so the lost memberships could not be traced directly to the SFI. But according to one industry participant, the defections occurred principally among small firms engaged in timber production, logging, and lumber manufacture in the American South, businesses whose independent owner-managers resented being "dictated to on how to manage their land" either by government agencies or by their trade group.[20] At the same time, however, all of the *Fortune* 500–sized, vertically integrated members of the AF&PA remained in the organization, and total acreage owned by members actually increased after the initiative began.

The AF&PA assembled a group of forest scientists from universities, government, and environmental groups to serve as an expert review panel on SFI. These foresters express cautious optimism about the program in statements in the SFI's annual reports: "Those panel members who have been involved throughout the process have become convinced that the majority of the forest products industry has genuinely committed to achieving the goals of the SFI."[21] The panel members also observe that more information is necessary to assess progress toward sustainability, however that term is defined. They stress the need both for "performance measures relating to wildlife habitat and biodiversity considerations" and for "credible verification" of companies' forest management practices. Finally, the panel members call attention to the "need for the SFI program to relate to the international community" in developing internationally applicable standards and indicators for sustainable forestry. AF&PA members and staff are working in all of these areas.

Meanwhile, environmentalists have criticized the AF&PA program on substantive and procedural grounds. Paul Ketcham of the Audubon Society told a reporter that the association set too low a hurdle for its members, arguing that the initiative "does nothing to address the abuses and damages of clear-cutting practices." He further argued that the expert panel drew its environmental members from "extremely conservative" groups like the Izaak Walton League of America and the Conservation Fund rather than from organizations like his own.[22]

INDUSTRY STRUCTURE AND COLLECTIVE ACTION

The AF&PA's initiative provides an interesting counterpoint to Responsible Care. The wood products industry resembles the chemical

business in several ways that facilitate collective action. In both industries, a few very large firms coexist with a large number of midsize and
much smaller ones. In the forest products business, these large firms
bore the start-up costs—both in out-of-pocket cash and in management
time and expertise—necessary to get the SFI off the ground. Furthermore, in forest products, as in chemicals, the collective action proposed
by the large firms has been found (so far at least) to be consistent with
other rules of behavior like the antitrust laws.

At the same time, other factors make the forest products executives' collective action problem thornier than the one faced by the
chemical executives. First, compared with the public affairs crisis in the
aftermath of Bhopal, the foresters' public relations problems are not
nearly so critical, diminishing the incentive for firms to play along. Second, the firms in the American forest products business do not have the
geographic scope that facilitated the efforts of their chemicals counterparts to export Responsible Care to other nations. In chemicals, a few
large firms are active in North America, Europe, Asia, and the developing countries. In forest products, although the products are heavily traded and markets are global, most firms serve the world market from a
geographically well-defined base. Although a few large American forest
products firms have operations in Latin America, most confine their
operations to North America; and although they sell products in Europe
and Asia, none is active in production on either continent. This situation makes the international transfer of any management ideas difficult,
especially those involving collective action.

Further, standard setting is inherently more difficult in forestry
than in chemical manufacturing. As mentioned earlier, a chemical
plant in Oregon can be virtually identical to one in Alabama or Maine
(or Sweden or Malaysia). Because of the differences in forest ecology
among these areas, by contrast, forest practice standards in different
regions will differ widely, making standard setting more difficult. If the
objective of the SFI is to improve the environmental performance of
firms while avoiding new rules that are so tight that firms simply give
up the effort, a more diverse mix of production processes and management styles—not surprising in an industry where practices are driven
largely by natural forest conditions—makes this task more difficult.

This is a particular example of a more general problem that any
private regulatory initiative will encounter. Some firms will have to bear
higher costs than others to comply with any regulation, public or pri-

vate. The architects of private regulatory programs need to consider the costs that different possible rules will impose on various firms. Private rules that err on the side of laxity may not accomplish their objectives, whether these include improving the industry's reputation, forestalling government regulation, imposing asymmetrical costs on rivals, or all three. On the other hand, private rules that impose extremely high costs on the laggards in the industry may trigger widespread defections from the coalition. This, too, may lead to a failure of the regulatory initiative if the accomplishment of its goals requires universal or near-universal compliance. Successful standard setting thus demands constant attention to the costs imposed on firms, even though these may not be precisely knowable.

Related problems arise with respect to enforcement. The forest products trade association has already lost several members over the SFI; no one has yet lost CMA membership because of Responsible Care infractions. The ultimate enforcement mechanism for the chemical firms is the threat that the established firms, in compliance with Responsible Care codes, will refuse to do business with violators. The forest products firms' ability to make a similar threat is limited because business among firms is much smaller than in chemicals. They can expel violators from the trade association, but the penalty to the expelled firm will be bad publicity, rather than bad publicity plus loss of markets for inputs and outputs. Despite this apparent advantage, however, the chemical firms' ability to invoke these ultimate sanctions may be constrained by antitrust considerations. In other words, the more credible and fierce the enforcement mechanism of a private regulatory program, the more likely it is to attract unfavorable attention from government regulators.

It is clear from these examples that firms' ability to make private regulation work depends on the structure of their industries and on the nature of the problems they confront. It depends, as well, on the institutional structures that govern environmental decision making and on the relationships between the private and public sectors. Executives thinking of initiating a private regulatory program need to consider carefully the conditions for success that are discussed here, and to decide whether the fundamental economic characteristics of their industries are conducive to a successful private regulatory program. The idea that an industry's basic structure constrains the ability of its firms to reach collaborative solutions to joint problems, first studied by

business historian Alfred Chandler in the context of nineteenth-century trusts, is no less applicable to environmental collaboration at the beginning of the twenty-first century.[23]

RAISING THE BAR FOR COMPETITORS: THE STRATEGIC USE OF GOVERNMENT REGULATION

Instead of trying to solve collective action problems without relying on the government, a firm might seek to achieve both financial and environmental objectives by actively managing the government regulatory system. The stereotype that business executives dislike all regulation is incorrect. Business executives have long been aware that government intervention in markets can benefit particular firms, and students of government behavior have contributed to our understanding of the interplay between business people and government officials. In the late 1950s, Anthony Downs analyzed the processes of democratic government as arising from the rational, self-interested behavior of politicians, just as economists analyze market performance as arising from the self-interested behavior of entrepreneurs.[24] University of Chicago economists George Stigler and Sam Peltzman developed this line of reasoning into what has come to be called the economic or positive theory of regulation.[25] For example, Stigler noted that both doctors and beauticians are able to charge higher prices than they could if state licensing requirements did not restrict entry into their professions. Stigler pointed out that both groups receive this sort of regulatory protection even though the normative public policy case for licensing might be somewhat stronger for doctors. Stanford economist and former World Bank official Anne Krueger coined the term "rent-seeking" to describe the efforts of business people to skew government policies in ways favorable to themselves.[26]

In this context, political debates about environmental policy resemble debates about any other public policy: they are opportunities for firms to capture value. Recall from chapter 1 that any government intervention in markets will increase or decrease social well-being and at the same time will bring about transfers of wealth from one group to another. From the viewpoint of the positive theorists of regulation, environmental regulation can help firms by restricting entry, by imposing disproportionate cost penalties on competitors, or both. And the firms

seeking environmental regulation find themselves in de facto alliances with their putative enemies, the environmentalists, a phenomenon labeled "Bootleggers and Baptists" by economist Bruce Yandle.[27]

Many firms and industry associations hire advocates to make their cases to legislators, regulators, and judges, and they commission studies to persuade these government officials of the virtue of their positions. The focus here, however, is not on routine lobbying operations, although these may be important in protecting a firm's interests. Instead, this discussion concentrates on marketplace activities that make it easier for government regulators to adopt policies that benefit the firm that initiated the changes. By demonstrating the feasibility of a particular technology, for example, firms can sometimes induce regulators to require it of competitors, who are unlikely to be able to match the cost of the first mover.[28]

This cost asymmetry could exist for several reasons. New entrants, in particular, might find it easier to install a particular technology than incumbent firms that would need to retrofit equipment. More generally, the selection of technologies is not random but is based on conscious selection by the first mover. Presumably, that firm will not engage in this tactic unless it has found a technology at which it is better than its competitors.

The technology in question could be a tangible mechanism for reducing pollution, like a device that removes sulfur dioxide from the gas leaving a boiler. The same logic would apply, however, if the technology were less tangible than machinery or equipment; it might, for example, be a practice of information disclosure, or a process for public participation in resource allocation decisions. In the case of these intangible technologies, the arguments about the higher cost of retrofitting still apply, although what raises the costs for followers is not a technical limitation but the cost of changing established ways of doing business. So we can define "technology" very broadly. What matters is that the technology is less expensive for the original firm than for its competitors, and that it fosters meaningful pressure for industry-wide adoption.

DUPONT: CHLOROFLUOROCARBONS

In the late 1980s, E.I. DuPont de Nemours and Company (DuPont) worked to bring about changes in the regulation of ozone-depleting chlorofluorocarbons (CFCs) that transformed a crowded,

low-margin commodity chemical business into a potentially much more lucrative business in CFC substitutes. It is not yet clear whether this approach has been entirely successful, since so far the structure of those new markets is not as favorable as DuPont and its large competitors might reasonably have anticipated. The history of CFCs and their substitutes shows both the importance of government regulatory structures in influencing commercial opportunities for companies and the difficulty in analyzing the relationships between regulation and market structure.

DuPont invented most of the CFCs beginning in the 1930s. Chemically stable, low in toxicity, and nonflammable, these compounds were seen as an almost miraculous improvement over many of the substances in use at the time as refrigerants, blowing agents, aerosol propellants, and solvents.

DuPont's CFC patents expired in the 1960s and early 1970s. The compounds were fairly easy to make, and by the early 1970s the CFC markets were crowded with producers. Fixed costs were high, and once the new entrants had crashed the party, the companies' ability to compete on any basis but price was limited. Then, in 1974, Sherry Rowland and Mario Molina, atmospheric chemists at the University of California at Irvine, hypothesized for the first time that CFCs could drift upward and catalyze the destruction of ozone molecules in the stratosphere. Because stratospheric ozone screens the Earth's inhabitants from ultraviolet (UV) radiation, and because such radiation contributes to the incidence of skin cancer, regulators in the United States reacted to this information by banning the use of CFCs as aerosols as of 1978.[29]

At the time, American use of CFCs accounted for about half the world total, and about half of American CFCs were used in aerosols. The demand-side restriction of EPA's aerosol ban led to a collapse in CFC prices as American firms scrambled to keep their plants running full. The ban worsened the already unappealing economics of CFC manufacture in the United States, as the excess capacity exacerbated price competition. Although in the mid-1980s DuPont had a 50 percent American market share and a 25 percent share of worldwide CFC capacity, selling roughly $600 million worth of CFCs a year, its margins were miserable, limping along below 3 percent of sales.[30] To take a specific example, CFC-12, the dominant compound in refrigeration and air-conditioning applications, was selling for about sixty-five cents per pound in 1985; per-pound production costs for DuPont, an efficient producer, came to about sixty-four cents.

Meanwhile, only Canada, Norway, and Sweden followed the U.S. regulators' lead in banning aerosols. Demand, especially for refrigeration and foam blowing, continued to grow. By the mid-1980s, world CFC production had again risen above the levels it had attained before the initial regulation, and the U.S. EPA was again predicting significant increases in skin cancer incidence and other adverse consequences from heightened UV exposure.[31]

In 1974, shortly after Rowland and Molina first published their findings, DuPont's CEO took out newspaper ads to promise that DuPont would stop production of the compounds "should reputable evidence show . . . a health hazard."[32] After the 1978 aerosol ban, however, DuPont led an unusual consortium of American CFC producers and consumers, called the Alliance for Responsible CFC Policy. The alliance opposed further regulation in general and unilateral U.S. action in particular. During the early 1980s, DuPont continued to invest in basic ozone science to better predict future regulatory developments, but its research on substitutes for CFCs was limited, since preliminary results showed them to be considerably more expensive and less effective than CFCs.

In 1986, more sophisticated atmospheric models and new empirical evidence strengthened the scientific case for ozone depletion by CFCs. The critical event from a public policy standpoint came in 1985, when British scientists found a "hole" in the ozone layer above Antarctica (not literally a hole, but a large region over which the stratospheric ozone concentrations were markedly lower). In light of this evidence, the EPA projected that increased UV exposure could doom up to 3 million Americans to premature death from skin cancer over the next 150 years or so.[33] DuPont persuaded its partners in the alliance to change their position and to support the Montreal Protocol, an international accord that called for a 50 percent cutback of CFC production, from a 1986 baseline, by the end of the century.

The Montreal Protocol, negotiated in 1987, was international rather than domestic, and it restricted CFC supply rather than demand. CFC prices were expected to spike wildly in response to regulatorily driven shortages, attaining values ten to fifteen times higher than the pre-Protocol levels.[34] This could occur because, even though their prices had been driven all the way down to production costs by competitive pressure, the compounds were enormously valuable in use: for example, unless it was replenished with CFCs that cost a few

dollars to make, a commercial air-conditioning system that cost many thousands of dollars would be useless to its owners. Because so many varieties of capital-intensive equipment—household refrigerators, the cooling systems in grocery stores and warehouses, air conditioners for buildings and vehicles—were designed to use CFCs, the Montreal Protocol promised to transform an unattractive business into a gold mine, with a structure so lucrative that the U.S. Congress started talking about taxing the windfall profits of the producers.[35]

But DuPont was not yet finished. In March 1988, new scientific findings came to light establishing a definitive causal link between CFCs and the ozone hole over Antarctica, and revealing thinning of the ozone layer above temperate (and populated) regions as well. DuPont responded to these findings by announcing that it was living up to its 1974 promise and getting out of CFC manufacturing altogether. Instead, the firm said, it planned to focus on substitute products. This announcement accelerated the market's transition from CFCs to a new generation of products that were far less damaging to stratospheric ozone but cost considerably more to make. And because DuPont possessed both patents and unpatentable know-how relating to these new products, it was able to shut many of its old CFC competitors out of these new markets. By 1990, diplomats and regulators were convinced of the technological feasibility of comprehensive substitution out of CFCs; they amended the Montreal Protocol to require industrial countries to phase out all CFC production by the end of the century, with developing countries following shortly thereafter. The same year, the U.S. Congress passed a tax on CFCs of several dollars per pound, effectively confiscating the windfall that DuPont would have reaped had it attempted to milk the CFC markets.

More recent developments in the markets for CFC substitutes have been much less favorable to the substitutes' producers. Technological barriers to entry into the substitutes business were lower than DuPont anticipated. In addition, instead of converting to non-chlorinated fluorocarbons, as DuPont and other producers hoped, some users made more radical changes to "not in kind" substitutes.[36] For example, instead of changing from CFC-113 to other fluorocarbons, some manufacturers of printed circuit boards started cleaning the boards with pressurized carbon dioxide. Moreover, illegal CFC imports from countries where production is still allowed under the protocol and its successor treaties have depressed the prices of CFC substitutes. In

1995, American law enforcement officials described CFCs as "the most lucrative contraband after illicit drugs."[37] These factors have depressed the returns on investments in CFC substitutes to which DuPont, along with other large CFC producers like AlliedSignal, ICI, and Elf Atochem, committed themselves in the late 1980s and early 1990s.[38]

NECESSARY CONDITIONS
FOR THE STRATEGIC USE OF REGULATION

As before, we can study this case for clues about the factors that influence the likelihood that a firm can successfully use government regulation as a source of strategic advantage. Obviously, the option of putting pressure on one's competitors by influencing the behavior of government regulators or other groups is not open to all firms. We want to know what conditions are sufficient or necessary for this approach to be successful. It turns out that these are closely related to the conditions for successful private regulatory initiatives discussed earlier in this chapter.

First and most straightforward, a firm that tries to pursue this approach must have some competitive advantage under the new regime. DuPont reasonably expected to enjoy such an advantage, since it had invested more heavily in CFC substitutes than its competitors. In the absence of some prospective competitive advantage, on the other hand, there is no reason for a firm to pursue regulatory intervention in the first place. Put another way, there is no long-term benefit in a strategy of pure rent-seeking. Without some complementary investment in the marketplace or some preexisting source of competitive advantage, the payoff to an investment in regulatory change will be zero: the firm and its rivals will compete away the economic surplus they are trying to divert into their own pockets.

Second, a firm that uses government regulation as a competitive weapon must be able to convince customers, rivals, and regulators that the underlying technological innovation is workable. DuPont was able single-handedly to move the markets served by CFCs toward a new set of products in part because it had long held a position of technological leadership, lending credibility to its announcements about finding substitutes and withdrawing from CFC production.

Technological credibility, however, is not enough. Strategies of this sort will succeed only if the regulators in question have jurisdiction

over the entire group of competitors. DuPont's announcement came only after the Montreal Protocol had established a regulatory framework that affected all CFC producers. An effort to tighten CFC regulation in the United States alone, even if successful, would not have allowed DuPont to introduce its higher-priced substitutes. And one of the main difficulties for DuPont's strategy has arisen because the protocol allows developing countries to wait several years before ceasing production of CFCs: once the CFCs are legally produced in those nations, it is difficult to prevent their illegal importation into the United States and other industrialized countries.

More generally, attempts to "raise the bar" for competitors by exerting pressure for changes in domestic regulation will succeed only if the product in question is not traded, if foreign producers' offerings can somehow be excluded, or if the regulatory effort can be coordinated with similar (and successful) regulatory efforts in other nations. To provide a counterexample, a Canadian producer of wood pulp may be able to change provincial or even Canadian regulations in ways that enhance its cost position relative to domestic competitors, but it is unlikely to be able to increase the costs of rivals located in Brazil or Indonesia. To the extent that such a firm competes with products from countries with lighter regulatory standards, its tactics, from a collective action standpoint, seem unlikely to be successful.[39]

FACTORS INFLUENCING GOVERNMENT INTERVENTION

DuPont relied on its credibility as a source of information about the technical feasibility of its innovation and on the existence of a regulatory entity that could control the whole market. But another condition was necessary as well, and is necessary more generally if strategies involving regulation are to succeed. It is analogous to one of the conditions considered in the last chapter: product differentiation strategies succeed only if customers are willing to pay. Likewise, strategies involving government regulatory change can succeed only if the government is willing to regulate. The question becomes: what will influence this willingness? The answers involve the distribution and magnitude of the costs and benefits of the regulatory program.

Clearly, groups that would be adversely affected by a proposed rule change can be expected to try to prevent it. In the environmental arena, political opposition to rules often takes the form of questioning

the scientific basis for a proposed rule, or of arguing that the benefits of the rule are oversold. But in the environmental arena or elsewhere, such opposition may also take the form of more naked power politics. In evaluating the probability that a regulatory initiative will be successful, one must understand how widely its costs and benefits are distributed. Individual people weigh their own costs and benefits of participating in political decision making. Other things being equal, government initiatives whose costs are spread over a large group of people are more likely to succeed than those whose costs are concentrated, a fact that has been noted and studied by political scientists. By the same token, initiatives whose benefits are narrowly concentrated have a better chance of succeeding than those whose benefits are widely shared.[40]

A classic example of this phenomenon arises in international trade. The group of producers that benefits from an import quota or a prohibitively high tariff is small relative to the number of consumers who will be adversely affected. Suppose that millions of consumers of sugar pay a nickel extra per pound because of import quotas or tariffs; they will not spend much time lobbying for the trade restrictions' abolition. But for the domestic producers of sugar, the extra nickel of revenue per pound is worth spending massive amounts of time and money to maintain. Hence even if the trade restrictions result in an overall loss of social well-being, government officials might retain the quotas and tariffs.

Manifestations of similar logic in the environmental field are numerous. For example, legislation to reduce acid rain by controlling sulfur dioxide emissions finally passed at about the time that people in Congress realized that tradable permits could be a mechanism for spreading costs over a larger number of utility ratepayers, as discussed in chapter 7.

It follows from this argument that policy initiatives whose costs are hidden from those who bear them will be more likely to succeed than those whose costs are readily visible. For example, in the United States in the 1970s, sewage treatment plants were funded from the general federal revenue in a way that spread the costs of construction over all taxpayers; taxpayers in Maine helped fund treatment of Missouri sewage, and vice versa, and the costs were effectively hidden from both groups. Laggard regions like the Boston area, which failed to take full advantage of this funding mechanism, are now paying for construction

of their sewage treatment plants with increases in water fees, presented in a highly visible manner directly to residential and commercial water users. This is proving to be a significant political problem.[41]

To return to the CFC case, the ability of refrigerator manufacturers, automobile companies, and other users of CFCs or their substitutes to pass on these costs to their own customers meant that the costs of the CFC phaseout were distributed widely. The producers of the substitutes were in an ideal position to pass on the cost increases: their products (e.g., the new refrigerants) accounted for a small fraction of their customers' total costs, yet they were essential to the performance of the customers' own products. Furthermore, the industries that used CFCs either were oligopolistic (like the auto industry) or faced very inelastic demand for their outputs (like providers of industrial refrigeration equipment) and so could reasonably expect to pass on their cost increases to their end consumers. Hence, the costs of the CFC phaseout were spread across a large number of ultimate consumers.

The distribution of the costs and benefits of a regulatory program is not, however, the only factor affecting the likelihood that the government will regulate. The magnitude of those costs and benefits matters as well. If the net social benefits (i.e., social benefits minus social costs) of a regulatory proposal are large, governments will be more likely to enact it. Given the immediately preceding discussion of distributional consequences, any mention of net social benefits may seem unduly idealistic about government motives. But the idea that regulatory initiatives whose benefits greatly exceed their costs are more likely to succeed finds both logical and empirical support.

For example, by the mid-1980s the problem of stratospheric ozone depletion was clearly a likely candidate for further regulation, and not only because the costs of a CFC phaseout would be widely spread. Beyond those distributional considerations, there was a near-unanimous scientific consensus that depletion of stratospheric ozone was occurring and that CFCs were responsible. Furthermore, the benefits of protecting stratospheric ozone were considered substantial, especially because there was a reasonable basis to conclude that cancer incidence would increase as a result of the depletion of the ozone layer. Given conventional ideas about the value of human life, the benefits of slowing ozone depletion outweighed the costs by a huge margin.[42]

The magnitude of costs and benefits determines the value that can be created by a regulatory program, and a scientific consensus about the

underlying problem strengthens government policy makers' beliefs in their estimates of those benefits and costs. A scientific and social consensus that a problem is serious is not a sufficient condition for a government intervention to take hold, exactly because of the distributional questions just discussed. Nonetheless, one does not have to be a Pollyanna to think that in the long run, on average, in democratic societies, government programs that actually increase social well-being are more likely to arise and persist than those that do not. Governments can use their power to effect wealth transfers, and do so consistently. They do so in the environmental arena and elsewhere, sometimes deliberately (e.g., through food stamp programs) and very often as an unintended consequence of pursuing some other objective (as when government programs to reduce acid rain increase the profits of railroads that transport low-sulfur coal). But, as University of Chicago Nobel Prize winner Gary Becker pointed out, governments have a better chance of implementing a particular program and ensuring its continuation if it actually creates value, because by definition such a program will generate more benefits for its beneficiaries than it will generate costs for those who must pay for it.[43] Problems whose potential solutions have high benefit-cost ratios are, by definition, opportunities for government to create value. On the other hand, problems whose solutions have significant benefits are commonly, and appropriately, left unaddressed if the costs of the solutions are also extremely high.

No one knows whether the case he or she is managing is the average case, and no one gets to manage the long run without surviving the short run. A political assessment of whose ox will be gored cannot be omitted, and is likely to be the best predictor of short-run government behavior and the constraints on executives' ability to influence it. At the same time, however, a realistic assessment of the science and economics of a particular problem is also essential in trying to predict government policy, in part for the reasons sketched out by Becker. The story of DuPont and the Montreal Protocol shows the importance both of the overall costs and benefits of a particular kind of government intervention, and of its distributional consequences and short-run political implications.

More generally, the same story is commonly cited as a cause for optimism about the ability of governments and companies to address complicated environmental problems. The Montreal Protocol was an impressive accomplishment, although this chapter has set out a number

of preconditions for its success that might not be common in other industrial and environmental settings. It is important, however, not to oversell the story: it is not one of the fabled "win-win-win" situations that some observers hold to be common in the environmental arena, in which producers, consumers, and the environment all benefit.[44] The producers and the environment certainly benefit. Consumers of refrigerators and air conditioners win in the sense that they will benefit from the "services" provided by an undepleted layer of ozone in the stratosphere. But consumers of refrigerators and air conditioners, seen only as consumers of those products, cannot be better off after the Montreal Protocol than before: they will have to spend more to obtain the same service. Even this success story is not really a "triple win."

This chapter concludes with an even more complicated example of regulatory policy and strategic advantage.

REFORMULATED GASOLINE IN CALIFORNIA

In August 1989 the Atlantic Richfield Company (ARCO), headquartered in Los Angeles, announced that its California retail outlets would start selling a reformulated gasoline designed to produce lower emissions of carbon monoxide and hydrocarbons. Nearly a decade later, ARCO and the other companies active in the refining and marketing businesses in California continue to cooperate with federal, state, and local regulators in the search for "cleaner" gasolines, a search in which narrow technical regulatory decisions can have significant impacts not only on air quality but also on barriers to mobility, market shares, and profit. But more recent scientific and political developments have created significant problems for this approach.

Vehicles contribute substantially to the air pollution levels in most major cities. Regulators distinguish two interrelated pollution problems. The first involves carbon monoxide, which is formed when fuels fail to burn completely. The second involves ground-level ozone, or smog, which is caused when hydrocarbons and oxides of nitrogen react in the presence of sunlight. (Ozone in the stratosphere, as discussed in the previous case example, is a naturally occurring and critically important environmental asset, but the same compound at ground level causes damage to human respiratory systems and to plant life.) Vehicle exhaust contains both oxides of nitrogen and hydrocarbons, and the hydrocarbons can also evaporate from the tank when no combustion is taking place.

To control the seemingly intractable smog problems of cities like Los Angeles, legislators and regulators have undertaken a series of increasingly expensive measures. federal legislation in 1970 gave important roles to regulators at both the federal and the state level. Federal officials set national ambient air quality standards for pollutants like carbon monoxide and ozone. They also established emissions standards in particular cases where national uniformity was considered important: factories constructed after the legislation was passed, for example, had to adhere to national standards to avoid competition among states for new investment through lenient regulation. State officials, meanwhile, were responsible for devising programs to make sure they reached the federal ambient standards. In California, this responsibility was further delegated to county-level or regional single-purpose agencies, of which the South Coast Air Quality Management District (SCAQMD), with authority over the Los Angeles region, was the most important. Air pollution programs in the 1970s and 1980s targeted stationary sources like electric power plants, where initial potential improvements were dramatic and where command-and-control regulation could be easily administered. But they also sought to control pollution from mobile sources: first, the federal government imposed tight restrictions on emissions from new vehicles, and many states later required emissions tests for cars and trucks already on the road.[45]

Despite this aggressive governmental behavior, many urban areas in the late 1980s were not close to meeting the ambient standards for ozone and carbon monoxide. Hence, governments at several levels began considering regulatory proposals that would have engineered large-scale switches toward methanol, ethanol, electricity, or other ways of powering vehicles. In March 1989, regulators at the SCAQMD announced a twenty-year plan to phase out gasoline-powered cars in the Los Angeles area. The California Air Resources Board, the state agency in Sacramento, was contemplating mandated use of methanol for smog control in Los Angeles. And the Bush administration, beginning its work to amend the Clean Air Act, was known to be contemplating an ethanol or methanol requirement.[46]

Each of these alternatives would address the ozone and carbon monoxide problems to varying degrees and in different ways, and each presented its own problems. Electric vehicles decouple the combustion that powers a car from the car itself, so that the combustion can take place at a power plant in Bakersfield while the car is in Los Angeles. (If the power plant is hydroelectric or nuclear, combustion can be avoided

altogether, although dams and reactors present their own environmental and public relations problems.) Electric vehicles are expensive, however, and their introduction does nothing to control the emissions of existing cars. Turning to alternative fuels, we find important similarities and differences between methanol and ethanol. Both are oxygenates; they contain oxygen as well as carbon and hydrogen, and fuels that contain them will generate less carbon monoxide and unburned hydrocarbons when burned. But methanol, made from natural gas, causes corrosion problems in vehicle fuel lines and engines; it also contributes to the volatility of fuels, and hence to their propensity to evaporate and contribute to ozone levels. Further, it absorbs water when transported in pipelines, so it cannot be blended with the gasoline at a central refinery; instead, it must be blended closer to the end consumer, which increases transportation and storage costs.[47] Ethanol, while less corrosive, has the same volatility and water absorption problems, and the additional difficulty (from the point of view of an oil company) that it is made from vegetable materials in facilities dedicated to this process. (This last characteristic is, of course, exactly what makes ethanol appealing to farmers, agribusiness giant Archer Daniels Midland, and politicians who represent those interests.)

ARCO's first reformulated gasoline (RFG), introduced in 1989, and called Emission Control One (EC-1), was intended to substitute for leaded gasoline in older automobiles. Over the next year both ARCO and its principal California retail competitors, including Chevron, Shell, and Exxon, introduced RFG products to replace premium unleaded fuel burned in newer cars.[48] Instead of methanol or ethanol, these gasolines use an alternative oxygenate called methyl tertiary butyl ether (MTBE). Unlike ethanol, MTBE is made from petroleum feedstocks in traditional refineries; also unlike ethanol, it can be blended directly into gasoline at a refinery before the fuel is transmitted by pipeline to distribution centers. ARCO initially estimated that EC-1 would cost two cents per gallon more to make than traditional leaded gasoline, but that the company would absorb this cost.[49]

The RFGs eased regulatory and legislative pressure toward the compulsory introduction of electric vehicles or the mandated use of methanol or ethanol fuels, any of which would have been undesirable from the gasoline marketers' point of view. Further, the RFGs created a new barrier to participation in the California market. Producing MTBE is not a difficult operation technically, but an existing refinery requires some modification to produce the ether. The addition of oxygenates

requires other changes in the gasoline recipe which require further refinery modifications. ARCO estimated in 1990 that it would spend "$300 million to $400 million in refinery changes" to make RFG.[50]

In November 1990, Congress passed amendments to the Clean Air Act that stipulated that all gasoline sold in nine designated urban areas after January 1, 1995, would have to be reformulated to contain less than 1 percent benzene, less than 25 percent total aromatic compounds, and at least 2 percent oxygen (measured by aggregated molecular weight). The federal RFG standards were aimed at reducing ground-level ozone, and the nine areas were those with the highest ozone levels: Baltimore, Chicago, Hartford, Houston, Los Angeles, Milwaukee, New York, Philadelphia, and San Diego. The U.S. EPA regulations implementing this legislation went further, requiring gasoline sold in these areas to meet even tighter standards starting in the year 2000. The 1990 Clean Air Act Amendments also specified that gasoline sold in the large number of urban areas that are out of compliance with ambient standards for carbon monoxide be at least 2.7 percent oxygen by weight.[51]

In November 1991, the California Air Resources Board announced its own standards for RFG. Because so much of the state was required under the federal rules to sell reformulated and oxygenated gasoline, the board simplified things by requiring a single type of fuel statewide beginning in the spring of 1996. Compared with the federal standards for reformulated gasolines, the California gasoline requirements allow fewer total aromatics, lower vapor pressures, and lower distillation temperatures. The latter two requirements make the use of ethanol difficult, and almost all California RFG uses MTBE. California RFG costs five to fifteen cents more per gallon to produce than conventional gasolines, compared with an increased cost of two to five cents per gallon for federal RFG. Even after the federal standards tighten in the year 2000, the California standards will be stricter still: California gasolines will satisfy the federal requirements, but not vice versa.[52] After the new rules went into effect, about 95 percent of California gasoline contained MTBE, which made up about 10 percent of the total volume of gasoline in the state.[53]

In the spring of 1996, as the California RFG standards went into effect, gasoline prices in California spiked markedly. Initially ARCO attributed the price increases in part to RFG production cost increases, but it later retreated from this position. Weather conditions, uncertainty about crude oil supplies, and technical problems that caused cutbacks in refinery operations made the effect of the regulatory change on

prices extremely difficult to determine.[54]

In 1997, MTBE was found to have contaminated municipal drinking water wells in the affluent City of Santa Monica, and officials predicted that the compound would contaminate groundwater supplies elsewhere in the state.[55] Since MTBE can cause cancer in laboratory animals, the Santa Monica findings led to ongoing uncertainty about the future regulatory climate for gasoline in California. Ethanol producers sensed an opportunity to invade the California markets, and third-place retailer Tosco sensed an opportunity to take market share from ARCO and Chevron by becoming the first company to introduce ethanol fuels.[56] ARCO and Chevron themselves split on federal legislation that would make it easier for California refiners to substitute other oxygenates for MTBE.[57] Opponents of MTBE use supported state-level legislation banning the substance. In August 1998, an environmental group called Communities for a Better Environment filed a suit against the major oil companies, seeking an immediate cessation of MTBE use and compensation by the companies for groundwater contamination.[58]

THE CONDITIONS FOR SUCCESS REVISITED

The State of California's RFG rules appear to provide a strategic advantage for in-state refiners collectively. Producing California RFG requires dedicated assets, so that regulatory segmentation of the gasoline market is a technical possibility. Because of distance and pipeline constraints, an increase in gasoline prices in California would not have brought an immediate influx of supply from other states, even before the RFG standards were imposed. The Air Resources Board's rules make the substitution of non-California gasoline for California gasoline more difficult and hence increase the collective pricing power of the California marketers.

The conditions under which such an approach can succeed, discussed earlier in connection with the DuPont case, all apply in the case of the California gasoline refiners, although in a less splashy way. In the RFG case, the technological feasibility of the innovation was not disputed: MTBE is a well-known compound, and its production involves standard chemical engineering techniques. The relevant regulatory authority—the California Air Resources Board—holds sway over a distinct market differentiated by geographic reality as well as political constructs. In California, refinery capacity somewhat exceeds demand for gasoline, so that ordinarily the state is a net exporter. If the California

companies were to increase the prices of California RFG too far, they would provoke entry, but otherwise it may not pay out-of-state refiners to invest in the capacity to produce gasoline for the California market. Finally, willingness to regulate was clearly present: smog problems in Los Angeles have been a high-priority item on environmental agendas for decades, the costs of RFG were spread widely among the drivers of cars and the consumers of goods transported by truck (which is to say practically everyone in California), and at least initially it seemed to California politicians that the net effects of RFG were positive. It is impossible to verify that ARCO and its California competitors are benefiting from the regulations, since none of the companies publishes cost and profit data disaggregated by regional market, but the information that is publicly available is highly suggestive. On the other hand, the discovery of groundwater contamination by MTBE in the late 1990s creates doubts about the future of that particular compound in California and raises the possibility that the regulatory deck will be reshuffled.

Is the RFG story an example of a "win-win-win" situation? Even leaving the groundwater problems aside, the answer is no. To the extent that the California Air Resources Board standards benefit indigenous California refiners, they do so by transferring dollars from consumers of gasoline. California consumers of gasoline, considered only as consumers of gasoline, cannot be better off than they were before the introduction of RFG or than they would be under a single, less restrictive national standard, just as consumers of refrigerators and air conditioners, considered only as consumers of those goods, cannot be better off after the Montreal Protocol than before. On the other hand, while a national standard would increase competition in California, it would also impose unnecessary costs on areas with cleaner air and hence less pressing needs for reformulated gasolines. Further, the situation does have the desirable attribute that the consumers of the more expensive gasoline are also the consumers of the cleaner air, just as the consumers of more expensive air conditioners also benefit from the maintenance of the stratospheric ozone layer.

MULTIPLE MOTIVES
FOR CORPORATE ENVIRONMENTAL POLICY

As with the other cases in this chapter, it is possible to read several motives into ARCO's actions. Like DuPont, and like the leaders of

the CMA or the AF&PA, ARCO was motivated in part by a desire to manage regulatory risk: industry analysts noted that the introduction of RFG reduced the chance that "something would be rammed down [the oil companies'] throats."[59]

It is possible that ARCO and the other California refiners did not intend or even foresee the economic results of the state's gasoline policy. Simple positive models of government behavior, in which producers and consumers fully understand their interests and the amount of regulatory rents to be captured and then devote resources to capturing those rents, are useful first approximations. They understate, however, the difficulty of understanding how a regulatory proposal may alter markets. ARCO may have engineered its economic and political activity to bring about a more favorable market structure. But an alternative explanation, impossible to rule out, is that ARCO initiated its RFG policy as a device for regulatory risk management and discovered its consequences for value only by experience. Here, as elsewhere, motive is difficult to impute, but the story remains an enlightening example of the distributional consequences of environmental regulation, of the relationships between industry structure and the success of firms' environmental policies, and of the ways in which firms and governments can effectively collaborate for commercial and environmental benefit.

FORCING RIVALS to match one's own behavior is fundamentally different from environmental product differentiation (the topic of chapter 2). Which approach an innovator should adopt depends on the fundamental economic characteristics of the business, and in particular on the willingness of customers to pay for public goods. For example, DuPont executives responsible for chlorofluorocarbons could not realistically expect to differentiate their CFC substitutes. In the absence of regulation, willingness to pay the production cost differential was absent: DuPont's customers would not pay five dollars a pound for CFC substitutes when the CFCs themselves sold for under a dollar. So DuPont worked to bring about a regulatory solution. Monsanto and Ciba, with products that would reduce their customers' overall costs even in the absence of regulation, could create willingness to pay, so they chose differentiation strategies. Managers choosing between the two approaches must consider both industry economics and political circumstances to determine which is more likely to succeed.

In both cases on the strategic use of regulation in this chapter, the success of the strategies still was not clear as of mid-1999. In the case of DuPont, the threats to the approach arose partly because of the design and enforcement of the regulations. The Montreal Protocol and its successor treaties permitted CFC production in developing countries; it proved difficult for developed countries like the United States to prevent the illegal importation of these CFCs, and the illegal imports undercut the market for substitutes. Other threats to DuPont's approach, however, have arisen in the marketplace, independent of the regulatory structure. "Not in kind" substitutes have turned out to be more widely available and less expensive than DuPont and the other substitute manufacturers predicted. In the case of the California RFG producers, the use of MTBE turned out to be more problematic from an environmental and business standpoint than the companies anticipated when looking for ways to reduce air pollution from vehicles.

Similarly, the ultimate success of the private regulatory initiatives studied in this chapter cannot be guaranteed. Both Responsible Care and the Sustainable Forestry Initiative face unresolved questions about monitoring and enforcement: How can trade associations that lack formal regulatory authority create credible verification schemes for the rules they write? The forestry initiative faces, in addition, the problem that any standards tough enough to satisfy environmentalist pressures may lead to defections from the trade association, thus defeating one purpose of the initiative. It also faces the problem of how to move its standards into the international arena to avoid a competitive disadvantage with respect to forestry firms abroad.

Clearly, the successful implementation of strategies involving government regulation demands constant monitoring of interrelated developments in science, the regulatory arena, and the marketplace. The same caveat applies to the strategies, considered earlier in this chapter, that involve new private regulatory institutions that tie competitors' hands. Neither type of approach is easy to implement successfully. But the payoffs to a successful approach of this sort—in the form of an improved cost position and an enhanced ability to deliver environmental services—are significant enough that it makes sense for executives to analyze carefully the possibilities for their own firms.

Reducing Costs within the Firm

MOST DISCUSSIONS of business and the environment presuppose that a firm must incur extra costs to improve its environmental performance. That has been the premise of chapters 2 and 3 of this book: I have been assuming that it costs money to provide environmental benefits, and have considered how firms can recover this extra cost. The assumption that environmental quality costs money might seem so clearly valid as not to require scrutiny. If it turns out not to be universally valid, then this is a discovery of considerable value to managers.

The idea that companies can simultaneously reduce their costs and improve their environmental performance is undisputed in environmental circles and has proven attractive to some managers as well. Minnesota Mining and Manufacturing, better known as 3M, began its Pollution Prevention Pays (3P) program in 1975. Numerous other initiatives, like Dow Chemical's Waste Reduction Always Pays (WRAP), have followed.[1] The very titles of such programs telegraph their underlying assumptions: that by scrutinizing their operations and investments in the light of environmental considerations, firms can realize cost savings that will more than offset the additional cost of providing higher levels of environmental goods.

In the short term, according to advocates of this view, a firm can realize cost savings by reducing expenditures on waste treatment and disposal, and by using fewer raw materials to produce the same outputs; legal expenses and pollution-related fines might also decline.

Even more significant benefits can occur over the longer term, as environmental pressure forces "innovation that delivers other competitive benefits" like continuing cost reduction and quality improvements.[2] This line of argument is reminiscent of the familiar idea that "quality is free," or the related notion that concern for product quality can transform companies into learning organizations capable of continuous improvement.[3]

These arguments seem to violate the economists' truism that there is no free lunch; they even seem to imply that there are lunches that one gets paid to eat. For this reason, economists and many managers have sharply criticized the notion that the increased provision of environmental goods can decrease a company's overall costs. Economists have been critical, too, of the more general idea that increased attention to environmental matters may result in overall productivity improvements.[4] In this view, competitive pressures already force managers to identify and exploit any available opportunities for savings, and it is impossible to increase the savings by adding new constraints.

Meanwhile, advocates of the ideas about cost savings, including a number of business executives, respond that the economists are proving only that economists are naive. In the view of these advocates, the economists would fail to pick up ten-dollar bills lying on factory floors on the supposition that, if the money were real, someone else would have picked it up already.[5]

If opportunities to reduce costs by improving environmental performance are in fact widespread, then tighter government regulation may actually benefit firms in the long run, and even create an advantage for an entire industry in a particular nation relative to the firms based in other countries.[6] This notion has proven appealing to some regulators, but appalling to people who are skeptical about the prevalence of cost savings.[7] The skeptics argue that the "no-cost paradigm" may be detrimental to the creation of sensible government policy with respect to the environment. In their view, this paradigm, by promising easy and costless environmental improvement, erodes any political consensus that exists for imposing real costs on private actors in the economy, costs that we may need to incur to solve environmental problems.[8]

From a normative public policy standpoint, this is an important debate. Creating expectations that environmental quality can be obtained painlessly may set the stage for disappointment and a weakened ability to implement tough policies. From a business policy stand-

point, though, there is no reason for firms not to look for free lunches—as long as there is a reasonable chance of finding them.

To shed some new light on this debate from a business perspective, this chapter first presents three case examples about companies whose managers have apparently succeeded in finding private cost savings while delivering more public goods. Next, it considers the kinds of cost savings that seem most likely to arise from concern about the environment. Then it analyzes the conditions that appear to favor the success of environmental cost-savings initiatives, looking, as in previous chapters, at how the economics, technology, and social context of a company create or constrain opportunities to create value. Finally, it pulls back the lens to think about the general lessons of the case examples and the analysis.

In other words, the approach in this chapter is similar in spirit to that of previous chapters. It will look for the circumstances under which advocates of the cost-savings hypothesis are more or less likely to be correct, rather than staking out and trying to defend a categorical answer. It turns out that the prevalence of opportunities for private cost savings in a particular business will be influenced by the structure of the industry in which the business is competing and the changes that this structure is undergoing; by the importance of human capital to the business's success; and by the time horizon over which the business evaluates its progress.

Two additional conclusions emerge from this analysis. First, some of the controversies over whether free lunches exist boil down to a disagreement over the appropriate baseline for comparing costs. Regulatory and other external environmental pressure is intensifying over time, and this pressure raises the prices of environmental goods. Firms used to be able to regard air and water as free, but they can no longer do so. As the price of environmental resources rises, it clearly makes economic sense to use less of them than it did when they were cheap; and doing so will lower costs relative to what they would have been if the firm had continued to operate in the old way under the new prices. Whether this is a free lunch depends on the baseline one chooses for comparison. To a manager, however, "Is it a free lunch?" is a less important question than "Is it a sensible policy?" And reducing use of inputs that have just become more expensive clearly makes sense.

Second, if we leave aside these cases where a moving target creates confusion about what is and is not a free lunch, then the narrowly

defined economic view—that few private cost savings are available as a result of environmental improvements—is likely to be true for most companies in the short run. Over the longer term, however, opportunities to reduce costs may be more widespread. While ten-dollar bills on factory floors might be relatively rare, the chance of finding hundred-dollar bills in corporate boardrooms may be considerably greater. That is, significantly different ways of approaching the business may be a more important source of cost savings than incremental cost reductions in existing technologies at existing facilities. If these larger, discontinuous improvements in cost position require significant investments, they can be hard to implement in firms focused only on short-term cash flow. Questions about cost savings in firms are thus inextricably connected with questions of time horizons, discounting, and trade-offs between the short term and the long, which will be important not only in this chapter but in the ones that follow.

ENVIRONMENTAL PRESSURE
AS A SOURCE OF COST REDUCTION

Before considering these questions further, this chapter presents three examples of industries or firms that are trying to find "free lunches." It first examines a service business—hotels—and then considers the manufacturing operations of Dow Chemical Company and the Xerox Corporation. Together, these case examples give a sense of the scope and diversity of environmental cost-savings opportunities, and of the difficulties involved in seizing them.

LODGING COMPANIES' ENVIRONMENTAL INITIATIVES

Visitors to hotels know from experience that many of the major firms in the lodging industry, over the past decade, have tried to reduce costs while improving environmental performance. The hotels' primary tactics include reducing solid waste and cutting usage of water and energy.

Many hotels replaced small bottles of shampoo, lotion, and other "amenities" with bulk dispensers, saving money and reducing solid waste. One such firm installed dispensers at a cost of $91,000; the expenditure led to savings of $36,725 per year.[9] Other firms use recycled and recyclable packaging for amenities: Inter-Continental Hotels

reportedly saved $300,000 per year in this manner at its ten properties in the United States and Canada.[10]

HVS Eco Services, a hotel consulting firm based on Long Island, reports that its clients have achieved substantial savings in solid waste management from simple recycling programs and renegotiation of waste-hauling contracts. Paybacks on investments in waste minimization have ranged from just over 3 to 6.5 months, implying returns on investment from 180 to 380 percent.[11]

Hotel firms have for decades tracked water consumption per room, but water conservation efforts took on new urgency in the 1990s, sparked in part by increases in the water rates charged by municipalities. For example, the Boston Park Plaza Hotel & Towers reported that it "renovated eighty-seven bathrooms and retrofitted them with new 1.6 gallons-per-flush water-saving toilets at a cost of $26,000 and a two-and-a-half year payback." A few years later, the same hotel reported savings of 17 million gallons of water, and $122,202, per year.[12] But because water rates are particularly steep in Boston, these results might not be indicative of such extensive cost-saving opportunities nationwide. HVS Eco Services reports payback periods of twenty-five and thirty-six days on faucet aerators and low-flow showerheads at a Caribbean resort, and paybacks of 0.9 years for faucet aerators and 3.5 years for low-flow toilets at a Howard Johnson hotel in New Jersey.[13]

The Boston Park Plaza Hotel & Towers also spent $1.2 million dollars to install 1,686 energy-saving windows in its 977 guest rooms. According to hotelier Tedd Saunders, "These windows not only save approximately $50 per window annually but also open easier and cut back on both noise and indoor air pollution."[14] The York Hotel in San Francisco achieved much higher returns on smaller investments in lighting, with paybacks ranging from 1.1 to 6.1 years.[15]

For hotels, if environmental investments don't earn returns in the form of cost reduction, it is difficult to recover the cost of the investment in price increases. Price, location, and service remain the primary decision criteria for hotel customers. In other words, opportunities to differentiate hotel services along environmental lines are limited. USA Today quoted one business traveler as saying, "I feel good when I hear hotels are [reducing environmental impacts]. But it would never be a reason for me to select or de-select a hotel because of that."[16]

Relationships among environmental cost savings, marketing, and employee relations remain problematic. HVS Eco Services offers the

following advice to hotel managers about positioning environmental initiatives: "It's very important that you market the program correctly to the employees in order for it to be successful with the guest, because the employees really need to buy into the program. It must come across as something that top management supports, that it's not just cost savings. Then, you have to execute the program in a manner that you want to portray to the guest. For example, in a five-star hotel, you're not going to want big stickers on the bathroom mirror saying 'Hang up your towel.'"[17]

At the same time, properly positioned environmental programs can enhance a company's standing in the eyes of its own staff. Ann Checkley manages environmental affairs for Canadian Pacific Hotels, which owns some of Canada's most famous properties. She says that a survey of staff revealed that "80 percent said they would be more proud to work for the hotel if there was an environmental programme in place."[18]

Hotel executives therefore need to reconcile cost savings and environmental performance with traditional imperatives of customer satisfaction; there is little reason to think that customers will tolerate higher prices or reduced service in order to patronize environmentally friendly hotels, so to make environmental improvements the hotels need to find "free lunches." If low-flow showers in a luxury hotel deter even a small number of potential return visitors, the cost savings on the water bill will not make up the lost revenues. According to a business correspondent for the *San Francisco Examiner,* "The trick is to conserve and recycle and still make guests feel pampered."[19]

WASTE REDUCTION AT DOW CHEMICAL

Dow Chemical Company, a $20 billion firm headquartered in Midland, Michigan, has long been a champion of the idea that increased attention to environmental matters saves a company money. Dow chemists and executives were working on yield improvements in their manufacturing processes (i.e., trying to increase ratios of product output to input) long before the initiation of the company's formal pollution prevention program, Waste Reduction Always Pays (WRAP), in 1986.[20]

Like other environmental initiatives in the chemical industry, including the collective Responsible Care program discussed in chapter 3, the WRAP program closely followed a series of well-publicized

disasters and legislative setbacks in the late 1970s and early 1980s. Like other large chemical firms, Dow was worried that Love Canal, Bhopal, and other calamities would so besmirch its reputation that it would be unable to recruit and retain talented employees, construct new facilities, or even operate the plants it had already built. WRAP, like Responsible Care, was a way of signaling both to outside parties and to employees that an intensified focus on environmental performance was required.

Under WRAP, individual Dow facilities are required to inventory and monitor their emissions to air, water, and land. At the same time, employees propose waste reduction projects that may involve changes in operating procedures, changes in administration, or capital investments. Employees who make outstanding suggestions are honored at an annual formal awards ceremony. According to materials written by the company, "A major goal of the WRAP program is to broaden the thinking of employees so that they look beyond individual plant boundaries and understand the total environmental impact of their chemical processes."[21]

In 1988, Dow executives described to researchers from an environmental group the economics of a project that recycled waste materials at a chlorinated solvents plant in Pittsburg, California. The manufacturing process at this facility produced hydrochloric acid gas as a by-product. Dow had formerly reacted this acid with sodium hydroxide, electrolyzed some of the resultant brine to make chlorine gas, and sent the rest of the brine to evaporation ponds. In response to a California law that required the closing of the evaporation ponds, Dow reengineered its waste treatment procedures so as to reuse some of the hydrochloric acid, recycle the stream of spent sodium hydroxide, and use all of the brine to make chlorine gas. The change, which reduced both the amount of hydrochloric acid waste and the amount of spent sodium hydroxide to be treated, cost $250,000 and was reported to save $2.4 million per year.[22] More recently, an operation making agricultural products at the Pittsburg complex fine-tuned a manufacturing process to increase yields of useful product, resulting in an 80 percent reduction in the use of a particular reactant, much of which had previously been incinerated as waste. This change reportedly saved $750,000 annually.[23] Because waste treatment rules were changing significantly when Dow was making these investments, however, the baseline against which these savings should be evaluated is unclear.

Company officials have also publicized information on waste reduction projects at Dow's Louisiana Division, a group of twenty plants that make a wide variety of organic and inorganic commodity chemicals. In that division, WRAP efforts followed naturally from contests begun in 1981 to develop ideas to save energy in manufacturing processes. During the first few years of this contest, engineers in Louisiana came up with thirty to forty projects a year that collectively earned triple-digit returns on investment: 173 percent in 1982, 340 percent in 1983, and 208 percent the following year. The returns to investments selected in the contest remained at or near 100 percent through 1987. Then, in 1988, the contest was expanded to include waste reduction projects under WRAP. In each of the next half dozen years, twenty to forty projects per year delivered an average return on investment at or near 100 percent.[24] Again, rapid changes in regulatory requirements make the choice of baseline both difficult and important.

Dow asserted that "in North America alone, WRAP projects reduced waste by about 45 million lbs a year and saved Dow more than $20 million a year in both 1993 and 1994."[25] During this period, North American operations accounted for slightly over half of Dow's revenues, and more than half of the operating profits of $1.1 billion in 1993 and $1.8 billion the following year.

Seven years after the WRAP program began, Dow Vice President Dave Buzzelli told management consultants at McKinsey & Company that it was still delivering a 55 percent return on new investments of capital: "Last year we spent about $200 million on the environment from our capital budget. If you look at the whole $200 million it earned us a negative 16 percent return on investment. But if you take that part of the $200 million that went into the WRAP program and pollution prevention, we got a 55 percent ROI on pollution prevention in 1992. So we made money on those initiatives, but lost it on end-of-pipe treatment."[26] According to Dow executives, opportunities of this sort persisted even ten years after WRAP began: "In 1996, for example, Dow announced plans to spend $1 billion to achieve new environmental, health and safety targets over the next decade—including further waste reduction initiatives—and that it expects to generate a return on that investment of 30% to 40%."[27] CEO William Stavrapoulos explicitly called attention to the rate of return figures in a press conference announcing the investment program.[28]

Despite the splashy title of its pollution prevention program, Dow

does undertake environmental projects that do not appear to pay for themselves. In 1992, Dow executives wrote, "Ideally, WRAP projects save the company money, but Dow realizes that some projects may not offer a return on investment that can be quantified."[29] The same year, a Dow spokesman told a journalist that "a good number of WRAP projects actually cost more to implement than they save."[30]

The WRAP program was an initial step in a program of environmental management that has become more comprehensive and aggressive over time. In the mid-1990s, Dow established numerical targets for the year 2005 for several environmental and safety-related measures, with a commitment to track its progress toward the goals and disseminate the results to the public. For example, Dow pledged to reduce emissions of a group of twenty-nine priority compounds by a factor of four from 1993 levels, and to cut total waste production per pound of product output from 0.027 pounds to 0.014. Dow's environmental policy states that "protecting people and the environment will be part of everything we do and every decision we make. . . . Our goal is to eliminate all injuries, prevent adverse environmental and health impacts, reduce wastes and emissions and promote resource conservation at every stage of the life cycle of our products."[31]

XEROX: COST SAVINGS
FROM ENVIRONMENTAL ENHANCEMENT

Xerox Corporation introduced the photocopier in 1959; over the next several years, it enjoyed enormous market power. The company protected this power with a thicket of technological patents and erected other barriers to entry as well. It chose, for example, to lease copiers rather than sell them, raising capital barriers to entry into the business.[32] But these secondary impediments could not deter rivals from invading Xerox's enormously lucrative turf once the patents expired in the early 1970s. By the end of the decade, Xerox's traditional markets were crowded with well-funded new entrants, including Canon and Ricoh in low- and medium-volume copier markets and Eastman Kodak and IBM at the high-volume end. In this newly competitive environment, Xerox's market share declined and its margins eroded precipitously: returns on sales, 11 percent in 1971, were in the 4 percent range in the late 1980s.[33]

In 1990, Xerox managers undertook a new environmental management initiative, called the Environmental Leadership Program, that

eventually included waste reduction efforts, product takeback schemes, and design-for-environment initiatives.[34] The reduction of waste from the company's manufacturing operations and administrative offices was a central feature of this program. Xerox's Waste-Free Factory program, initiated in 1993, sets goals of 90 percent reductions in air emissions, solid waste, and hazardous waste, and qualitative goals in other areas like "environmental communications." The program requires managers to use a self-assessment matrix to track their progress and compare it with that of other facilities. A similar program for Xerox offices began in 1995, with the idea of reducing waste to landfills by 90 percent, energy consumption by 50 percent, and so on. The company is implementing both initiatives worldwide, with factories and offices in India, Mexico, Brazil, and elsewhere meeting the "waste-free" targets.[35]

Waste that is designated "hazardous" is especially costly to incinerate or to deposit in landfills, creating unusually strong incentives for waste reduction. By the mid-1990s, Xerox's large manufacturing complex in Webster, New York, sent only 2 percent of its hazardous waste to landfills.[36]

To be successful, the Waste-Free Office and Waste-Free Factory initiatives require widespread employee participation. Internal audits of the office program show that about three-quarters of employees recycle paper and beverage containers, and about seven-eighths contribute to energy conservation by complying with "power-down efforts" for lights and office equipment.[37] Employee education efforts, whether through simple postings on the company Intranet or multiday "Ecology of Empowerment" training programs, are seen as critical to the success of the Environmental Leadership Program. At the same time, Xerox has made capital investments in energy conservation equipment intended to reinforce employee involvement efforts. For example, at its large facility in Webster it invested substantially in sensing equipment that automatically turns off lights in unoccupied rooms.[38]

The waste reduction schemes at Xerox's own facilities complement two other components of the Environmental Leadership Program, a product recycling program and a design-for-environment initiative. Xerox encourages its customers to return copiers, cartridges, and other products once the products' useful lives are over, so that Xerox can reuse them or recycle the constituent materials. Application of design-for-environment principles can increase the efficiency of this process. These extensions of waste minimization principles beyond the

company's own facilities have changed the economics of the copier business dramatically, in ways that are examined in chapter 5.

From its inception, the Environmental Leadership Program enjoyed the visible support of Xerox's chairman and chief executive. In 1990, Paul Allaire reportedly told the architects of the program, "Not only do I approve it, but you are mandated to do it." Allaire said in a public statement, "We've pledged ourselves to a never-ending search of things that we—as one company—can do to protect the environment. Moreover, this promise is something we take every bit as seriously as the business commitments we make to our customers and our shareholders."[39]

Even in the early 1990s, before these more ambitious components of the Environmental Leadership Program had a chance to bear much fruit, Xerox executives were already labeling the program an unqualified success. While Xerox did not publicize cost savings data, Allaire said that "there are good reasons to protect the Earth. . . . it's the safest and surest way to long-term profitability"; one of his managers asserted that "there are no conflicting motives—what is ecologically sensible gives you the best value."[40]

TYPES OF POTENTIAL SAVINGS

Before analyzing these case examples, it makes sense to think about the types of cost savings that environmental concern might produce. The four basic inputs to any production process are capital equipment, labor, purchased materials and services, and information. A firm uses a particular quantity of each of its inputs and pays a particular price per unit for each of them (information is unusual in this respect because it is hard to identify its price). At the most basic level, cost savings can arise because the firm needs less of a particular input, or because it pays less for each unit of the input that it uses.

Most of the immediately evident forms of environmental cost savings that firms can capture in the short run—like the reduced water use in hotels, or the reduced waste at a Dow factory—take the form of reductions of quantities of purchased materials and services. Firms that produce less waste need to buy fewer waste management services, and perhaps fewer raw materials as well. As one chemical plant manager put it in an interview, "We know that every raw material that enters this factory leaves the factory in one of two forms: as waste that we

have to pay to get rid of, or as product for which we get paid."[41] To reduce the quantities of purchased inputs, firms substitute some other input, usually capital or information. The examples of Xerox, Dow, and the hotels suggest that most short-run cost savings come from reduced purchases of materials and services rather than from reductions in capital or labor used.

The same examples further suggest that short-run environmental cost savings ordinarily arise from reductions in quantities rather than from reductions in price. Improved environmental performance may lead to lower per-unit costs for certain specialized purchased services, like purchased environmental impairment liability insurance. More commonly, though, quantity reductions drive the short-term cost savings.

These reductions in the quantities of materials and services used may not be current or even certain. Reductions in future costs or contingent costs are still cost savings. When managers at Xerox, Dow, or other firms reduce the amount of hazardous waste sent to landfills, they do so in part to save disposal costs today, but they also are trying to reduce the contingent costs of cleanups a year or a decade from now. These contingent future savings may be even more important than the savings of current disposal costs. The possibility of saving future and uncertain costs creates some difficult problems in incentive design: the manager making the decisions today may not anticipate contingent costs a decade from now, and may have a high tolerance for such risk even if he or she anticipates it.[42]

Savings from capital, labor, and information are harder to capture in the short run than savings from purchased materials and services; in the short run, it is easier to bring about savings by reducing quantities than reducing prices. In the longer term, the firm may be able to capture savings in some of these other categories—but not all.

Some observers have argued that better environmental performance lowers the price that firms have to pay for capital. Such arguments fall into three categories. One might think that environmental enhancement is good for the bottom line and hence drives share price upward.[43] One might think that the securities of environmentally aggressive companies are less risky and therefore can pay lower returns.[44] Finally, one might think that some providers of capital will shun companies whose environmental records don't comply with minimum quality standards, thus driving the securities prices of those firms down.[45] Unfortunately for advocates of these views, the evidence on all

of these points is unconvincing. As we have seen repeatedly, being "green" doesn't always pay: whether it does depends on the industry, the firm, and the acumen of the managers. Hence there is no simple relationship between environmental friendliness (however defined) and financial performance, much less a causal relationship from environmental to financial performance. Similarly, some investments in risk reduction may make sense from a financial perspective, but others may not (a topic discussed in chapter 6). And despite the presence of investment funds that hold only the securities of companies that are thought to be preferable from an environmental standpoint, the prices of securities are still made at the margin by traders interested in discounted cash flow rather than in environmental performance for its own sake.[46]

The analysis gets more complicated when we turn to labor and information; here the advocates of long-term free lunch programs tell stories that are not so easily discounted. It is possible, for example, that improved environmental performance could free up labor that was formerly used for waste management and waste treatment, the in-house equivalent of contracted waste management services. It is also possible that environmentally benign firms are better able to recruit talented people who care about their employers' environmental performance, to elicit more effort from workers of this sort, or both. Effects like these would play out only in the long term. Finally, it is possible that environmental pressure can serve, like quality or safety, as a prod to change managerial behavior and create a company culture that allows continuous innovation and learning. This is the most difficult of the sources of potential savings to pin down or measure, but it may be the most important over the long term.

CONDITIONS FAVORING COST-SAVING OPPORTUNITIES IN THE SHORT RUN

Three conditions must apply if environmental concern is to reveal private cost savings within the firm. First, the opportunities for the cost savings have to exist: that is, the firm must be flexible enough to change its operating procedures if it makes sense to do so. Second, the company's managers must be able to recognize opportunities for savings; that is, they must be able to obtain access to relevant information. Third, these managers must have an incentive to make the changes

necessary to capture the cost savings. In practice, of course, none of these is a binary variable, like the position of a switch; in any situation, flexibility, information, and incentives will be present to some degree.

This section examines the relationship of these variables to the identification and capture of environmental cost savings. It also examines the effects of changes in social expectations about firm performance on the firms' opportunities to identify environmental cost savings. Throughout, I analyze the search for these cost savings as I would other investment opportunities available to the firm. The capture of these cost savings typically requires some initial outlay of capital, management attention, or both. The payoffs come later. And there is usually at least some uncertainty about the value of those payoffs, because the value depends on prices—for waste disposal, raw materials, management talent, and so on—that are moving in response to regulatory changes and changes in the marketplace.

THE CRITICAL ROLE OF FLEXIBILITY

Clearly, if a company is to improve its cost position, it needs to have the flexibility to implement changes in its purchasing and production. The ability to improve environmental performance is only one manifestation of managerial discretion. Companies that are locked into particular modes of operation, whether by market pressures or by internal administrative dynamics, will not be able to realize cost savings.

Some firms have deliberately designed flexibility into their operations. At Xerox, for example, various outputs are produced at any given manufacturing facility. Manufacturing equipment is not specialized to a particular product. In chemicals manufacturing, similarly, processes often involve production of a complex mix of outputs in any given facility, physical and managerial assets that are useful for any of a number of products, and substantial amounts of learning by doing.

Similarly, hotels and many other service businesses can maintain inherently flexible production processes because their product is less narrowly and explicitly defined by physical characteristics. A hotel is selling comfort, convenience, cleanliness, and a restful atmosphere, which can be made from a huge variety of inputs. If you want to produce jet fuel, by contrast, you must start with oil.

The same logic appears to apply in the restaurant business. For example, McDonald's Corporation apparently generated considerable

cost savings in a waste management project conducted jointly with the Environmental Defense Fund in the early 1990s. In a partnership that was widely touted as an example both of successful waste reduction and of fruitful collaboration between business and environmentalists, McDonald's executives and researchers from the environmental group identified ways to reduce solid waste generated at McDonald's restaurants.[47] One reason that the project succeeded from a waste management standpoint is that McDonald's deliberately designs flexibility into its processes: equipment is not dedicated to a single process, and the mix of outputs changes from minute to minute and from month to month.[48]

Capital investments that are dedicated to a particular means of production constrain managers' flexibility. From this perspective, the investments at a typical specialty chemical plant are inherently more flexible than those at a typical pulp mill or electric power station because they can economically be used to produce a greater variety of outputs with a broader range of possible inputs. This does not mean that cost savings can never be realized in industries, such as pulp and electric power, where capital is more specialized. But managers in such industries may need to be more patient about the time frame over which they obtain the savings.

Some researchers have identified a second source of inflexibility in management structures and even in managerial attitudes. From this perspective, an undue insistence on traditional ways of conducting business can blind managers to possible cost savings. If this is accurate, it provides a reason to suppose that regulatory pressure, by forcing managers to view their operations in a different light, can bring about cost savings that otherwise would have escaped the attention of the firm.[49]

THE IMPORTANCE OF INFORMATION FLOWS

If environmental considerations are to serve as a source of ideas about cost reduction, it must be the case that the company is not currently minimizing its costs, perhaps because its managers do not possess the relevant information or appropriate incentives.

Information does not flow with complete freedom between managers on different levels or between managers and shareholders. In particular, the firm's senior managers know less about environmental costs and opportunities than do the frontline and middle-level managers, and

the company's shareholders know even less. If information flowed freely within the firm, senior managers and shareholders could detect opportunities for cost savings as easily as the managers who are immediately responsible for the operations, and could make sure that such opportunities were exploited. In other words, the bosses would be able to ensure that the managers behaved in accordance with their superiors' objectives.

In the special case where markets are perfectly competitive, on the other hand, the relevant information about the managers' behavior is revealed in the marketplace. In a perfectly competitive market, only firms that minimize costs can remain in business. In such a market, any management inefficiency is punished. So, if the market is perfectly competitive, information about the managers' performance is revealed in the market outcomes.

Opportunities to save costs will exist only if there are impediments to the free flow of information and if it is possible to remove some of those impediments. If the relevant information is already available, as it is in perfect markets, there is no way that environmental scrutiny (or any other kind of scrutiny) is going to divulge additional relevant information. If, on the other hand, the relevant information is buried but there is no way to disinter it, environmental pressure cannot drive cost savings.

"Information systems" may connote massive investments in software and consulting, implemented over considerable time periods. But systems for gathering information about potential cost savings need not be elaborate or expensive. In the examples from the hotel industry, for instance, some of the cost calculations could be done literally on the back of an envelope. More systematic analysis of costs may reveal more savings, but the initial savings may be accessible with very modest investments in information.

The logic of this chapter implies that opportunities for environmental cost savings should be treated like other investment opportunities. Any firm needs a capital budgeting system that can identify investments with rates of return in the triple digits and fund them, regardless of overall spending targets, and regardless of whether the project delivers its returns by saving environmental costs or in some other fashion. At the same time, some environmental "success stories" actually entail quite low rates of return. For example, the Boston Park Plaza's window renovation program, discussed previously, entails rates

of return of 3.5 percent on investment: unless intangible benefits like noise reduction are extremely important, the project isn't delivering the opportunity cost of the capital. The resource allocation system must avoid problems of this sort, too.

The idea that environmental improvements are investments provides a rationale for government programs that require companies to disclose certain kinds of environmental information. Initiatives like the EPA's Toxics Release Inventory, mandated by the Superfund Amendments and Reauthorization Act of 1986 (SARA), were initially intended as mechanisms by which environmentalists and community groups could obtain access to systematically gathered data on releases of environmental contaminants, factory by factory. It turned out, however, that executives of the companies concerned benefited from the provision of this information. A manager at one of Dow's large competitors, AlliedSignal, remembered that top executives had not anticipated how high the company's emissions numbers would be compared with those of other firms: "It just hit us, in comparison to our peers and the rest of the universe that submitted these numbers, how big [Allied's numbers] were. I and everyone else thought that this was the way everyone did business. Then it turned out it was an aberration."[50] Such accounts do not prove, of course, that government programs for mandatory disclosure of information always pay for themselves in improved performance. They do suggest, however, that potentially useful information can remain buried within the firm unless some incentive—whether a government rule or an internal executive initiative—brings it to light.

THE IMPORTANCE OF INCENTIVE DESIGN

Academics who study company behavior often assume that the principals of the firm (the shareholders) are interested solely in profits and hence in cost minimization, but that their agents (the managers) have other interests as well. For example, the managers might want to avoid the effort and stress that squeezing costs out of a system inevitably entails. If, by contrast, the managers had the same interests as the shareholders, one would expect they already would have seized any opportunities to save costs that they could identify, and that environmental scrutiny would not reveal any additional opportunities. As with information, then, we must be assuming that incentives are imperfect but that they can be improved.

Here, too, the degree of competition in the firm's markets is important. If the firm operates in perfectly competitive markets, incentives for managers will automatically be aligned with those of shareholders, since managers will preserve the firm's existence, and their own jobs, only if they minimize costs.

To summarize, if shareholders and managers have the same interests, the managers will seize every opportunity to save costs. Even if their interests diverge, the managers will seize every opportunity for cost savings if they operate in perfectly competitive markets. And even with divergent interests and imperfect markets, the managers will seize every opportunity to save costs as long as they know that their shareholders have the same information about the opportunities as they do. But if none of the three conditions holds, the incentives of the managers are not fully aligned with those of the shareholders, and neither the markets nor the shareholders themselves can prevent the managers from pursuing their own agendas. Because it requires time and effort to implement cost reduction programs, and because the managers will not capture all of the benefits of cost savings, they may be better off if they leave some of these opportunities untapped. In these circumstances, increased environmental attention, whether driven indirectly by regulation or directly by owners or senior managers, may benefit both the environment and the firm by effectively raising the benefits to the managers of seizing the opportunities.[51]

Shareholders, upper management, and line managers at the facility level may also not share the same attitude toward time horizons and discount rates. Line managers who are evaluated on the basis of short-term profits may pass up opportunities for long-term cost savings. This is a particular example of a more general and very important problem of incentive design. Many companies have attempted to solve it by relying more heavily on qualitative factors (like senior managers' appraisal of a plant managers' focus on improvements that may not pay off in the short run) in performance evaluation and promotion decisions. If taken too far, however, this shift in focus can also be problematic, blunting the other incentives more than is desirable.[52]

If we examine any business closely, we are bound to find imperfections in the markets in which the firm competes, impediments to the free flow of information within the organization, and divergences among the objectives of managers, senior executives, and shareholders. This implies, at a basic theoretical level, that any firm ought to consid-

er the possibility that it can save costs by scrutinizing environmental performance. It also suggests that we should look at the degree to which these conditions hold in a particular firm or industry to assess the likelihood that its managers can find free environmental lunches.

Firms that have historically enjoyed market power and hence evaded cost-reduction imperatives might be more likely to find numerous opportunities to use the environment as a tool for cost reduction. Xerox provides a striking example of this phenomenon. It had enormous market power in its main line of business until the 1970s. After the entry of new competitors, cost pressures on Xerox mounted, and the firm discovered cost savings opportunities in part through its environmental initiatives. There may not be anything unique about the environment in this regard. Xerox found cost savings by shining an environmental flashlight around its factories, but other firms have used different flashlights. Alcoa CEO Paul O'Neill, for example, used quality as a tool for identifying cost savings in the short run and changing the corporate culture over the long term.[53]

This example suggests that electric utilities, now facing competitive pressure for the first time in their organizational lives, might find environmental considerations a useful catalyst for cost reduction. Electric utilities facing deregulation now need to make sure that their cost structures can stand up to the test of market competition as well as the scrutiny of state regulatory officials. Although their flexibility is constrained by the single-purpose nature of their generating plants and the long lives of their capital equipment, electric utilities may well benefit from the sort of search for environmental cost-savings opportunities that proved profitable at Xerox and Dow.

THE ROLE OF CHANGING EXPECTATIONS

Operating flexibility, relevant information, and appropriate incentives must all be present if firms are to capitalize on environmental cost-savings opportunities. We now turn to a fourth factor that, while not necessary for the existence of those opportunities, appears to enhance the probability that they will exist.

Firms for which social expectations about environmental performance are changing rapidly may find unusually large opportunities for cost savings. In particular, firms for which environmental issues have been historically unimportant are more likely to have embedded

environmental costs in overhead accounts that spread the costs evenly across products, and are likely to have devoted relatively little management attention to cost-saving opportunities of this sort. Thus there may be more "low hanging fruit" in such firms. Xerox again provides an example.

The fact that social expectations of corporate environmental performance are changing is at the root of much of the misunderstanding between economists and the advocates of the free lunch. Suppose that new regulations raise the cost of treating water pollution. A business whose operations generate water pollution may now find it profitable to reduce the amount of pollution it creates (by using different inputs, for example). This change will reduce the business's costs relative to what they would have been had it not made this change—otherwise, the change would not be made. But the costs might still rise relative to their level before the regulation was passed in the first place. Is this an example of environmental concern serving as a catalyst for cost reduction? It looks like that to advocates of the "win-win" approach. To gloomy economists, it appears as a much less inspiring story about a company responding rationally to an external shock.

Public discussions about the existence of free lunches often fail to set the baseline for comparison explicitly. In the stories about Dow Chemical cited earlier, it is not clear whether the Dow executives are reporting savings against a baseline of the status quo or whether the baseline reflects new regulatory requirements that will raise the costs of business-as-usual. This ambiguity may be desirable to firm managers from a public relations standpoint, but in internal discussions about possible investments, managers need to be sure what the baseline is.

Along similar lines, the stories about cost savings assume that managers are leaving some opportunities for cost savings unexploited. But given that the managers' own time is costly, this may be a perfectly rational thing to do. Suppose, for example, that increased regulatory scrutiny diverts a manager's attention away from other opportunities and into a more diligent search for pollution reduction (as it will). Suppose further that this increased attention produces results (as one would expect). To someone predisposed to asserting that "free lunches" are widespread, it will look as though the manager found a free lunch. To others, it looks like a diversion of resources from private good provision to public good provision: the new state of affairs may be preferable from a social point of view, but "preferable from a social point of view" and "free from a private cost

standpoint" are not the same thing. The time and attention of competent managers are among the most valuable and scarce resources in any organization, no matter how well run; environmental initiatives need to take account of the costs of those managerial resources.

CONDITIONS FAVORING COST-SAVING OPPORTUNITIES IN THE LONGER TERM

The long-term challenge in cost management is to move beyond one-shot reductions in the quantities of purchased materials and services to some more persistent and durable source of cost savings. The analysis of opportunities for short-run cost savings focused on three factors: flexibility, information, and incentives. These same three factors turn out to be critical in the long term as well.

Flexibility is a function of time. Other things being equal, an organization has more flexibility in the long run than in the short run. Recall that the main impediments to flexibility are a capital stock that is chosen to do certain things optimally and may not be so useful for other purposes, and managerial attitudes and procedures that were designed for one set of external circumstances and may also be resistant to short-run change. In the long run, neither constrains organizational flexibility to the extent that each does in the near term.

The set of feasible and appropriate investments in information systems also depends on the time horizon. Simple, ad hoc cost measurement systems will capture low-hanging fruit of the sort available at Xerox and in the hotels. Over the longer term, investments in more elaborate systems may pay.

Changes in information systems aimed at cost reduction within the firm also may unearth opportunities to create value for customers, and hence enable companies to implement other strategies that reconcile environmental and economic performance. For example, the waste reduction efforts at Xerox complement larger initiatives aimed at restructuring the company's relationships with its customers. Conversely, efforts to restructure relationships with customers and suppliers can have important effects on cost structures within the firm. These relationships will be examined in chapter 5.

Even leaving these kinds of opportunities aside, however, an information system that encourages repeated scrutiny of environmental costs

is likely to pay dividends simply because the costs of environmental pollution are changing over time. Regulatory changes, in particular, can affect the costs of both raw materials and waste disposal. Thus if a firm finds that reducing a waste stream saves money, it does not necessarily follow that the company had been neglecting cost-saving opportunities beforehand. It might be that the waste reduction didn't pay for itself when disposal was cheaper. As noted earlier, this line of argument implies that firms whose regulatory constraints are changing rapidly, or whose input costs are subject to environmentally related shocks, are more likely to benefit from a search for cost savings.

The time horizon matters for incentive design as well. It might seem obvious that it is important to provide financial incentives to managers so that they will take their environmental responsibilities seriously, and to reward managers and workers financially for environmental innovations that save money. Dow Chemical has explicitly rejected cash awards for such innovations, however, fearing that they would trigger disputes over authorship, stifle teamwork, and send the message that "finding significant improvements is not part of the regular job."[54] In other words, there is some reason for executives to be cautious about using economic incentives to motivate what they hope will be a cultural change. I will return to this topic in chapter 7. For now, note that the time horizon matters in incentive design as in other aspects of operations. If the time horizon for a cost-savings project is one year, it makes no sense to toy with the incentive structure. It will take nearly that long to design a new system and announce its formal adoption, and considerably longer for managers to alter their behavior in response to the new incentives. But if the time horizon is ten years, new incentive systems can be very powerful instruments of change.

Flexibility, information, and incentive design are all critical in bringing about the successful recruitment, retention, and effort of committed employees, a critically important source of long-term cost savings for the firm. Particularly for companies whose competitive edge comes largely from innovation, managerial acumen, and other capabilities that reside in people (rather than static economies of scale like plant size or power in distribution channels), the ability to attract and retain superior talent is critical. And that ability can be related to environmental performance. The effects of environmental performance on employee recruitment, retention, and effort are extremely difficult to measure, but numerous senior managers assert that a reputation for

environmental probity helps them attract and retain good employees. An executive at the Chemical Manufacturers Association put it this way: "By the year 2000 we will be 400,000 short of scientifically and technically trained people in the United States. Where will the precious few who have that training want to work? In the industry with a reputation for screwing everything up and causing all the problems? . . . The long-term health of this industry depends on who we can attract to its ranks."[55] As noted elsewhere in this book, it takes time and investment to acquire such reputations; because of the long time horizons and the difficulties in quantification, it may require a leap of faith by senior executives to decide that the investments are worth making.

In the long term, one of the most significant benefits of policies aimed at using the environment to find cost savings (as well as the least tangible, and most difficult to translate into cash flows) may be their role in helping companies learn. That is, it may be possible to use concern about the environment as a tool in efforts to transform the firm into an organization capable of continuous learning and improvement, repeatedly pushing out the production frontier. For advocates of the learning organization approach, the search for internal cost savings can pay for itself in part because it entails an investment in organizational capabilities, intangible assets that will yield dividends over the long term. Here, as with the creation of reputational assets, time horizons are long, and benefits are all but impossible to quantify. But some executives will find the logic compelling and will conclude that investments in organizational learning make sense for their firms.

THE DEBATE about cost savings through environmental scrutiny, like the more general debate about business and the environment, is polarized. On one side, we hear that "there is no free lunch," and that it is ridiculous to suppose that competent managers leave ten-dollar bills lying around on the floors of their factories. On the other side, we hear that economists believe so fervently in efficiency that they would fail to pick up a ten-dollar bill even if they saw one in the street. To reconcile these views, consider the possibility that the sidewalks are littered with pieces of colored paper, some of which are genuine currency but most of which are valueless. Managers rushing to get somewhere else can, if they choose, stop to scrutinize these pieces of paper, but spending time this way may interfere with other duties. Environmental pressure, in this

story, has the effect of increasing the worth of some of the slips of paper, or of making it easier for managers to locate those that are valuable.

An alternative way of reconciling the apparently divergent ideas about the ten-dollar bills is to note the possibility that a firm might be operating at a local optimum that is not a global optimum. To see this, consider the following analogy to the geography of New England.

Mount Lincoln and Mount Lafayette dominate the Franconia Ridge in the White Mountains of New Hampshire. The slopes of Mount Lincoln fall off steeply from its summit, and the narrow Franconia Ridge, running due north, descends to a saddle before rising to the top of Mount Lafayette a couple of miles away. Lafayette is higher than Lincoln, but from the summit of Lincoln there is nowhere to go but down. Mount Lincoln is a local optimum. From there, whether and how you can gain elevation depends on how much time you have, and how far you are willing to descend before climbing again. If you want to be at the highest possible elevation fifteen minutes from now, you should stay put on top of Lincoln. But to maximize your elevation an hour from now, you should start descending now along the ridge to Lafayette. If your time horizon is somewhat longer, say a few hours, you could attain even higher elevations by descending from the ridge altogether and driving to Mount Washington. And if you have a day, you could be in the Rockies, or the Sierra Nevada, or the Alps.

Managers of plants get paid, in part, to minimize costs. If there are ten-dollar bills on the factory floor, they usually have been left there for a good reason. On the other hand, the plant managers and their bosses and their bosses' bosses all operate in a system that was almost certainly designed when environmental costs represented a significantly lower fraction of total costs and when the business risks arising from inferior environmental performance were considerably lower than they are now. Redesigning information and incentive systems to reflect this new state of affairs may be like picking up hundred-dollar bills in the boardroom rather than tens on the factory floor, but it is also likely to entail considerable investments of time and executive effort in the short run and considerable waiting before results become manifest.

A third perspective on the ten-dollar bills comes from the analogy between environmental management and quality management. For decades most American managers assumed that quality cost money. This seemed to them the intuitive conclusion to reach, and they did not question their intuition. Then, in the 1970s, these managers were

confronted by competition from Japanese firms that seemed to be capable of matching or beating American firms on cost while producing goods of vastly superior quality. The conventional wisdom was turned on its head, and many managers decided that "quality was free."

Only after another two decades have we reached what now seems the logical conclusion: the cost of quality depends on the circumstances of the firm. For some firms in some industries, quality may indeed be free; for some, its cost may even be negative, creating a sort of qualitative free lunch. For others, its cost is positive, but what continues to matter is its cost to a given firm relative to its cost to that firm's competitors.

A similar learning process may now be occurring with respect to environmental costs. At first, the conventional wisdom held that environmental improvements cost money. After all, the reasoning went, the environment is a public good; if pollution prevention were free, we would already be doing it. Why waste time examining the obvious? Next, some serious scholars, politicians, and businesspeople began advocating the notion that the environment is free, often explicitly invoking analogies to the quality revolution. Now, we should be able to reach the logical middle ground in this debate as well: the environment is not free for everyone, but all executives should take a look at how much it will cost them and their firms; and environmental quality looks cheaper the further into the future one is able to look.

Redefining Markets

THIS CHAPTER is about trying to do it all. The firms discussed here are attempting simultaneously to increase revenues, reduce costs, and improve performance in the environmental arena. Observers with environmentalist leanings call approaches of this sort "win-win-win" strategies because customers, shareholders, and the environment are all supposed to benefit.[1] Clearly, if a business can devise and implement such a strategy, it should.

The question is whether the approach is realistic. The answer, of course, is that it depends on the basic economic context in which the strategy is executed. The success of such ambitious strategies requires some unusual economic circumstances and managerial approaches.

Previous chapters have examined the basic ways in which companies can reconcile demands for environmental quality with their traditional imperative of delivering value to shareholders. Chapter 2 analyzed attempts to recover the costs of environmental quality from customers by differentiating products; chapter 3 examined attempts to manage competition through collaborative arrangements or through the strategic use of government regulation; and chapter 4 analyzed attempts to use environmental concern to identify or create private cost savings within the firm. We observed that the success of a particular approach depends on the structure of the industry in which it is implemented, on the position of the firm within that industry, and on the organizational capabilities of the firm. We also observed that while

the firms following these approaches do so with the primary objective of increasing profitability, the approaches can yield additional benefits in the form of improved risk management. Both of these observations apply to the more ambitious approaches discussed in this chapter.

We have already seen that the basic approaches that can permit a business to reconcile shareholder value with environmental quality—differentiating products, managing competitors, and reducing internal costs—are not always mutually exclusive. The case examples in the previous chapter, while focused on cost reduction in the firm, had competitive overtones as well. Dow's initiatives to reduce solid waste, for example, both lowered the company's own costs and put pressure on rivals to follow suit; Dow reinforced this pressure on competitors by playing an active role in the Responsible Care initiative. Cost-saving environmental measures in fast food, lodging, and other service businesses can put pressure on competitors as well.

Some approaches to environmental management are designed with this kind of synergy explicitly in mind. That is, they are intended to serve several objectives at once, differentiating products or managing competitors while simultaneously reducing internal costs and improving environmental performance. This chapter focuses on approaches of this sort.

To succeed in delivering more value to customers and improving environmental performance while simultaneously reducing costs, firms need to redefine the markets in which they compete. By thinking creatively about the fundamental nature of their business, executives in certain firms have been able to find ways to reconfigure the whole system by which they create value and deliver it to customers. In so doing, these firms can reduce the total social costs of the activities in which they and their customers are engaged, increase the private value that they provide to customers, and make life very difficult for their competitors.

For example, makers of consumer durables may commit to taking their used products back for remanufacturing or recycling. This phenomenon is spreading from electronics firms like Xerox and Hewlett-Packard to other manufacturers, notably European carmakers. Some American electric utilities have tried to change the way they serve their customers by instituting demand-side management programs: a utility may install insulation in a customer's home, retaining it for accounting purposes as a capital asset on which the regulators will allow it to earn a return. As a third example, Monsanto and some of its competitors in agricultural biotechnology have been changing the entire system that farmers use to protect their crops from

pests, substituting genetic information for a complicated delivery system involving the manufacture and dissemination of synthetic pesticides.

All of these innovations involve a redefinition of property rights within the commercial system. Thinking systematically about property rights is a useful way for managers to make sense of possible opportunities to redefine environmentally salient markets to their firms' own advantage. For example, instead of transferring all rights and responsibilities of ownership to their customers, Xerox and other manufacturers retain some of the obligations that go with ownership of the product even while the product is in use or when its useful life is over. Utilities' demand-side management programs also involve a rearrangement of property rights, with the insulation physically installed in the customer's house but retained as an asset on the company's books. Companies that combine innovations in property rights with technological innovation, as Monsanto and its competitors have been attempting to do in agricultural biotechnology, may be able to create even stronger positions to profit from concern about the environment.

Realistically, not all firms are in a position to succeed with ambitious strategies of market redefinition, because not all possess the requisite market and financial power. Still, by thinking about the circumstances under which such strategies can succeed, executives in smaller or less lavishly endowed businesses can learn more about their own firms and understand the factors that influence corporate success.

To set the stage for the case examples that follow, this chapter first presents some basic ideas about property rights. The cases cover initiatives in electrical equipment manufacturing, the electric utility industry, and agricultural biotechnology. Next, the chapter examines the circumstances that contributed to the success or failure of these and other efforts to redefine markets to the mutual benefit of the environment and the innovative firm. As in earlier chapters, the aim here is to discern the conditions under which such strategies can succeed. Also as in earlier chapters, we will see that these conditions are closely related to those that determine corporate success more generally.

PROPERTY RIGHTS AND THE CREATION OF VALUE

Property rights include the right to the use and enjoyment of an asset, the right to alter the use of the asset, the right to exclude use by others,

and the right to transfer these property rights to another party. Usually, all of these rights are bundled together; when one is transferred, all are transferred simultaneously to the same person. For example, when Smith buys a house, she obtains the right to enjoy the asset (i.e., to live in it, or to collect rent from tenants), the right to change its use (within the constraints imposed by government regulations, she can renovate it, turn it into a restaurant, or tear it down), and the right to resell it.

We are used to thinking of certain bundles of property rights as "natural." At the same time, much business activity involves the bundling and unbundling of property rights so that people who are interested in a particular right can enjoy it without incurring the expense of acquiring other rights that are less valuable to them. If Jones leases a car, he obtains the right to use the car. He does not obtain the right to change its use or to resell it, but he may be uninterested in having those rights and unwilling to pay the extra money that it would cost to acquire them. A car lease is a straightforward example of a rearrangement of property rights to mutual benefit. Transactions that are far more complicated but nonetheless similar in their basic purpose occur continuously in ordinary business practice and especially in the financial markets. Since not every person has the same willingness to pay for various property rights, the unbundling of the rights enables each to get those in which he is most interested, making the overall use of resources more efficient.

These beneficial effects can extend to the environmental arena as well. In real estate, for example, the unbundling of property rights can lead to the preservation of environmental and aesthetic value that might otherwise be lost. Numerous land trusts and other conservation organizations arrange for landowners to donate conservation easements on their real estate. The easements typically preclude subdevelopment, strip-mining, and other land uses that have detrimental environmental or aesthetic impacts. The easement donors are unbundling the various rights to the land, separating the use, enjoyment, and resale rights from some of the rights to change the use of the asset. Then they are destroying a property right—for example, the option to create a housing development—which they have no intention of exercising anyway. The easement becomes an encumbrance on the property and remains in place even if the property changes hands.

EXAMPLES OF MARKET REDEFINITION

Thinking systematically about the bundling and unbundling of property rights can lead to some innovative business practices. We first consider the case of product takeback initiatives implemented by Xerox and other electronics manufacturers, and then turn to examples from electric utility and biotechnology companies.

PRODUCT TAKEBACK INITIATIVES AT XEROX CORPORATION

The acquisition of property usually entails obligations as well as rights. The owner of a vehicle, for example, is legally obligated to dispose of it properly when it is no longer useful, and cannot simply abandon it. Increasingly, manufacturers of durable goods like photocopiers and computers are encouraging or even requiring customers to return end-of-life products to the manufacturers. The manufacturers are retaining the responsibility for disposal instead of transferring it to customers along with the other property rights.

In the early 1990s, for example, Xerox Corporation began to take back old copiers from its customers' offices, dismantle the machines, "remanufacture" modern copiers using the constituents of the old ones, and sell these remanufactured machines with a guarantee that they, too, could be returned at the end of their useful lives. Remanufactured machines now carry the same guarantees, and sell for the same prices, as machines made in the traditional manner.

Xerox executives assert that it is considerably cheaper to collect and reengineer such machines than to build them in the traditional way. Savings from the product takeback initiative arise from reduced logistics, inventory, and raw material purchasing costs. During the first twelve months of the initiative, cost savings reportedly amounted to $50 million.[2] This figure represented a mere sliver of revenues: during 1991, the year of the program's initiation, Xerox's revenues in its core document-processing business were over $13 billion. But the more relevant comparison may be to post-tax profits, which that year were only $254 million. Of these cost savings, avoided raw material purchases were probably the most significant.

Copy cartridges were an early target for recycling at Xerox. A company publication reads, "Designed for use in our smaller conventional copiers, the copy cartridge contains the main xerographic elements crit-

ical to the copying process—photoreceptor, electrical charging devices, and a cleaning mechanism."[3] As it figured out how to recycle these cartridges, Xerox improved its understanding of the remanufacturing of large machines. By 1996, cartridge return rates were 65 percent.[4] Xerox also aggressively recycled toner containers for larger machines: according to a company document, "Similar to copy cartridge return programs, customers re-box empty toner containers in their original packaging and return them with the shipping costs paid by Xerox. The containers are then cleaned, inspected and refilled or recycled."[5]

At least some of the recovered cartridges were diverted from small independent businesses that had previously collected, refilled, and resold them. Xerox's scale economies, and later changes in the cartridges' design, made these firms' operations increasingly difficult.[6]

As time passes, Xerox is integrating takeback systems more tightly into its mainstream business operations. For example, the company initially conducted its remanufacturing activities at sites separate from the new-product assembly lines, but later it began conducting both operations together to exploit economies of scale and standardize product quality procedures.[7]

Even more important, according to Xerox executives, is the incorporation of design-for-environment principles into the takeback initiative. Initially, of course, the products collected and reused in the program were not specifically designed to facilitate this process. But now the company is altering the design of its original products to make recycling easier at the end of the products' lives. Xerox executives anticipate that as design-for-environment ideas are implemented the benefits of the program will increase.

In addition, Xerox is engaged in broader initiatives to increase the amount of recycled plastic in its copy and print cartridges, equipment panels, and other components. It is working with other electronics firms and with suppliers to accomplish this goal.[8]

As a result of product takeback initiatives, Xerox reported "estimated savings to Xerox exceeding several hundred million dollars in 1995."[9] That year, revenues from continuing operations in Xerox's core document-processing businesses amounted to $16.6 billion, on which the company earned $1.17 billion after tax.[10]

Other manufacturers of electronic equipment have undertaken similar initiatives. Kodak, IBM, Canon, and other manufacturers track each other's progress in the field and imitate successful innovations.

For example, Canon's cartridge recycling initiative predated Xerox's; Hewlett-Packard encourages customers to return cartridges from computer printers; Kodak also recycles cartridges and offers its customers both new and remanufactured machines.[11]

Manufacturers' desire to manage regulatory risk doubtless figures in their decision to set up product takeback programs. The manufacturers hope that by initiating voluntary programs to take back products, they will preempt mandatory government programs that might be inflexibly designed or unnecessarily expensive, or shape those government programs to their own benefit. In this respect the manufacturers resemble the chemical companies implementing Responsible Care. Like the chemical firms, however, the manufacturers have other motives besides regulatory risk management. Takeback schemes enable the companies to increase the total amount of value they create, capture, and deliver to shareholders.

Takeback schemes can help firms financially with respect to both costs and revenues. On the cost side, takeback initiatives represent a straightforward extension of the logic of waste reduction beyond the traditional boundaries of the firm. Chapter 4 discussed companies (including Xerox) that discovered cost savings through improved efficiency in their internal operations. Takeback initiatives allow the firm to pursue similar cost savings that may exist downstream.

On the revenue side, product takeback initiatives can have important strategic implications of the sort discussed in chapter 3. Economies of scale exist in networks for product takeback, just as they do in product distribution. Further, Xerox and other established firms can use product takeback initiatives to capture business from competitors—in this case, the small companies that collected, refilled, and resold used copy cartridges. Finally, firms like Xerox may find it useful to try to manage government regulation to their own advantage: having invested in design changes that will make its products easier to disassemble than those of its competitors, Xerox could pressure regulators to require the same practices of all competing firms, as DuPont did with chlorofluorocarbon substitutes.

ELECTRIC UTILITIES AND DEMAND-SIDE MANAGEMENT

Simultaneous reductions in costs and increases in revenues may also be possible for electric utility companies. If they can creatively

restructure their own property rights and those of their customers, they can deliver more value to those customers at lower costs to themselves while reducing their environmental impacts.

Since the 1970s, American electric utilities have initiated a variety of demand-side management (DSM) programs aimed at helping their customers reduce electricity consumption while still enjoying the same real benefits from the electricity they consume. Electric utilities in the United States and elsewhere operate under an unusual regulatory framework devised in response to the peculiar economics of the production and distribution of electricity, but the lessons of DSM extend to firms not covered by these idiosyncratic rules.

Historically, electric utilities have been seen as "natural monopolies." The fixed costs of constructing a network of wires that reaches every home and business in a community are extremely high; it would be inefficient for more than one company to make this investment. But if only one company did so, then in the absence of regulation it would charge monopoly prices. To avoid these two undesirable situations, governments have generally sanctioned a single company to serve each geographic area and then regulated the prices that the company can charge.

In the United States, electric utility companies are answerable to state public utility commissions or public service commissions. Periodically, the utility brings to the commissioners a plan for meeting the demand for electricity and a statement of the capital and operating costs of the plan. The commissioners then set prices for electricity that allow the utility to recover all of its operating expenses and to earn a return on the invested capital (the "rate base") consistent with similarly risky investments in other industries.[12]

The idea behind DSM is straightforward. Traditionally, utilities have forecast future demand for their electricity using relatively simple assumptions and then built the capacity required to meet that demand. Advocates of energy efficiency have argued for decades that numerous opportunities exist for households and firms to save money by saving energy. If it costs six cents to supply an extra kilowatt-hour of electricity, but only two cents to reduce demand by a kilowatt-hour, then electric utilities should not automatically respond to economic growth by building new generating capacity. They should consider, instead, the possibility of reducing demand and sharing the resultant four-cent gain with their customers. This would leave the

utility, the customer, and society as a whole better off than they were before.

One might wonder why the utility needs to get involved at all: if its customers can really knock six dollars off their electric bills by spending two dollars, why don't they just invest in conservation themselves? Advocates of utility DSM programs suggest two reasons. First, customers may find it difficult to obtain information about the savings opportunities or to understand the information they do obtain. Thus, most utilities disseminate information on the costs and benefits of conservation as part of their DSM programs. Second, customers may lack the financial wherewithal to invest in energy conservation. If it costs several thousand dollars to insulate an attic, some homeowners won't do so even if the investment would pay a very high rate of return. Thus, many utilities have made investments in insulation, energy-efficient windows, automatic timers and switches, and other apparatuses in their customers' houses. The capital so invested is included in the rate base, and the utility commissioners allow the company to raise electricity rates in order to earn a return on its investment. The out-of-pocket costs to the customer are zero.

Electric utility companies began analyzing DSM opportunities—and financing energy conservation investments for their customers—beginning in the late 1970s. The initiatives were spurred by rising energy prices, by an uncertain inflationary environment in which large-scale sunk-cost generating stations appeared risky, and, not least, by pressure from market-oriented environmental groups like the Environmental Defense Fund. In 1979, Oregon's Pacific Power & Light began offering its customers low-interest and interest-free loans for energy conservation. The following year, northern California's Pacific Gas & Electric Company initiated a "zero interest program" under which it financed $100 million in insulation, storm windows, and other conservation devices; energy savings enabled the firm to delay or altogether avoid the construction of new generating plants. This and related initiatives allowed ratepayers and the companies' shareholders to avoid the private costs of investment in new plants, and also avoided the social costs—mostly in the form of air pollution—that the new plants would have imposed.[13]

During the 1970s, utilities also invested heavily in new generating capacity to satisfy projected future demand for electricity. Cost overruns and construction delays, especially for nuclear capacity, drove utilities'

investment levels still higher. Then, in the 1980s, regulators in several states determined retrospectively that the utilities had incurred the costs of new generating capacity in an imprudent manner and refused to allow the companies to earn a return on this invested capital. These retrospective findings highlighted the risks to the utilities of relying exclusively on supply-side initiatives, and stimulated utility interest in DSM. In 1989, American electric utilities spent close to a billion dollars on DSM. The figure rose to $2.7 billion by 1993, or about 1 percent of the utilities' total revenues.[14]

Utility deregulation now poses a serious challenge to DSM as conventionally constructed. Policy makers have concluded that whereas transmission and distribution of electricity may still be natural monopolies, generation can no longer be regarded in that light. Deregulatory proposals differ from state to state, with some states planning to introduce competition at the wholesale level and others contemplating its introduction at the retail level as well. Under either scenario, the transmission grid that connects power plants to wholesale customers will remain a legal monopoly under traditional (probably federal) regulation. At the same time, generators will lose their monopoly status and will have to compete for customers' revenues (directly in the retail competition case, indirectly in the wholesale case). This will presumably increase generators' incentives to operate efficiently, to the ultimate benefit of consumers. It will also impose additional pressure on utilities to cut discretionary costs, perhaps including DSM programs. Utilities may not be able to recapture DSM-related investments from customers as they could in the regulatory climate of the 1980s and early 1990s.

Utilities in some states, including Massachusetts, have proposed that some DSM programs be funded through mandatory payments by all customers, as a surcharge on fees for the transmission of electricity. Other aspects of DSM, including investment in residential conservation, might be funded by third parties or by the utility companies through contractual arrangements with customers.[15]

A more general challenge to DSM, related to but distinct from the move toward deregulation, arises from changing conditions in electricity markets. Shortages of generating capacity, widely predicted in the early 1980s when many DSM programs were established, have turned at least temporarily into gluts. Further, the DSM incentive programs tended to be blunt instruments: they undoubtedly encouraged people to

install insulation or reduce consumption who otherwise would not have done so, but they also generated a significant response from consumers who, according to DSM opponents, would have happily paid for the insulation themselves. The charge for this insulation was passed on to all ratepayers. Businesses and individuals whose own conservation opportunities were limited had no wish to subsidize investment from which they did not directly benefit. They argued, and regulators, courts, or legislatures in several states agreed, that DSM programs are not justified if they merely lower overall costs of electricity. To survive, they must not result in any rate increase anywhere—clearly a much more difficult requirement. For example, Georgia utility commissioners terminated Georgia Power's DSM programs on these grounds in 1995; and Connecticut's state regulatory body reached a similar decision two years later.[16] By 1996, nationwide utility spending on DSM programs was $1.9 billion, down 31 percent from its 1993 peak.[17]

Like the electronics companies' product takeback initiatives, utilities' DSM programs are alterations of traditional allocations of property rights. In this case, insulation and storm windows go in the customer's house; if the house is sold, they will be sold with it. At the same time, however, the utility company retains ownership of the assets for the purposes of calculating the rate base on which it is allowed to earn a return. The rebundling of property rights permits the utility to deliver a superior service to its customers at a lower total cost to the firm and at a lower total social cost. This rebundling benefits the utility, its customers, and the environment.

The choice of a discount rate is critical in evaluating investments in energy conservation, as noted in the discussion of hotels in the previous chapter. In the absence of utility DSM programs, consumers who buy energy-saving equipment like storm windows incur the costs of the equipment when they purchase it, and then receive the benefits in the form of cost savings over the life of the equipment. Like the hotel managers discussed earlier, they need a discount rate to account for the time value of the money invested. One might expect this discount rate or hurdle rate to approximate the opportunity cost of money—the rate at which the economic actors can lend or borrow. Suppose for example that an American consumer, carrying credit card debt at 18 percent interest, is thinking about investing in energy-saving equipment. Unless the equipment delivers at least an 18 percent return, this person would be wiser to pay off the credit cards.

A lower discount rate represents a more patient attitude, a willingness to forego more consumption now to enhance future wealth. The lower the discount rate, the larger the group of possible investments that look attractive. Economists who have studied this behavior find that some consumers use very high discount rates in making decisions about whether to purchase energy-efficient appliances: at least 20 percent, and perhaps as high as 400 percent. Wealthier individuals were found to use lower discount rates.[18] In contrast to these figures, Amory Lovins and Hunter Lovins of the Rocky Mountain Institute estimated that more than half of American electricity consumption could be eliminated at a cost per kilowatt-hour of under two cents, compared with prevalent retail prices in the six- to eight-cent range. Lovins thought that one-sixth of American electricity consumption could be saved at a cost of less than zero. To obtain these estimates, however, Lovins and Lovins used a 5 percent discount rate to calculate the present value of the energy savings.[19] Researchers at the Lawrence Berkeley Laboratory estimated that American utilities' DSM programs saved 2.4 billion kilowatt-hours per year in 1992 at an average cost of 3.2 cents per kilowatt-hour (retail sales of electricity that year were 2,763 billion kilowatt-hours). In computing this average cost, the Berkeley scholars, like Lovins and Lovins, used a discount rate of 5 percent.[20] The rates of return allowed by regulators on utilities' investments have historically been higher than 5 percent, but are obviously well below the 20 percent or higher discount rates that emerge from analyses of consumer behavior. For example, the Southern Company, the utility serving Georgia and Alabama, uses an opportunity cost of capital of 10 percent in evaluating investments.[21]

The disparity between a 20 percent or much higher rate used by households and the considerably lower rates that utility investors can obtain represents an enormous opportunity. A discount rate is a price like other prices, and when two entities attach different prices or values to a good, this gives rise to an opportunity for a mutually beneficial bargain. The whole consumer credit industry is built on the discrepancy between consumers' willingness to trade off future income for present consumption and investors' attitudes toward the same trade-off. Utility managers may have similar opportunities. As we have seen, however, the institutional impediments to their capturing this value are considerable. I will reexamine them toward the end of the chapter in the light of the utilities' own experience and that of other firms that are attempting to redefine their markets.

THE REVOLUTION IN AGRICULTURAL BIOTECHNOLOGY

Innovations in biotechnology promise to transform agricultural markets, make parts of the existing agricultural chemicals business more valuable, render others obsolete, create entire new markets for innovators, and simultaneously reduce the environmental costs of growing food. Building on enormous long-term investments in biotechnology—Monsanto alone spent $1.5 billion over fifteen years—companies are betting that they can deliver more value to farmers and farmers' customers while reducing the environmental impact of the agricultural system.[22] Agricultural biotechnology remains enormously controversial, with wide disagreements about the environmental and social risks of the technological innovations. In order to succeed commercially, the companies in the industry must not only design products and services that enhance agricultural productivity and environmental performance, but also must persuade regulators, farmers, and the ultimate consumers of the food that the innovations increase economic and social well-being.

Like the regulatory structures in the electric utility example, the market characteristics of agricultural biotechnology may seem highly idiosyncratic. But the lessons of the biotechnologists, like those of the utility managers, are transferable to other industrial settings.

Chapter 2 examined Monsanto Company's successful efforts to position its Roundup glyphosate herbicide as a product that saves farmers money while simultaneously reducing their environmental impact. Monsanto sells Roundup as the logical complement to no-till agriculture, which reduces both soil erosion and the farmer's labor and energy costs. This product positioning has enabled Monsanto to expand its sales beyond the level that would otherwise have been attainable.

Building on their long-term investments in biotechnology, Monsanto and its competitors are introducing engineered crops that will further increase the demand for their herbicide products and further reduce environmental impacts. Monsanto sells seeds for plants that are resistant to Roundup, so that the herbicide can be used after the crop sprouts. In 1996, the firm introduced seeds for Roundup Ready soybeans and Roundup Ready canola. The economic benefits to farmers are significant: for canola, incremental returns averaged nearly twenty dollars per acre planted.[23] Social cost savings arise in the form of

reduced pollution from the manufacture, distribution, and use of alternative herbicides.

The U.S. patents on Roundup will soon expire, and competition from generic equivalents is already pervasive abroad. Monsanto's position in the markets for the seeds, protected by both patents and manufacturing know-how, is likely to be far easier to defend. Monsanto also produces Roundup Ready cotton, and plans to extend the line to encompass corn, oilseed rape, sugar beets, rice, and wheat.[24] Meanwhile, AgrEvo Canada, a joint venture of German companies Hoechst and Schering, sells both Liberty glufosinate herbicide and seeds for canola, corn, and soybeans engineered to be resistant to that herbicide. And Calgene (a California firm later bought by Monsanto) and Rhône-Poulenc of France developed a cotton plant that is tolerant of bromoxynil, sold by Rhône-Poulenc as Buctril herbicide.[25]

Monsanto, Novartis (the Swiss company formed by the 1997 merger of Ciba-Geigy and Sandoz), and other biotechnology companies are racing to disseminate similar innovations in pest management. A naturally occurring soil bacterium called *Bacillus thuringiensis* (Bt for short) produces proteins that are harmful to cotton budworms, the European corn borer, and the Colorado potato beetle. By transferring genetic material from the Bt organism to cotton, corn, and potato plants, the companies have created plants resistant to the insects. This innovation enables growers to use far less pesticide on their fields, and hence reduces both private costs (the costs of pesticide manufacture and distribution) and social costs (the environmental damage caused by pesticide use). Monsanto introduced Bollgard Bt cotton in 1996, and Novartis launched its Bt corn product, Maximizer, the same year. In 1997, Monsanto introduced Yieldgard corn and NewLeaf potatoes. Monsanto plans to introduce cotton resistant to boll weevils, wheat resistant to fungal and viral diseases, and other pest- and disease-resistant products early in the new century.[26]

In 1996, the first year it sold Bt cotton, Monsanto charged farmers a licensing fee of thirty-two dollars per acre but estimated that the farmers would save fifty to sixty dollars per acre because they would need to apply fewer pesticides.[27] Gains to the farmer can also occur in the form of yield increases. Seed accounts for a relatively small fraction of a grower's total costs, so that small increases in yield enable farmers to offset considerable increases in the price of the seed. For example, Novartis and Mycogen (a firm majority owned by Dow Chemical)

jointly sell a Bt corn product. The seed costs about forty dollars per acre sown, compared with thirty-two dollars for conventional seed corn, but this investment will pay for itself if yields increase by 2 percent.[28] By contrast, a light infestation of corn borers—too light to make spraying pesticides attractive—can reduce yields by over 10 percent.[29]

To bring these new technologies to market and to recover their investments in the underlying science, Monsanto and its competitors have imposed unusual restrictions on their customers' activities. The companies are especially anxious to prevent farmers from saving the seeds from plants grown one year and planting them the following spring, a practice known as "brown bagging." Farmers have to agree explicitly not to resell seeds, not to retain them without planting them, and not to collect seeds from the plants they grow. At the same time, they must tolerate regular inspections of their crops by the seed companies—a significant departure from previous practice.[30]

Despite these restrictions, and despite some performance problems in 1997 (about 10,000 acres' worth of Roundup Ready cotton did not grow properly, and Monsanto paid the would-be growers an undisclosed amount in compensation), American farmers have rapidly adopted these new technologies. By 1998, for example, herbicide-tolerant and Bt cotton accounted for 5.5 of the 12.2 million acres planted in cotton in the United States, up from 2.2 of 13.8 million the previous year. (Growers on the other 1.6 million acres switched to soybeans or corn in response to changes in the relative prices of these crops.)[31]

This favorable marketplace verdict stood in marked contrast to that of Monsanto's first serious foray into agricultural biotechnology: its 1994 introduction of bovine somatotropin (BST). This product, trademarked Posilac, increases milk yields when fed to cows. Monsanto developed BST over a dozen years at a cost of $500 million. Like the engineered seeds, BST was thought capable of reducing both private and social costs. The increase in milk yields of over 10 percent would allow current levels of milk production to be sustained with a 10 percent reduction in the total number of dairy cows if the remaining 90 percent were given BST. This, in turn, would reduce the amount of land, water, agricultural chemicals, and other inputs to the production of grain crops for cattle feed. Monsanto's marketing materials for BST explicitly stressed these productivity gains.[32]

Regulators in the United States were cooperative. In approving the product, Food and Drug Administration Commissioner David A.

Kessler said, "There is virtually no difference in milk from treated and untreated cows. In fact, it's not possible using current scientific techniques to tell them apart. We are confident this product is safe for consumers, for cows and for the environment."[33] But some consumers worried about the health consequences of drinking milk from BST-treated cows, grocers worried about scaring consumers out of their stores, farmers worried about the health of their animals, and government officials worried about the financial health of farmers in a business already plagued by overcapacity and complicated by price supports. A year after the product's introduction, about 10 percent of the 9.5 million American dairy cows were receiving a $5.80 injection of Posilac every twenty days, but this number failed to grow in later years.[34] As of 1996, the product was thought to be losing $10 million a year.[35] Meanwhile, the European Union, facing its own glut of dairy products and a public skeptical of biotechnology, placed a moratorium on the use of BST until the end of 1999.[36]

Like BST, the engineered crops remain subjects of bitter controversy among end consumers, environmentalists, and politicians. In 1996, for example, Monsanto began sending to Europe Roundup Ready soybeans that had been grown in the United States. Although regulatory officials at the European Union had approved the sale and distribution of the soybeans, public reaction to the soybeans' introduction was intensely negative. The beans were not labeled as genetically modified, so consumers could not assure themselves, if they wished to, that they were not directly or indirectly consuming engineered farm products. The European Union is now revisiting its regulations for cultivating, importing, and labeling such crops. Meanwhile, the regulators have approved the importation or cultivation of several other biotech products, including Bt corn.[37]

At the same time, however, Greenpeace, the Sierra Club, and other environmental organizations plan to sue the EPA unless it withdraws its approval of Bt crops.[38] Greenpeace argues that the introduction of the technology will accelerate pests' development of resistance to Bt, which is used in the organic farming industry as an alternative to synthetic pesticides. AgrEvo's product safety manager for biotechnology, Sue MacIntosh, told a conference of insect ecologists that the company was assuming that "delaying resistance through management for 20 years" was possible, but that insects would eventually develop resistance to Bt in plants.[39] One way to slow the development of resistance

is to plant non-Bt crops near the Bt crops so that insects that are not resistant to the toxin are able to survive. The Union of Concerned Scientists and other organizations would like the EPA to mandate the use of large "refuges" of this sort, constituting 20 percent to 50 percent of total crop average in corn, potatoes, and cotton. The EPA mandates a refuge strategy for cotton but not for the other crops.[40]

Despite these interrelated scientific and political problems, forecasts of revenues and profits in agricultural biotechnology remain extremely optimistic. Simon Best, chief executive of "Zeneca Plant Sciences," estimated that sales of engineered plants would reach $2 billion by the year 2000 and $20 billion ten years later. Traditional pesticides, by contrast, account for $25 billion in annual sales.[41] In July 1998, Monsanto stock was trading at eight times book value and more than a hundred times earnings, and bidding wars for smaller agricultural biotechnology companies pushed the multiples of these firms even higher.

Clearly, innovations in biotechnology need not be triggered by a conscious attempt to lower social costs; they may be motivated by traditional competitive concerns. "I don't think it ultimately matters whether my soul is pure or I want to make a lot of money for shareholders; we come out at the same place," says Monsanto chairman Robert Shapiro.[42]

ANALYZING THE ENVIRONMENTAL REDEFINITION OF MARKETS

All of these case examples involve the redefinition of the markets in which the companies are competing. In each case, the new definition is intended to allow the innovative firm simultaneously to lower its costs, deliver more private value to its customers, and improve its environmental performance.

Strategies that redefine markets are often characterized as "moving from a product to a service mentality."[43] Livio DeSimone of 3M and Frank Popoff of Dow Chemical, writing with the World Business Council for Sustainable Development, argued that "there is a growing realization that customers do not value physical goods—or ownership of them—for their own sake. The goods are merely a means to an end—satisfying customers' needs. The implication is that the best marketing approach will be the one that provides a complete service to

meet those needs. Taking ownership of physical goods might be a part of this service, but it might not."[44] As Monsanto chairman Robert Shapiro points out, "No one says, 'Gee, I'd like to put a cathode-ray tube and a lot of printed circuit boards in my living room.' People *might* say, 'I'd like to watch the ball game' or 'Let's turn on the soaps.'" [45]

In the three case examples just discussed, the firms' executives do not think of themselves as producing goods for sale to customers. Instead, they view their activities as providing customers with a service, using physical materials only insofar as this is the cheapest way to provide that service. Monsanto and its competitors no longer think of themselves as producers of agricultural chemicals but rather as providers of crop protection. Similarly, Xerox is trying to redefine its business as the service of manipulating printed and electronic information, rather than as the sale of copy machines; utility managers engaged in demand-side management see their business as energy services rather than the delivery of electricity. In each case, the redefinition allows the executives to imagine ways of delivering the service that result in increased value to customers (and hence increased willingness to pay), lower costs for the firm, and lower aggregate social costs.

In addition to redefining markets, the firms in these cases are altering the scope of their activities. The electronics firms are extending their reach into recycling, the utility companies into insulation and other services for consumers, and the agricultural biotechnology companies into completely new methods of crop protection. In each case, however, the initiative is more than just an expansion of the scope of the firm's operations. If the firm does no more than take over operations previously performed by others, it should not expect to be successful. Monsanto and its rivals clearly are engaging in new activities, not just supplanting other firms' existing operations. Xerox can extend its scope into the territory previously occupied by small recyclers only because it brings distinctive competence and cost advantage to that operation. The utilities assert that they, too, possess a cost advantage in their new demand-side endeavors, but their mettle will be tested in the deregulated markets.

SOURCES OF SUSTAINABLE ADVANTAGE

Like any competitive strategy, approaches involving a redefinition of markets along environmental lines must enjoy some protection from

competitive imitation. We already observed this problem in chapter 2, when we examined product differentiation strategies. Proprietary technology and economies of scale are familiar to corporate strategists as sources of protection from imitators, and they play important roles in the environmental arena as well.

The utility companies lack proprietary technology for DSM, and the economies of scale in that business are limited. One would expect that their DSM services would attract imitators, and this is in fact occurring. Utilities' DSM activity is being copied successfully by independent energy service companies (called ESCOs in the trade) that specialize in understanding energy customers' opportunities to save energy and money and in implementing schemes that will allow consumers and the ESCOs to split the savings. Utilities have benefited from direct government regulations that have buffered the firms from competitive forces and allowed them to provide environmental public goods through the redefinition of markets. As the deregulation of the industry progresses, though, the utilities will need some technological or economic barriers to replace the governmental one if they are to capture value in this way.

By contrast, Monsanto, Novartis, and the other agricultural biotechnology firms have more straightforward ways of maintaining a profitable redefinition of their markets. They are protected both by formal patents and by the huge investments that competitors would need to sink to replicate the first movers' capabilities. The companies supplement these technological barriers to competition with other barriers based on economies of scale in marketing, distribution, post-sale service, and business-government relations.

Xerox, too, is striving to create technological protection for its strategy by investing in environmental design changes that are difficult for competitors—especially small refillers of cartridges or toner containers—to replicate. Xerox also enjoys protection from its competitors in the form of scale economies and brand reputation. Its takeback initiatives depend on these advantages for success, but the initiatives themselves may improve both the cost position and the reputation over time.

RELATIONS WITH REGULATORS, CUSTOMERS, AND OTHER FIRMS

More broadly, all of the strategies discussed in this chapter benefit from the support or tacit approval of government agencies. Even if

the reorganizations of property rights on which they are based increase well-being in an aggregate sense, they will rarely leave everyone better off: one man's roast beef is another's gored ox.[46] Significant environmental initiatives are bound to be challenged in the political and legal arenas. This is exactly what has occurred, for example, with respect to DSM programs: consumers who are not direct beneficiaries have successfully complained that they should not have to subsidize other consumers. The introduction of product takeback schemes, too, has hurt some economic actors, and the small companies whose operations are threatened by the cartridge recycling programs of Xerox and others have sued the larger companies under antitrust laws. In the case of agricultural biotechnology, the actors most directly hurt are the makers of conventional pesticides and herbicides, often the same firms as those that are introducing the new technologies.

Innovative managers need to anticipate who may be hurt by their initiatives and the likely responses of those organizations in the marketplace and the political arena. That is, they must understand the economic effects of the changes on other actors and the abilities of those actors to affect political outcomes. If the parties that will be hurt are other divisions of the same company, managers can and should resolve the disputes internally. If the potential losers are outside the firm, then the managers' problem is the same as that confronted by DuPont, the California oil companies, and other firms described in chapter 3: the managers need to anticipate their adversaries' responses and formulate plans to counter them in the marketplace and the political arena.

In addition to these political issues, firms pursuing strategies of market redefinition face some interesting marketing challenges. Any firm proposing innovative rearrangements of property rights needs to persuade its customers that the changes will serve their interests. From one point of view, the marketing problems facing the companies discussed here are straightforward. The companies are making value propositions to their customers that do not depend on the customers' willingness to subsidize environmental quality: from the customers' standpoint, storm windows paid for by someone else, or an improved method of protecting crops, pay for themselves independent of their effect on social cost. From this perspective the initiatives are more like Ciba's introduction of bireactive dyestuffs than like the Heinz introduction of dolphin-safe tuna: they appeal directly to customers' economic interests.

One especially important challenge in persuading other firms to cooperate in redefining markets is that the redefinitions involve changes in the institutions that govern economic behavior—both formal rules and informal expectations about "normal" business practice. New allocations of property rights require new kinds of behavior with which customers may be unfamiliar and uncomfortable. This problem arises clearly in the case of agricultural biotechnology, where the new technology requires restrictions on traditional activities like the "brown bagging" of seeds, and also requires monitoring of the farmers by the seed companies. In the long run, these requirements will likely lead to an improved understanding by seed company managers of their customers' needs, and to closer relationships between producers and farmers, thus conferring additional benefits beyond the immediate benefits of the technology. But in the short run, the new requirements may increase farmers' resistance to the new products. The creation of new institutions is not a job for the impatient, but it is likely to be both necessary for the redefinition of markets and an important benefit of that redefinition.

THE ROLE OF INFORMATION

It is partly for this reason that investments in information are critical to the success of strategies involving the redefinition of markets. We have seen the importance of information in strategies involving cost reduction within the firm, and information becomes even more important when the firm is trying to economize over the entire value chain.

Companies undertaking strategies of market redefinition need to have a sound understanding of their own economics and the economics of their customers' businesses. As Xerox anticipated and is now verifying, designing products for easier takeback and disassembly can improve the economics of takeback initiatives. Meanwhile, as Monsanto discovered, the basic economics of the farm businesses to which the company is selling its biotechnological products are critical determinants of adoption and market penetration. And utility companies, by failing to separate customers who were willing to pay for home insulation from those who weren't, increased the tax they needed to levy on all households and therefore increased the political opposition to their innovations.

The design of product takeback systems, biotechnological innovations, or energy conservation programs involves trading off environmental

impacts at the end of a product's life against impacts at other stages of the life cycle. For this reason, firms with expertise in environmental cost accounting are more likely to succeed with design-for-environment initiatives. Conversely, such initiatives can also strengthen a firm's ability to analyze and understand its environmental costs by creating a demand for this kind of cost information and a demonstration of its usefulness.

Because successful design-for-environment programs weigh products' impacts during manufacture, use, and disposal using a common measure, they rarely involve complete recyclability of products. Indeed, the implication of systematic thinking about product costs and design-for-environment is that complete recyclability of products is not necessarily desirable. In the motor vehicle industry, for example, only one-sixth of the total energy consumed over the life of a car is used in production and recycling; the other five-sixths is used in driving.[47] Use of recyclable materials may increase the overall burden imposed on the environment if these materials are heavier and thus reduce fuel efficiency during the car's life.

From a wider perspective, it seems even more likely that investment in information would be critical to the success of strategies that redefine markets. The strategies involve shifting not only from the provision of goods to the provision of services, but also from capital, labor, and materials on one hand to information on the other. Monsanto executives stress that their strategy hinges on substituting information for materials. Information—the genetic instructions that enable plants to protect themselves against caterpillars—can replace a whole material-intensive value chain that uses capital, transportation systems, and the labor of farmers to apply pesticides to crops.

Why might this be sensible? At the most basic level, the optimal strategy for a firm—the best way for it to produce its outputs—depends in part on the relative prices of the inputs it uses to make them. The costs of labor are trending upward. The costs of capital and of basic materials seem likely to rise as the rate of savings in developed countries declines for demographic reasons, and as energy and natural resource prices rise to reflect increasing relative scarcity. Meanwhile, thanks to phenomenal advances in information technology, the costs of information continue to fall. Optimists in the debate about the "limits to growth" believe that improvements in information, and the attendant gains in total factor productivity, will offset any scarcity of nonrenewable natural resources and capital. As these resources and capital become more

scarce and hence more expensive, firms will face incentives to substitute renewable resources, of which knowledge is perhaps the purest example.[48] The structures of the markets in the information-based products may be considerably more favorable than those of the old nonrenewable resources, leading to a double benefit from the firms' point of view.

DEFINING THE BASELINE

In evaluating opportunities to redefine markets, managers need to be careful to define the baseline properly. The value of seeds engineered to be resistant to insect pests, as opposed to the traditional chemical methods of pest control, depends on many factors. Variables that will affect the seeds' value include the stringency of pesticide regulation, the costs of the fossil fuels used as feedstocks for the chemicals and as a source of energy for their transportation and application, the continued efficacy of traditional pesticides, and the externalities that may arise from the transgenic seeds. Monsanto and Novartis, for example, are betting that agricultural practices will have to change as insects increase their resistance to traditional pesticides, as fossil fuel prices rise, and as societal tolerance for widespread pesticide application becomes more and more strained. Their opponents are betting that the externalities from the genetically engineered seeds—in the form of accelerated resistance of insects to Bt—will prove far more expensive than the companies assert. Neither the firms nor their opponents think that the baseline against which the firms' investments should be evaluated is continued business as usual.

If redefining the value chain, as Monsanto and Xerox are trying to do, adds value, it might seem as though environmental concern should not be required for this restructuring to occur. As we have seen, though, there is nothing automatic about the creation of value, and this is especially true of redefinitions of the value system that require changes in the behavior of suppliers, distributors, and customers as well as changes within the firm. It may not be in these entities' interests, relative to the status quo, to have the value system restructured. Environmental concern may enable companies to move their suppliers, distributors, and customers away from the status quo to a new and (to the company initiating the change) more favorable situation, particularly if the initiating firm shares some of the benefits with those parties or if the change reduces those parties' environmental risk.

In other words, in the absence of environmental pressure, suppliers, distributors, or customers might successfully resist the substitution of information for materials if this does not favor their own short-term interests. In fact, one of the jobs for the firm undertaking the restructuring of the value system may be to persuade those whose interests will be affected that the status quo is not the relevant baseline for comparison. Innovators must persuade these other entities that some change is inevitable, and that the one proposed by the innovators is preferable to the ones that might otherwise be imposed by regulators or the courts. The other entities are more likely to be persuaded if the innovators can share some of the benefits of the change with these suppliers, distributors, or customers. Given the considerable value that can be created by redefinitions of markets and restructuring of property rights, the innovators may be able to appear fairly generous and still leave themselves with a substantially improved position.

THE CASE examples in this chapter are more complicated than those discussed in earlier chapters. They all involve strategies that pursue multiple objectives simultaneously, combining cost reduction within the firm, superior customer service, and improved environmental performance.

Most executives would be happy if they could improve their performance along any one of these three dimensions without suffering significant setbacks along one or both of the others. Given the difficulty of achieving even one of these objectives alone, it may seem surprising that companies can successfully pursue all at once. Of the cases studied here, it is still too early to tell whether utility DSM programs can survive the shareholder value test in the institutional climate of deregulation, or whether the agricultural biotechnology revolution can surmount the significant scientific, economic, and political obstacles it confronts. The product takeback initiative of the electronics companies is further advanced, but even it still confronts substantial regulatory and market uncertainty. In all of the cases examined in this book, there is no point at which the executives can conclude that they have succeeded and begin to relax. But the absence of any such hiatus is especially striking here.

At the same time, the stories in this chapter are encouraging. It is true that each of the stories is idiosyncratic: not all firms enjoy the market power wielded by Xerox, the unusual regulatory relationships of the

electric utilities, or the huge base of scientific expertise, product development, and government relations commanded by Monsanto and Novartis. But the examination of these unusual companies does yield more general insights into the management of environmental problems.

We have seen, for example, that inventors of a feasible way to deliver more well-being to customers at a lower social cost should be able to find ways to make that happen, although their ability to hold on to the value they create will depend, as always, on the economics of their business and on the institutional framework in which they operate. Institutions include the legal rules of the economic game, which clearly influence how much value companies can add and retain. Institutions also include social expectations about what sorts of allocations of property rights are "reasonable," and these, too, both create and limit opportunities to deliver and capture extra value.[49]

We have also seen that, to overcome obstacles, innovators need to consider sharing the value they create with customers and other parties. This makes institutional change easier as the number of beneficiaries grows. More radical technological changes are likely to require more such gain-sharing to overcome institutional resistance, but those radical changes are also more likely to give rise to large gains that can be widely shared.

Finally, as we have seen previously, time horizons are critical. Variations in time horizons can create opportunities to add value, as in the utility DSM case. More generally, firms with longer time horizons, unlike their less patient counterparts, are in a better position to build up the technological and economic power they need to redefine markets and benefit the environment and their own shareholders.

Managing Risk and Uncertainty

THE PRECEDING chapters have examined the ways in which some companies can improve their financial performance while responding to social and regulatory demands for increased environmental quality. To that end, they have considered approaches to environmental management that aim explicitly at creating competitive advantage. In many businesses, however, the explicit purpose of environmental management is not so much the creation of competitive advantage as the reduction of risk. This chapter examines firms' management of the business risk that can arise from concern about the environment.

While not every business should try to differentiate products along environmental lines or to use environmental concern as a way to tie its competitors' hands, every firm must manage environmental risk. In fact, much of what companies do in the environmental arena falls into the category of risk management: lowering the probability of accidents during operations, for example, or reducing the chances that activists will target the company. A more analytic and systematic approach to environmental risk management can benefit firms by revealing opportunities to reduce or shift risks cost-effectively. In fact, although it is natural to think of risk management as distinct from value creation, a business that manages risk better than its competitors will find this capability to be a source of competitive advantage over the long term.

Most firms do not manage environmental risks in the same ways as other business risks. The systems and procedures for managing

environmental risk are different, for example, from those for managing foreign exchange risk or risks of increases in the costs of raw materials. One question is whether companies could benefit from managing environmental risk in ways more similar to their other risk management activities.

This chapter begins with an overview of environmental risk and its management by firms. In the course of this discussion, we need to keep track of a number of alternative definitions of risk and risk management. "Environmental risk" can refer to the risk of damage to people's health or to natural systems that results from pollution or other environmental degradation. Alternatively, it can denote the risk of financial harm to a firm that can arise from its own environmental behavior and that of other economic actors, including regulators. The second category includes several kinds of risks, such as risk of legal liability for environmental damage and risk of business interruption in the aftermath of an environmental accident. This chapter will identify several tools that both governments and firms use to manage these risks; these tools reduce the risks, shift them to other parties, or both.

Following this introductory discussion of risk and risk management, I will turn to four cases about risk management in a variety of economic and institutional settings. The first two case studies pertain to manufacturing facilities in the North American pulp and paper industry. Alberta-Pacific Forest Industries and Champion International Corporation are attempting to reduce their mills' environmental impacts in order to manage the business risks of lawsuits, business interruptions, and punitive regulation. Because of their similarities, and because each involves a single industrial facility rather than a more complex industrial network, these cases provide an ideal introduction to the problems of risk assessment and risk management.

The next case, on Chevron Corporation, shows how the same problems play out in a more complicated setting involving decentralized management in a very large firm. In addition to risk assessment and risk management, this case raises problems of incentive design and information management. The final case example in the chapter, on the electronics manufacturing industry, shows the application of these same ideas in a setting where operations are beyond the direct control of the managers whose risk is being affected. The prevalence of contract manufacturing in electronics presents managers at firms like Xerox and Hewlett-Packard with some particularly challenging risk management problems.

Following these case studies, I return to the analysis of the management of environmental risk and uncertainty, assembling a picture of the most important considerations for managers. As before, I use the cases as touchstones to help us understand the underlying logic of sensible risk management. The cases show that a variety of risk management tools exist to affect different elements of environmental risk; executives need not make use of all of them, but they at least ought to be aware of their existence. The cases also show that, although risk management is traditionally seen as a necessary cost at odds with the spirit of value creation, superior risk management can actually contribute to the creation of value. Finally, we will see that environmental risk management should be related to other risk management activities within the firm, rather than be treated as an isolated or peripheral function.

THREE PERSPECTIVES ON ENVIRONMENTAL RISK

Risk exists when a decision maker confronts events that are contingent: events, that is, whose occurrence is possible but not certain. In financial textbooks, the word "risk" is often used to describe the variance of some return around its expected value.[1] That is, risk refers to the possibility of both undesirable and desirable events. In common English, "risk" is confined to events that are undesirable, and this is its usual meaning in business outside of financial circles. Executives at insurance companies, for example, would say that what they do for a living is to understand and manage risk. They mean that they will succeed only if they understand the probabilities and magnitudes of the financial losses that fall on households or companies, and use this information to create insurance products that are both attractive to their customers and profitable to supply.

In the context of business and the environment, "risk" has three related but distinct definitions. The first is the possibility of harm to human health and ecosystems that arises from some human activity. The second is the possibility of financial damage to a firm that arises from environmental change or from social concern about the environment. The third is the possibility of personal liability or criminal penalties for executives that arises from their firms' environmental activities.

When environmental regulators and activists speak of "risk," they are using the first of these three definitions: the possibility of harm to

human health and ecosystems that arises from some human activity. For instance, they might speak of the risk of cancer that arises from contamination of drinking water, or the risk of declining bird populations because of logging operations in a forest. The U.S. EPA does not explicitly define risk, but the government officials' implicit definition emerges clearly in reports like this one from an EPA advisory board: "Each environmental problem poses some possibility of harm to human health, the ecology, the economic system, or the quality of human life. . . . Risk assessment is the process by which the form, dimension, and characteristics of that risk are estimated."[2]

From the firm's perspective, it is important to distinguish between the possibility that the environment or human health will be damaged and the possibility that the firm will suffer financial loss. Either is commonly called "environmental risk," but the two are obviously not the same. They will not usually be equal in magnitude; either can be quite severe even if the other is small.

Consider the possibility of an oil spill. To a government official or a staffer at the Environmental Defense Fund, "environmental risk" would mean the risk to ecosystems or to human health that the spill would create. To a business executive or a banker, it might have this meaning as well, but it also might refer to the possibility of economic damage to the firm or the bank as a result of the spill.

This contingent economic damage could take several forms. Some are easier to quantify than others, but all could be considered environmental risk. The cost of the cleanup that regulators might require is one example; the liability for damages that the firm might incur is a second; the risk of a damaged reputation in the eyes of government officials, consumers, and the public is a third. These business risks are all related to one another, and to the risk of damage to the physical environment, about which the regulators and the environmentalists are concerned. But each is different from the others, and all of them are distinct from the risk of damage to the environment.

The total economic exposure of the company (i.e., the maximum amount it would lose if the adverse event occurred) can be either larger or smaller than the total social cost of the event. In general, the company's economic exposure will be smaller, because the company will not be liable for the entire social damage caused by an adverse event in which it is not the only actor. On the other hand, some methods of dispute resolution, like those under tort law in the United States, can

result in punitive damages greater than the total social damage caused by an incident. And the Comprehensive Environmental Response, Compensation, and Liability Act (better known as the Superfund law) establishes strict joint and several liability for companies that contributed hazardous waste to disposal sites that are later found to be creating hazards to human health. Under this law, any contributor of waste to a site can be held liable for the site's entire cleanup cost, regardless of the relative size of its own contributions of waste materials.

We also need to consider the environmental business risk that falls directly on individuals rather than on the firms for which they work. Since the 1980s, environmental regulators in the United States have been using criminal prosecutions for violations of environmental laws as supplements to the traditional civil and administrative law procedures. The major federal environmental statutes (the Clean Air Act, the Clean Water Act, the Resource Conservation and Recovery Act, the Superfund law, and so on) all create the risk of individual fines and imprisonment for corporate executives who knowingly violate the regulations written under them.[3] The possibility that executives can personally face criminal prosecution complicates risk management both for managers and for shareholders in the companies they run.

AN OVERVIEW OF RISK ASSESSMENT:
FOUR FACTORS THAT INFLUENCE RISK

Executives who manage environmental risk are ultimately interested in the probability distribution of some contingent cost. As an example, consider the oil spill again. To assess the probability distribution of the contingent costs of a spill, executives need to think systematically about the several elements that affect it. The first of these elements is the probability that the adverse event will occur; the second is the probability distribution of the total costs if it does occur; the third is the distribution of allocations of responsibility for those contingent costs. In the oil spill example, this last distribution depends on readily measurable quantities like the amount of insurance the firm has purchased, and on less easily measured factors like the probabilities of successful lawsuits against the firm.

Together, these three elements define a probability distribution for the contingent cost, also called a "risk profile."[4] This distribution

can be narrow or broad. In a narrow distribution, the possible outcomes are not too dissimilar from one another; in a broad distribution, the range of possible outcomes is extensive.

A fourth element that the executives need to consider is the solidity or robustness of their assessments of these probability distributions. A robust assessment is one about which the executives are relatively comfortable; that is, they think it unlikely that their assessment would be much affected by new information of any sort that they can imagine obtaining. A less robust assessment, by contrast, is one that is thought likely to be subject to considerable revision as new information arrives.

This robustness can be distinguished from the narrowness or breadth of the probability distribution itself.[5] For some risks, decision makers' assessments of the probability distributions can be quite robust even though the risks themselves have broad probability distributions. An extreme example is a state-run lottery. Here the probability distribution of prizes is very wide (with a few people winning millions and most getting nothing). But at the same time, an observer's assessment of that probability distribution is extremely robust, since the distribution of prizes is fully controlled by the lottery's organizers and hence can be exactly known by anyone. Fire insurance for houses provides a similar example: the variance of fire damage across houses is great, but the probabilities are very well understood. For other risks, by contrast, executives might think that their assessment is not very robust even though their best current understanding is that the probability distribution is narrow. This will often be the case for environmental risks because these depend not only on physical events (like fires or storms) but also on future regulatory and legal changes, which may be very difficult to predict.

Reflecting the importance of these considerations of robustness, some scholars have drawn a distinction between risk and uncertainty, defining risk as a situation in which it is possible to define probability distributions for the possible outcomes, and uncertainty as a situation in which it is not possible to define these probability distributions. Other scholars have argued that this distinction lacks both theoretical basis and practical implications, and that there is no sharp line to be drawn between uncertainty and risk.[6] It does seem clear, however, that the quality of information available to executives about a particular set of risks—that is, the robustness of their assessments of the risks—will affect the executives' risk management strategies. At the very least, a

low degree of robustness may indicate that it would be sensible to invest in more information about the probability and magnitude of the risk in question, especially if the risk is thought to be large. More generally, the quality of information available to executives about a given risk is likely to influence their choice of the mechanisms for managing that risk.

AN OVERVIEW OF RISK MANAGEMENT

Considering these four elements that together affect a particular risk suggests a natural way to think about risk management. When executives manage risk, they are trying to affect one or more of these four factors. They can change the probability distribution of the total costs, either by (1) changing the probability that the adverse event will occur or by (2) changing the total losses if it does occur. In the oil spill example, these changes can occur through physical investments: the executives can invest in double-hulled tankers, lowering the probability of a spill, or they can invest in rapid-response crews, reducing the costs if a spill occurs. In addition, they can invest in (3) changing the distribution of the allocation of responsibility for the costs or shifting the contingent costs from themselves to other parties. This can be done through contracts and other institutional mechanisms: the oil company executives can buy insurance or invest in legal help to shift the burden of the spill to other parties. Finally, executives can manage their risks by (4) obtaining more information about the probability of the event, the magnitude of its costs, and the distribution of those costs among the firm and other actors. This will permit them to make better decisions about the first three elements.[7]

In allocating risk reduction investments among the four elements of risk management, companies should invest capital where it will create the most benefit. One critical complication here is that investments made in any of the four elements may affect one or more of the others, reinforcing or, more often, offsetting the benefits of the investment. For example, if a firm invests in information about environmental risk, it may by this very act increase its likely share of whatever environmental damages have to be paid for. These relationships emerge in the Chevron and electronics industry examples later in this chapter, and are discussed in more detail following the cases.

GOVERNMENTAL TOOLS FOR MANAGING RISK, AND THEIR IMPLICATIONS FOR MANAGERS

Although this chapter focuses on the private management of private risk, the ways government manages social risk set the context for the private decisions.[8] Governments use a number of mechanisms to try to bring about a situation in which risk is managed appropriately. In practice, any government is likely to use almost all of them, although the mechanisms can conflict with one another and the presence of one can make others less effective. Among these mechanisms, command-and-control regulation receives particular attention in this book because its use in the environmental area is so widespread: government tries to reduce risk by requiring or prohibiting certain types of behavior. These regulations are aimed at reducing the probability of some bad event, at reducing the event's magnitude if it does occur, or at both objectives at once. For example, a speed limit reduces both the probability of car accidents and the likely consequences if one occurs.

Other governmental mechanisms for risk management abound. Voluntary insurance contracts are a traditional way of managing many risks, but government may find it desirable to compel people to enter into insurance contracts; along with command-and-control speed limits and product standards, this is a typical way to manage the risk of car accidents. The court system and the common law are additional risk management mechanisms: under tort law, courts assign responsibility for an adverse event after the event occurs, in keeping with principles and precedents from earlier cases. Governments also use direct subsidies to mitigate risks, for example, by insuring deposits in banks and in savings and loan institutions. Finally, governments can require private entities to provide additional information with the intention of altering risk management practices. In the environmental arena, for example, "right-to-know" laws require firms to publish data on the volumes and types of pollution they release.

Any step that the government takes to bring about risk reduction is likely to shift risk, and any action it takes to shift risk is likely to affect incentives and hence the amount of risk reduction that takes place. For example, implementing policies based on notions about the "fair" allocation of the contingent costs may result in a greater total risk level. If the government promises to subsidize certain risky behavior (i.e., to compensate actors after the fact for contingent costs), one

would expect people to engage in more of that behavior. This problem is widely thought to have contributed to the savings and loan crisis of the 1980s. At the same time, attempts to reduce the overall level of risk typically result in the transfer of risk from some parties to others. For example, product liability law is intended to lower the overall risk of unsafe products by making manufacturers responsible for any damages caused, deliberately shifting risk from consumers to producers to bring about lower levels of risk. (The underlying assumption is that producers are better able to analyze and manage product safety than consumers are.) The logic here is similar to that in chapter 3, which noted that any government program changes both overall social wealth and the way in which that wealth is distributed.

Risk reduction and risk shifting are interrelated for two reasons. First, information flows imperfectly within and among economic units like firms and government agencies. Individuals and firms that will directly be hurt by some adverse event often know more about the likelihood of that event, or about the magnitude of its consequences, than the insurance companies or government agencies that are interested in reducing or shifting these risks. For example, individuals know much more about their own health than insurance companies can: if health insurance were available to anyone at a set price that reflected average probabilities of disease, unhealthy individuals would be more likely to buy it than healthier ones. Also, the same individuals are likely to be in a position to change those risks in ways that the insurance companies or government agencies cannot detect.[9]

A second reason that risk reduction and risk shifting are related is that once an adverse event occurs, it changes the incentives for the parties concerned. This is a particular problem for governments. Once a flood happens, it is very difficult for Congress to withhold funds to help the victims reconstruct their homes and livelihoods, even if, prior to the flood, it explicitly stated that it would not make these expenditures.

Governments thus have a variety of mechanisms by which to manage risk. They can try directly to reduce the probabilities and magnitudes of adverse events through regulation. They can shift risk from one party to another in a deliberate attempt to create incentives for firms or individuals to reduce probabilities and magnitudes. They can create new requirements about the dissemination of information in order to achieve the same results. Finally, they can shift risk or impose information requirements without a well-defined goal of changing behavior, out

of a sense of fairness, for example—but this risk shifting, too, will have consequences, perhaps unintended, for the probabilities and magnitudes of the risks. And governments' ability to allocate responsibility for costs after the fact increases the risks for private firms.

PRIVATE MECHANISMS FOR RISK MANAGEMENT

Executives, especially in large and decentralized firms, confront two related problems in managing business risk, each of which resembles a problem confronted by government officials. The executives need to determine the right mix of risk reduction, risk shifting, and information acquisition. And they also need to devise incentive systems for other people or other firms whose behavior is not completely under the executives' control. These other agents can be managers of decentralized business operations, or companies with which the executives' firms do business. In either case, the executives, like the government officials, lack perfect knowledge of the technical circumstances facing those other people. They also cannot fully know the other people's objectives. The executives may worry that their employees and contract suppliers may overinvest or underinvest in risk management, thereby imposing on the executives' firms excessive risk, unnecessary costs, or both.

Before discussing these problems, we need to obtain a clear picture of the reasons that company executives manage risk in the first place. Remembering that managers serve the firm's shareholders, one might wonder whether risk management is an appropriate function from the shareholders' point of view. It is well known that shareholders can use diversification to protect themselves against many of the risks that managers face. A company that produces both potato chips and luxury cars will have more stable cash flows than firms that concentrate on making one or the other, since it is partially buffered from shocks to production costs or consumer demand for either product. But shareholders could easily replicate the cash flows of a chip-car conglomerate themselves, so there is no reason for managers to spend time and effort assembling one. Environmental risk can be thought of in the same way. Managers in a paper company may worry that new pollution control laws will reduce the private value of their operations. They may want to reduce this risk by lobbying for looser standards, by installing equipment in advance of the regulations, or by adopting some other procedure. Any of these operations, though, is likely to cost

money, and hence to reduce the expected value of the firm. Meanwhile, if a shareholder in the paper company worries about the effects of new pollution control laws, he or she can construct a portfolio that includes other stocks that will be unaffected by those laws (or even positively affected, like stock in a firm that makes pollution control equipment). Why should he or she want the company to reduce its expected value by buying insurance against this event?

Several related answers are possible, all focusing on imperfections in capital markets and the absence of free flows of complete information about firms and their prospects. Because the managers know the company's prospects better than external providers of capital can, externally provided capital is more expensive than internally generated funds. Further, by evening out its cash flows from year to year, the firm may reduce the risk of bankruptcy or other financial distress and avoid the considerable costs (in legal expenses, possible business interruption, and so on) that this distress would entail. For these reasons, and also because of tax considerations, strategies that even out cash flows from year to year can lower the company's overall costs. A related argument is that since managers cannot hedge their own risks of unemployment should catastrophe strike the firm, they will demand (and get) higher compensation if the firm's shareholders force them to bear this risk by barring them from buying insurance against it. Finally, in practice it might be difficult for a shareholder to use his or her portfolio to hedge environmental risks: time-consuming to acquire the relevant information, and expensive to engage in the right transactions. Hence the shareholder might be satisfied to let the executives reduce this risk even if there is some reduction in the stock's expected value.[10]

In practice, executives routinely manage risk, and shareholders are happy to let them do this. For example, most large companies buy general liability insurance, a purchase that reduces the variance of a company's cash flow but also reduces its expected value. It is easy for shareholders to observe such a purchase; it would be easy for them to restrict it, but they do not. Naturally there is a danger that managers will overinvest in risk management compared with what shareholders would want, but as we will observe, shareholders have other tools with which to control this kind of behavior.

Managers within firms have a broad array of tools for managing risk. The purchase of external insurance, to shift risk to other parties in return for payments of premiums, is one of the most common. A second common

tool is an internal subsidy to reduce the magnitude of undesirable events. Internal subsidies to operating units to help them manage environmental risk might include, for example, the maintenance of an emergency response unit. This lowers the contingent cost of an accident in the same way as flood relief programs implemented by the government.

A third device for risk management within firms is command-and-control regulation, whose purpose is to reduce the magnitude of adverse events, reduce their probability, or both. Although it is common to hear businesspeople complain about command-and-control regulation when it is put in place by governments, the same business-people often use private versions of it to reduce their own environmental risk. Company manuals that specify particular practices for fire safety or hazardous waste management are examples of internal command-and-control regulations.

Executives also use management evaluation and promotion to establish targets for risk management and to align managers' incentives with those of the firm. Because these systems always rely on executive judgment and other nonquantifiable factors, they are well suited to the management of risks that are difficult to analyze and quantify, such as those that arise from environmental concern.

Finally, managers seek to alter company culture and other intangible variables in order to change behavior. These incentive devices can complement the use of other tools, especially those relating to management evaluation and promotion criteria.

In theory, managers could also make use of price-based mechanisms to manage risk within the firm. For example, they could tie managerial bonuses more tightly to environmental performance, change transfer prices to reflect the environmental risks imposed by various flows of goods and services, or even set up internal insurance programs under which operating units would have to pay for environmental risk management. None of these mechanisms is in widespread use in companies today, for reasons explored in this chapter.

From the point of view of a senior executive, managers might either overinvest or underinvest in environmental risk management. Managers might be overly averse to environmental risk at their own facilities because they are not in a position to hedge it through diversification or because they have other reasons—their own status within the community, for example—to be especially anxious to avoid an environmental accident. On the other hand, managers face strong external pressures to

underinvest in risk management, especially if the reduction of risk requires the up-front expenditure of cash for later, uncertain returns. Corporate incentive systems ordinarily reward managers for reducing costs or increasing profits within their areas of responsibility, and therefore create incentives for managers not to overinvest in environmental risk management. Firms employ internal command-and-control regulation, and incorporate environmental goals into the criteria for evaluation and management promotion, in order to create some countervailing pressure and to reduce the chances of systematic underinvestment.

Risk Management at the Facility Level

To illustrate the complexities inherent in risk management, it is helpful to compare two cases drawn from the same industry—forest products—that are similar in many respects. In each, a company invests significant capital and effort to provide environmental goods in order to manage the risks of regulation and potential legal liability for pollution. In one of the cases, these initiatives seem to be having the desired effect, at least so far. In the other, similar initiatives seem to have been of less benefit to the company.

The lessons here are applicable far beyond the forest products industry. The stories raise basic questions about the management of environmental risk: what is the risk that executives are trying to manage? How will investments of different kinds affect that risk? And how does the risk management policy relate to the overall goals of the company?

ALBERTA-PACIFIC FOREST INDUSTRIES, INC.

Alberta-Pacific is a joint venture involving two Japanese firms, Mitsubishi Corporation and Oji Paper Company, Ltd. Its main assets are an enormous pulp mill in north central Alberta, Canada, and an agreement with the provincial government that allows the business to harvest government-owned trees to feed the mill. Alberta-Pacific managers have responded to environmental pressures by investing in pollution control equipment well beyond what is required by law, by changing forest management practices so that environmental values are protected, and by attempting to raise public expectations of the company's environmental performance.

After petroleum prices fell in the mid-1980s, politicians in the oil-rich province of Alberta looked for ways to diversify their economy. Along with a push into tourism centered on the 1988 winter Olympics in Calgary, they aggressively shopped the province's timber resources to forest products firms around the world. Agencies of the provincial government provided harvest rights at rock-bottom prices, sank public money in infrastructure, and even loaned their own funds to private entities willing to invest in the pulp and paper industry in Alberta.

This government intervention stimulated the expansion of an existing mill owned by Champion International Corporation in Hinton, on the Athabasca River in west central Alberta, and the construction of a new mill by Daishowa-Marubeni International Limited in the town of Peace River, in the northwestern part of the province. (Figure 6-1 shows the pulp mills in Alberta as of 1991.) Following these commitments, Mitsubishi and Oji Paper formed a joint venture with Crestbrook Forest Industries, a small forest products firm based in southeastern British Columbia. The purpose of the joint venture was to build a large pulp mill near Boyle, Alberta, in almost uninhabited country 350 miles downstream from Hinton on the Athabasca River and a hundred miles north of the provincial capital of Edmonton.

From a business perspective, this project enjoyed raw material costs of the level one might find in Indonesia or Brazil, but with far lower political and exchange rate risk. It also seemed a good strategic fit for all three participants. Crestbrook wanted to expand but lacked the capital to do so on its own. Mitsubishi, a giant trading company with 1992 revenues of $155 billion but just a 0.3 percent return on assets, was looking for opportunities to produce some of the commodities it traded, since the margins in trading had been eroding. For Mitsubishi and Oji Paper, the project also made sense as a way of locking in raw material supplies for paper mills in Japan.

Like the chlorofluorocarbon business discussed in the DuPont case example of chapter 3, the market pulp industry in which Alberta-Pacific competes is a commodity business. Alberta-Pacific and other makers of market pulp sell their dried, baled output to paper mills, which convert the pulp into final products. At any given time, hardwood pulp (made from deciduous trees like eucalyptus or the aspen that grows in northern Alberta) may sell at a higher or lower price than softwood pulp (made from coniferous trees), but competition within either product category is based mostly on price. Demand is cyclical and price

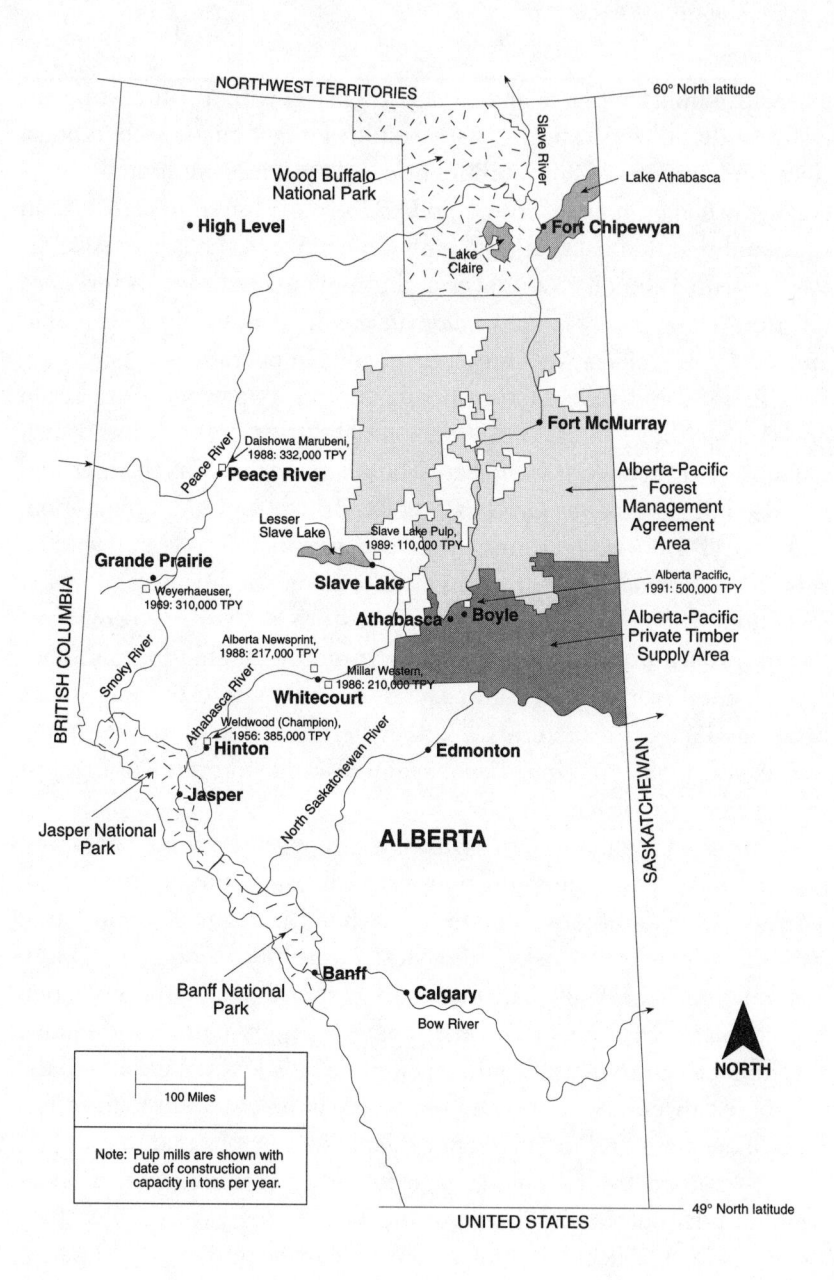

Figure 6-1. Alberta, Showing Pulp Mills as of 1991

1 4 5

insensitive; mills are large and capital intensive, with a stiff cost penalty for underutilized capacity. As a result of these market conditions, price competition is fierce and the prices themselves are brutally cyclical; hardwood pulp prices rose from U.S.$400 per ton in 1986 to $750 in 1989, and then fell back below $500 by 1993. A mill the size of Alberta-Pacific, with a capital cost of over U.S.$1 billion, could see its revenues fall from close to U.S.$500 million in good times to about half that amount in recessions, with very little change in operating costs.

In 1988 and 1989, when Mitsubishi and its partners first began envisioning their operations, they brought in a team from British Columbia to manage the project. These included Gerry Fenner and Bob Ruault, executives in Crestbrook's British Columbia operation, and Darryl Hebert, recruited from the provincial fish and wildlife agency to oversee the environmental aspects of the business's forestry operation. Mitsubishi, Oji Paper, and Crestbrook planned to construct a conventional pulp mill, bleaching their pulp with chlorine gas. They also planned to run their forests more or less as forestry had always been conducted in western Canada, where, as Hebert put it, "there was never a plan for forest management, and 'forest planning' just meant 'fiber extraction.'"[11]

But the project ran into a buzzsaw of opposition from local farmers, aboriginal residents of northern Alberta, and environmental activists from southern Alberta, elsewhere in Canada, and other nations. To handle the risks of business interruption and bad community relations, the Canadian managers responsible for the operation shifted gears. They persuaded the Japanese equity partners to modify the mill's design so that it would put significantly less pollution into the Athabasca River, and they promised to break new ground both in forest management and in public and stakeholder involvement.

To reduce the risk of damage to the river ecosystem, Alberta-Pacific undertook to eliminate the use of chlorine gas as a bleaching agent. Instead, it decided to use chlorine dioxide and hydrogen peroxide to bleach the pulp. This change required significant modifications not only in the bleach plant but also in the earlier stages of pulpmaking. In the vocabulary of the industry, Alberta-Pacific's original proposal was for a mill that made "standard" pulp (i.e., pulp bleached with elemental chlorine gas). The mill as it was eventually constructed makes elemental chlorine free (ECF) pulp, with chlorine dioxide as the main bleaching agent.[12]

Compared with the initial design, the new configuration entailed only a modest increase in investment costs, perhaps 2 percent of the capital cost of the mill as initially planned.[13] But it reduced the discharge of chlorinated organic compounds to the river by a factor of fifteen, to 0.08 kilograms per metric ton of pulp produced. Alberta-Pacific's water pollution in the form of biological oxygen demand was one-twentieth of the amounts per ton of output released by some other mills in western Canada.[14]

In response to the initial opposition to the project, Alberta-Pacific also proposed modifications of forest practices and of public involvement in decisions about forestry. In this new regime, Alberta-Pacific promised to eschew traditional wide-scale clear-cutting in favor of more numerous "cutblocks" that would vary widely in size and shape, mimicking the patterns left by naturally occurring forest fires.

The company also decided to take the interests of its neighbors systematically into account in conducting its planning for forest management. The area from which the trees are harvested is roughly the size of Ireland, and less than 1 percent of this acreage is slated for logging each year. This leaves large areas that are useful for hunting, fishing, camping, and other outdoor recreation. Through an ongoing series of public meetings and informal contacts, the company seeks to make sure that those recreational opportunities are protected.

In addition, Alberta-Pacific conducts an ongoing program of collaborative research with environmental groups and professors from local universities, applying techniques from forestry, biology, river ecology, and other disciplines to shed light on the relationships between the industrial operation and the ecosystem. These efforts require some management time, although not much money. "We spend maybe half a million [Canadian dollars] on that kind of research a year," said one manager. "That's a hell of a lot less than lawyers cost."[15]

Darryl Hebert, the biologist recruited from the British Columbia wildlife agency to oversee Alberta-Pacific's environmental forestry practices, elaborated on the relationships between ecological risk and business risk:

What is acceptable in the public view is what is "natural," but nobody, including us, knows what "natural" forests in northern Alberta look like. The forests that people see today aren't natural. They're the result of a hundred years of fire suppression. We have forty to fifty people, under

various cooperative arrangements, doing forest research so that we'll know what the forests need, and so we'll earn the trust of people to manage them the way the research says they should be managed. This may mean bigger cutblocks; the scientists tend to favor larger, irregularly shaped cutblocks, not uniform in size, that replicate fire patterns. To do this, we need the public trust. And to get the public trust, we have to deserve it.[16]

Most cutblocks in Alberta-Pacific's aspen stands are about forty hectares (100 acres), but some are half that size and some are considerably larger.

The Alberta-Pacific mill enjoys extremely low raw material costs. As is customary in Canadian forestry, the provincial government retains title to the land and sells timber on the stump to the company. Fees paid to the province are forty Canadian cents per cubic meter of wood, or less than two Canadian dollars per ton of pulp. Because the forests are scattered over such a vast area, road-building, harvesting, and hauling costs are relatively high, but the total delivered wood costs are comparable to those of the plantation forests of Brazil or the intensively managed forests of the American South. Overall, Alberta-Pacific has among the world's lowest variable costs in its category of bleached kraft hardwood pulp mills. On the other hand, in the weak pulp markets of the late 1990s it had difficulty covering its high capital costs, which are attributable in part to its aggressive environmental investments. In 1998, the joint venture partners repaid the principal on C$250 million loans granted by the Province of Alberta when the mill was constructed; the province forgave all but C$10 million of the interest that had been accruing since that time. Also in 1998, Oji Paper and Mitsubishi bought out Crestbrook, since the Canadian firm's equity base was too small to weather the cycles of the pulp markets.[17]

It is not clear to all observers that Alberta-Pacific's aggressive efforts in pollution control and forest management are a sensible approach to risk management. The company's efforts to take seriously the views of stakeholders other than its shareholders also draw criticism. "You can talk all you want about different sized cutblocks to replicate fire patterns, but when push comes to shove, the environmentalists will never let you make a 200-hectare cutblock," one industry representative from British Columbia told Fenner and Hebert at a meeting in 1993.[18] Fenner remarked that "we have shown people,

within the company and outside of it, that they can have real input into the way we manage the ecosystem. If we decide, now, to deny them that input, they will turn on us. At the same time, many in industry, and in government as well, would like us to stop involving the public in decisions: they know that if we do it, they will have to eventually, too. They will put pressure on Crestbrook and Mitsubishi to try to get us to change our behavior. But we have started across a very swift river. If we stop moving ahead, we will drown."[19]

CHAMPION INTERNATIONAL CORPORATION'S CANTON MILL

The town of Canton (1990 population: 3,800) sits in the Smoky Mountains near Asheville, at the western end of North Carolina. Champion International Corporation, headquartered in Stamford, Connecticut, has operated a pulp and paper mill at Canton since 1908. Champion sells about $6 billion in pulp, paper, paperboard, and building materials annually, of which about $200 million is attributable to the Canton mill.

The mill's environmental impacts have been controversial ever since its construction. Champion executives have spent hundreds of millions of dollars in attempts to manage these impacts and the resultant business risk.

Like the Weyerhaeuser Company, International Paper, Georgia-Pacific, Boise Cascade, and other old, established firms in the American forest products industry, Champion has been criticized by environmentalists for aggressive harvesting of timber and for the pollution emitted from its mills. Like many paper companies, Champion has been the target not only of environmentalists' displeasure and regulators' scrutiny but also of multimillion-dollar lawsuits, filed by people who say their health or property values have suffered because of pollution from mills. Meanwhile, also like those other firms, it has been criticized by Wall Street analysts for failing to deliver adequate returns to shareholders, and for tying up too much capital in low-yielding timberlands and the capacity to make commodity products.[20] Champion likely would not have retained its independence through the takeover years of the 1980s had it not concluded its own takeover of St. Regis Corporation in 1984, which raised Champion's debt levels and made the company less palatable to raiders, and had it not implemented a series of other anti-takeover financial measures.[21]

Champion's operation in Canton encompasses a bleached kraft pulp mill (similar to the one operated by Alberta-Pacific, but about half the size), paper machines with a collective annual capacity of 250,000 tons, and other machines that can produce 250,000 tons of bleached paperboard yearly. The paper is used in photocopying machines and computer printers, the paperboard for milk and juice cartons.[22]

To make this paper and paperboard, Champion draws timber from its own lands in the Carolinas and from other private timberland owners. The mill is located in Canton because Champion owned large tracts of timberland in the area around the turn of the century, although much of this land was sold to the federal government during the 1930s so it could be included in Great Smoky Mountains National Park. Besides timber, pulp and paper mills need huge quantities of water, and for this reason are typically built on large rivers. The medium-sized mill at Canton withdraws up to 29 million gallons of Pigeon River water each day, uses it in pulp- and papermaking, treats it to remove pollutants, and puts it back in the river.

Champion opened its Canton mill in 1908. Many decades later, old-timers recalled that the effluent from the mill, which in those days entered the river without treatment of any kind, took a heavy toll on the fish in the local stretch of the Pigeon River.[23] Over the ensuing decades, pollution from the mill, as for other facilities in this and other industries, became increasingly controversial as prosperity raised the demand for environmental quality and as social expectations about companies' environmental performance heightened.

Geographic circumstances have played an important role in the controversies over pollution in the Pigeon River, in two important respects. The first has to do with political boundaries. Almost immediately after flowing through Canton and receiving the wastewater from the mill, the Pigeon River enters a gorge in which few people live; the nearest downstream town, called Newport (1990 population: 7,100), is forty miles away in Tennessee. Thus, while most of the jobs at the mill are filled by North Carolinians, the environmental costs fall largely on residents of another state. (Figure 6-2 maps the path of the Pigeon River.)

The second geographic circumstance is the size of the river. A river's ability to absorb pollution flows increases with its size. The flow of the Pigeon averages about 200 million gallons per day at Canton, but under low flow conditions it is as little as 40 million gallons. By contrast, the Athabasca River near the Alberta-Pacific mill just discussed

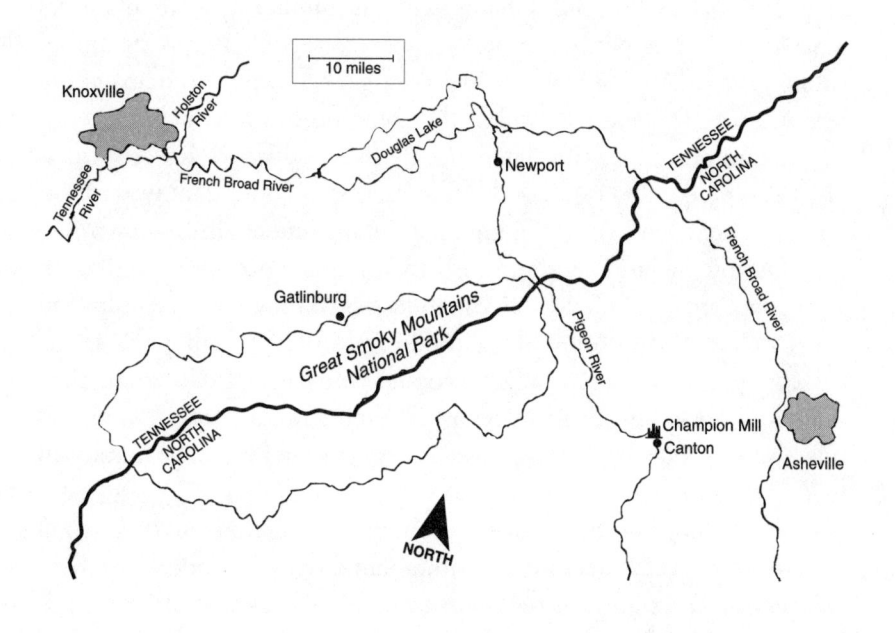

Figure 6-2. The Pigeon River and Adjacent Areas

runs at 2,000 million gallons a day even during low flow in the subarctic winter and at over ten times that rate during the spring; and the Ohio River at its mouth flows at a rate of about 180,000 million gallons per day.[24] Both Champion executives and critics of the mill point out that the construction of a large pulp mill on a stream as small as the Pigeon would be unlikely today.

Because the Canton mill's river is small, the mill's contribution to the river's color became a controversial issue. Water pollution controversies at most pulp mills, including Alberta-Pacific's, focus on biological oxygen demand and chemical oxygen demand (which lead to eutrophication and inhibit the water's ability to support fish and other animals), and on chlorinated organic compounds. But if a pulp mill uses a significant fraction of the total river water, dissolved organic compounds from the mill affect the downstream river's color, tending it to brown or black. This issue never arose in the Alberta case because the Athabasca is so much larger than the Pigeon.

Champion's first major pollution control investments occurred in the early 1960s, when the company installed primary wastewater treat-

ment facilities at the mill. Champion made similar investments at its other mills in this period, in part to manage regulatory risk by anticipating government agencies' requirements, and in part to manage the risk of lost or forgone goodwill in the communities in which it operated. At Canton, Champion later installed secondary wastewater treatment equipment and expanded its facilities so it could treat water from the households and small commercial establishments in the town.

During the late 1980s and early 1990s, Champion embarked on an aggressive program of capital expenditures throughout its pulp and paper mills as CEO Andy Sigler tried to position the company as the low-cost producer in certain key product categories. Despite criticism from Wall Street, Sigler invested over $6 billion in modernizations and selective capacity expansions over an eight-year period beginning in 1986.[25]

This emphasis on capital expenditures affected environmental decisions as well. In 1995, environmental vice president Richard Diforio told the trade journal *American Papermaker* that about $1 billion of the $6 billion in capital investment during the late 1980s and early 1990s went to environmental management.[26] Diforio later noted that Champion pollution control policies during the late 1980s and early 1990s were based on the assumption that regulators would eventually force companies to "close their mills," that is, to operate without any effluent to nearby streams. "It made sense in our judgment to anticipate the regulations, although the regulations to date have not gone in that direction."[27] In other words, Champion embarked on a very aggressive policy for managing both regulatory risk and the business risk inherent in antagonistic relations with downstream neighbors.

As part of this initiative, Champion announced in 1990 that it would spend $300 million to improve the environmental performance of the Canton mill's pulping and bleaching operations. The old bleach plant, where the wood pulp is bleached white with chemicals in a multistep, capital-intensive process, had used chlorine gas as the bleaching agent. The newly configured bleach plant included oxygen delignification and substituted chlorine dioxide for chlorine gas. The changes in technology at Canton were thus very similar to the changes made at Alberta-Pacific's mill, with the important difference that Alberta-Pacific was modifying the plans for a mill that had not yet been built and Champion was retrofitting a mill that was eighty years old. In this case, as elsewhere, it can be difficult to draw a sharp line between cap-

ital expenditures for environmental purposes and capital expenditures for productivity and quality improvements. But under North Carolina state regulations that allow preferential tax treatment for environmental capital investments, about two-thirds of the investment at Canton was "environmental." Champion executives expected that the changes would cut pollution loadings by one-half to three-quarters, and in this they were not disappointed.

This aggressive spending did not, however, prevent the 1991 filing of a $5 billion class action lawsuit by residents of Newport, Tennessee, while the oxygen delignification and chlorine dioxide equipment was being installed. The suit charged that pollution from Champion had lowered property values and contributed to allegedly higher incidences of cancer in downstream communities. In 1992, after a mistrial, Champion settled the suit for $6.5 million.

In the mid-1990s, Champion decided to spend an additional $30 million to reduce pollution still further at the Canton mill. The motive here was regulatory risk management at the firm level, not at the level of the mill. Champion executives expected that the EPA, in its "cluster rule" for pulp and paper mills, would impose very tough standards for chlorinated organic compounds released to waterways.[28] Following the $30 million investment at Canton, mill managers could recycle part of the wastewater from the bleaching process, recirculating it through the pulping and bleaching process rather than returning it to the river. The company intended to show the EPA that it was not necessary from an environmental standpoint to require a complete phaseout of all chlorine compounds in bleaching. Champion may also have been partly motivated by the thought that it might make some money licensing its Bleach Filtrate Recycle equipment should the EPA require its competitors to adopt that technology.

Champion needed a mill at which to demonstrate the technology. It chose Canton because that mill was equipped to accommodate a demonstration project of that size, and because a demonstration there would not require significant capital beyond what was required for the Bleach Filtrate Recycle equipment. "BFR has been a boon to color in the Pigeon River," said Champion's Diforio, "but that's not why we did it."[29] As it turned out, the EPA required neither a complete chlorine phaseout nor bleach filtrate recycling in the final version of the cluster rule.

As a result of all this investment, the Canton mill dramatically reduced its pollutant loadings. With respect to color, Champion's con-

tribution to the Pigeon declined from 375,000 color units per day before the modernization to about 83,000 afterward, and below 60,000 following the successful demonstration of Bleach Filtrate Recycle. The mill now easily complies with the standards established in the EPA's cluster rule. The rule allows bleached kraft mills to produce 0.62 kilograms of total adsorbable organic halides (AOX for short) per metric ton of pulp. Canton is now producing 0.1 kilograms per ton, one-sixth of the maximum allowed and near the level achieved by the new Alberta-Pacific mill.

Because of this investment in the bleach line, the Canton mill carries a large capital burden relative to other paper and paperboard manufacturing sites. "We were forced at a time when we were not making money to invest a lot of capital in the plant," said Diforio about the investments of the early 1990s. The switch to oxygen delignification and chlorine dioxide yielded significant environmental benefits and some improvements in product quality, but it did not increase the mill's capacity. Further, the small size of the river and hence the volume of discharge acceptable to the regulators and the community meant that capacity expansion was constrained, precluding the achievement of scale economies that would have driven down costs. Champion executives report, however, that in 1990 they saw investments in oxygen and chlorine dioxide as the most cost-effective way to get the levels of color necessary to satisfy the company's critics. As Diforio put it, "We could not have stayed in the same business of bleached board and uncoated paper at that location without an investment of this sort."[30]

Meanwhile, in September 1997, Tennessee residents filed another class action suit against Champion to recover nuisance damages arising from pollution from the Canton mill.[31] Champion put the Canton mill up for sale in 1997, and sold it in 1999 to a newly created company owned by a New York investment fund and the mill's employees and managers.[32] The rationale for the divestiture was a strategic one: the mill was part of an interlinked set of assets for the manufacture of paper and paperboard products that were not integral to the company's desired focus. Champion executives stated that the pollution controversies were unrelated to the sale. Diforio said, "We have addressed the problems, and given today's technology, that mill can live on that river. Further, from an operating cost standpoint its competitive position is viable."[33]

THE IMPLICATIONS OF THE PULP MILL CASES

An obvious conclusion to draw from these two stories is that context matters. In the case of water pollution, the size of the river influences the relationships between firm behavior (pollutant loadings) and risk of environmental damage (ecological and aesthetic conditions in the river). More generally, the social context influences the relationship between the risk of environmental damage and the business risk to the firm. Alberta-Pacific was entering a province with a long pro-business tradition stretching back to the oil booms of the early decades of the twentieth century, and social expectations of the mill's environmental performance were tempered by the presence of several other mills on the river. Meanwhile, when Champion decided to invest aggressively in water pollution control at Canton, it had to overcome eighty years of bad relations with downstream communities.

But behavior matters as well. Alberta-Pacific's managers proposed the switch to bleaching practices that do not use elemental chlorine as part of an integrated strategy of environmental risk management and value creation. Besides ECF bleaching, the strategy also included a new approach to forest management, new ideas about the role of local organizations and other affected parties in determining the company's operations, and collaborative efforts in scientific research. Champion's installation of the same technology was conducted in the context of traditional relationships between the company and government, between the company and environmental advocates, and even within the company itself. Like StarKist's switch to dolphin-safe tuna, the move was not fully integrated with the overall strategy of the firm.

RISK MANAGEMENT IN DECENTRALIZED FIRMS

We will consider these forest products case examples in more detail following the introduction of two others. These next examples are more complicated than the Alberta and Champion cases. Besides questions about risk assessment and risk management within a single hierarchical structure, they also raise questions about the management of risk in far-flung business systems over which the corporate center has imperfect control. These circumstances make environmental risk management both more difficult and more important.

CHEVRON CORPORATION'S
SYSTEMS FOR INTERNAL RISK MANAGEMENT

Chevron Corporation, headquartered in San Francisco, made $1.34 billion in profit in 1998 on revenues of just under $30 billion. Like Exxon, British Petroleum, Texaco, and other large oil companies, Chevron is integrated from the well to the gasoline pump, with activities encompassing exploration, production, refining, distribution, and marketing. And like those other firms, it owns or has owned a number of related businesses, like coal mining and the manufacture of organic chemicals, in which environmental risk is also significant.

The 1989 *Exxon Valdez* oil spill serves as an expensive reminder of the environmental risks that confront oil executives and their shareholders. The total costs of the spill to Exxon shareholders remain uncertain a decade later, primarily because an award of $269 million in compensatory damages to commercial fishermen and a $5 billion award of punitive damages remain under appeal. Even leaving these numbers aside, however, Exxon pledged nearly $1 billion over a ten-year period in a settlement with the U.S. government and the State of Alaska, and apparently spent over $1 billion in direct cleanup costs.[34] Of these amounts, Exxon recovered $480 million from its insurers by January 1997.[35]

Aside from the risk that they will be forced to incur cleanup costs, third-party damage costs, and even punitive damages like those that arose in the aftermath of the Exxon spill, oil company executives are concerned about risk of business interruption stemming from accidents in transportation and refining. They worry, too, about the loss of reputation that would arise from a newsworthy environmental event like the *Valdez* oil spill or the discovery of widespread groundwater contamination, despite the difficulty in attaching a dollar figure to this exposure. Chevron's most important retail market is California, and Chevron executives believe that public expectations about corporate environmental performance are unusually high in that state. Hence they feel particularly sensitive to reputational risks.

Because of Chevron's large presence in California, regulatory risk and regulatory opportunity are especially important for the company as well. The adoption of reformulated gasoline for smog control, discussed in chapter 3, is an example of a regulatory risk that Chevron and the other California refiners were able to turn at least temporarily to opportunity.

As would be expected, Chevron manages environmental risk by try-ing to reduce the probability of adverse events, by trying to lower the total costs of any such events if they occur, by shifting some of this risk to other parties through insurance contracts, and by investing in additional information about the nature and magnitude of the risks it confronts.

Like other large, decentralized firms, Chevron faces the problem of how to align individual managers' risk management incentives with those of the corporation. To do so, the company makes extensive use of internal command-and-control regulation, and of its systems for managerial performance evaluation and promotion. Chevron's internal risk management program is based on Policy 530, "Protecting People and the Environment," which briefly sets out the company's environ-mental objectives and guiding philosophies: "It is the policy of Chevron Corporation to conduct its business in a socially responsible and ethi-cal manner that protects safety, health and the environment. The goal is to be a leader within industry by emphasizing innovation and encour-aging creative solutions, both of which will improve our competitive position."[36] Based on this broad policy framework, environmental staff at corporate headquarters is responsible for developing requirements for specific management practices, and line managers are responsible for implementing these practices within their authority limits. Risk management is mentioned explicitly only once in Policy 530: "The Company will . . . follow relevant standards, good engineering practices and principles of risk management to ensure Chevron's safety, fire, health and environmental protection activities are conducted responsi-bly." But the implementation guide written by environmental staffers under the authority of Policy 530, which covers such topics as pollution prevention and emergency preparedness and response, makes clear that improved management of environmental risk is an important goal. Ad hoc teams of managers and experts, recruited from within the com-pany, conduct periodic audits of all operations to ensure compliance both with applicable government standards and with the rules written under Policy 530.[37]

In keeping with a tradition of decentralized management, Chevron's internal environmental regulation tends toward specification of management practices rather than specific technical measures or performance standards. For example, the manager of every Chevron facility in the world is required to "provide a current, written facility-specific emergency-response plan that addresses, among other things,

communication to employees, contractors and the public and, where appropriate, the recovery needs of the community after an emergency."[38] That is, the rules specify the risks that managers must address, and lay out processes and procedures for doing so, but they ordinarily do not specify required levels of performance. Instead, performance levels are negotiated between the manager and his or her supervisor, and evaluation of the manager's performance in this area takes place during the annual cycle of management evaluation and periodic decisions about the manager's promotion within the firm.

Because the firm can use evaluation and promotion processes to help create the desired incentives for managers' handling of risk, it does not need to rely so heavily on command and control. This enables the company to retain flexibility that would be lost under a pure command-and-control system. Different situations can be handled differently, and individual managers retain considerable ability to manage risks as they deem most appropriate.

For some other risks, however, Chevron uses tools that look much more like conventional command-and-control regulations. An example is its management of the risk of spills during transportation, where probabilities of accidents are low but the potential impact of any one incident is high. After the *Exxon Valdez* accident, some oil companies sold their tanker fleets and contracted with other firms for oil transportation. Chevron remained in the transportation business, but to manage the risks of spills more tightly, it instituted detailed rules and procedures that all ship captains must follow. The rules are similar in scope, purpose, and level of detail to the government rules that regulate procedures at potentially dangerous facilities like nuclear reactors.

The company uses other management tools to reduce the risk of oil spills. One of these is to personalize the risks. Several of the company's supertankers are named after senior executives or other members of the board of directors; another supertanker is called the *Chevron Employee Pride*. At first blush this choice of names looks like a rash assumption of additional risk to the company's reputation. For that very reason, however, it sends strong messages about avoiding accidents and spills both to the company's employees and to its directors.

Chevron further raised the stakes in its management of marine transportation risks by announcing and publicizing a goal of "incident-free operations." It has placed advertisements in *Time, Harper's,* and other magazines calling attention to its transportation record: "It's

appalling how much oil our ships spilled last year. Four barrels. Out of nearly 500 million barrels we shipped around the world. To put that in perspective, it would be the same as filling a 16-gallon gas tank 200 times and spilling just one drop. Impressive? Not to us. Because while Chevron may have one of the best environmental safety records in the shipping industry, our top priority is to have a perfect one."[39] To make good on these assertions, Chevron maintains an aggressive program of auditing and inspection both for its own ships and for those it charters to move oil. Its retention of its own ships enables its managers to develop their understanding of technical and organizational devices for oil spill prevention, which can then be applied not just on Chevron ships but also on ships owned by others that move Chevron oil. Chevron executives would like their auditing and inspection programs to become industry standards.

In addition, Chevron has made complementary investments in reducing the cost of a spill should one occur. Chevron participates in industry-wide joint ventures that maintain rapid-response crews for spills in various regions. For example, the oil industry's Marine Spill Response Corporation maintains sixteen vessels at sixteen harbors along American coastlines; the corporation's investment and operating expenses have totaled about $1 billion since its establishment after the *Valdez* spill. Chevron also maintains its own rapid-response crews; while these engineers and technicians hold other jobs within the company, they conduct frequent spill simulations and other training exercises and are on permanent standby so they can reach any oil spill site on the globe within twenty-four hours.

From the perspective of a line manager in one of the Chevron operating companies, corporate-level initiatives like the rapid-response crews provide a free service of risk reduction, since they reduce the cost of an accident to the operating company. Conceptually this looks like the federal government's deposit insurance programs because it cushions the managers from the consequences of adverse events. That is, it is a form of subsidy to the operating companies. It does not appear, however, to give rise to the kinds of problems the government encountered in deposit insurance because the company can complement it with effective command-and-control regulation and a credible commitment to punish managers responsible for spills. In other words, the company can shift risk from the operating companies to the corporate level without creating the kinds of perverse incentives that would arise if risk were shifted between

two otherwise unrelated parties. The same logic applies to Chevron's purchases of liability insurance at the corporate level: although this constitutes a subsidy to the operating companies, other incentive mechanisms and command-and-control rules can prevent line managers from exploiting this subsidy by reducing their attention to environmental risk.

Chevron has also undertaken initiatives to identify risks arising from discontinued operations, even though such activities could expose the company to common law liability or to the retroactive liability provisions of the Superfund law. For example, the company's chemical subsidiary, Chevron Chemical Company, identified several hundred sites that had been used as distribution centers for fertilizers and pesticides in the earlier decades of this century, and then inspected those sites in search of potential contamination problems. "Our belief was that, first, it was the right thing to do," said one manager involved in project. "Second, we could do voluntary cleanup if that was warranted, which involves much less red tape and allows us to do what makes common sense. The reduction in costs that arises from this flexibility is greater than the increase in costs that arises because we clean up a few sites that otherwise we might not have to."[40]

Chevron has undertaken attempts to make risk management more systematic and analytical. Decision tools, basically simple spreadsheet programs developed by company staff and consultants, help managers identify the benefits of the risk reductions that the company is buying, and therefore to set priorities among possible investments. To evaluate a particular investment—say, the installation of extra pumps that reduce the probability of a spill at a refinery—managers input the cost of the investment, and their assessments of the probability of the adverse event before and after the investment is made. They also input the different kinds of damage the adverse event could create for the company, including adverse publicity, environmental harm, and so on, as well as more readily quantifiable impacts like out-of-pocket costs. The spreadsheet, by assigning risk "weights" that roughly reflect the costs to the company of these different types of damage, computes ratios of benefits to costs for each possible investment. This procedure allows managers to compare "prevention" investments (i.e., those that reduce the probability of an adverse event) against "mitigation" investments (those that reduce its costs). Further, it allows managers to compare environmental risk management options against risk management opportunities in other arenas in terms of overall cost-effectiveness in reducing risk.[41]

One of the important risk management questions facing Chevron and similar firms is the degree to which such systems ought to be implemented company-wide and used as the basis for allocating environmental investments. On one hand, at least in theory, this would allow the company to maximize the returns to all of its environmental risk management activities; it would bring a consistent approach across the company, and force managers to justify their expenditures in terms of actual risk reduction or value creation. At the same time, implementation difficulties would be severe: one might argue that the company lacks the information on risks and benefits that is required to make such systems useful. Further, cost-benefit analysis of this kind works best when applied to risks characterized by relatively high frequency and a relatively low cost per incident, not for events like the *Exxon Valdez*; we do not know whether a single system should be used to analyze risks of both types.

Echoing their company's Policy 530, senior executives and environmental staff managers at Chevron assert that their aggressive but systematic approach to environmental risk management can contribute to their competitive advantage in the oil business. At the same time, they recognize that delivering on this promise will remain a difficult and complicated challenge. The relationships between risk management and value creation will be explored in this chapter following the last of the four cases, and then discussed further in chapter 7.

THE ELECTRONICS INDUSTRY:
MANAGING SUPPLIER BEHAVIOR AND BUSINESS RISK

We have studied electronics manufacturing operations twice before in this book. Chapter 4 examined Xerox Corporation's efforts to locate private cost savings using the environment as a search engine. Chapter 5 analyzed how Xerox and other firms use product takeback strategies to deliver the same services at lower social cost and simultaneously improve their own market positions. I now turn to these same firms again in order to learn from their approaches to the management of environmental business risk in a highly dynamic industry where the traditional levers of control are difficult to use.

Price competition is intensifying in the electronics field as the boundaries that separate product categories become more porous, as sophisticated and well-funded firms invade each other's turf, and as

production capabilities become more widely dispersed across continents. To maintain flexibility and lower their costs, many large electronics companies have "dis-integrated," exiting those parts of the value chain in which they feel they have no clear advantage and focusing on those in which some special ability or competence allows them to stake out and defend their position. Much of the manufacturing of products that bear such famous names as IBM, Xerox, and Hewlett-Packard (HP) is conducted by contract manufacturers, often operating overseas, whose names are unknown to most of the big firms' customers.

This dis-integration creates some special problems for managers of environmental risk. The Chevron example focused on the problem of assessing risks accurately and then creating rules and other incentives so that managers throughout the corporate hierarchy will manage them appropriately. Managers in the electronics business also need to assess risks and then create rules and incentives. Their concern is that suppliers will underinvest in protection against environmental risks, imposing business risk on the larger, more famous firms. But in designing programs to manage these risks, the companies lack the coercive power that government regulators enjoy. Further, they have no hierarchical authority over the people whose behavior they are trying to influence; hence they cannot use the evaluation and promotion processes that Chevron and other firms employ to shape incentives within the firm.

Procurement managers and environmental risk managers at companies like Xerox, IBM, and HP are concerned with different kinds of risk in the supply chain. Business interruption risk, risk of liability, reputational risk, and regulatory risk are the most prominent. Environmental emergencies or regulatory difficulties at a supplier's plant can interrupt the flow of components and products, a concern intensified by concurrent efforts, also driven by cost considerations, to reduce work-in-process inventories. Managers at brand-name high-tech manufacturers also worry that liability for an upset at a supplier's plant will generate liability for them as well, even if they have no formal authority over the supplier's operations. They worry, too, about damage to their corporate reputations that might result from environmental damage at a supplier's plant; they are especially concerned about their ability to recruit talented (and environmentally conscious) young people to work for them should one of their suppliers make headlines for environmental problems.

As at many firms, management of environmental risks in electronics firms tends to be carried out by a different set of executives from those who manage other business risks. Both Xerox and HP, for example, maintain risk management offices responsible for the purchase of insurance policies and the management of business risk outside the environmental arena. In both cases the activities of these executives are formally separate from those of environmental risk managers, although there is some informal communication between the two units. Environmental risk is thought to be qualitatively different from other risks against which the companies buy insurance, and to require special expertise to analyze and manage. On the other hand, both the environmental staff office and managers specializing in procurement issues clearly have roles in the management of environmental risk that arises from suppliers' operations. At HP, Xerox, and other electronics firms, managers from procurement and the environmental office have worked closely on strategies for managing this risk.

The electronics industry's first forays into the management of its suppliers' environmental behavior were driven directly by regulatory requirements. The systems the electronics companies have put in place to manage risks involving their suppliers have their roots in the international agreements to end the production of ozone-depleting substances (ODSs), most notably chlorofluorocarbons (CFCs). Prior to the 1987 Montreal Protocol, manufacturers of consumer and defense electronic products bought over 100 million pounds of CFCs a year, and their consumption was increasing more rapidly than that of other industry segments like refrigeration. The electronics firms used the CFCs to clean printed circuit boards and other components.

The Montreal Protocol, and its revisions in London three years later, allowed developing countries to produce ODSs after they were to be phased out in industrial countries, so in theory the companies and their subcontractors could have continued to use CFCs. But regulations written by the U.S. Environmental Protection Agency to implement the protocol in the United States required manufacturers to label products manufactured using ODSs.[42] Further, the protocol made ODSs increasingly expensive, if not entirely unavailable. In response, companies began regulating not only their own use of the compounds but also the behavior of their suppliers. They developed systems for monitoring supplier behavior, sharing technical expertise, and phasing out ODSs throughout the supply chain, either unilaterally (as in the

case, for example, of Xerox) or under the auspices of an industry consortium, established in 1989, called the International Cooperative for Ozone Layer Protection (ICOLP).[43]

Once this risk management apparatus was in place, it was relatively inexpensive for individual firms to use it, in modified form, to specify other product characteristics and to manage other environmental risks. Xerox, HP, and other firms in the industry have periodically expanded their requirements for suppliers. For example, in December 1997 Xerox issued new instructions to its suppliers: in addition to blanket prohibitions on ODSs and heavy metals, Xerox required suppliers to "agree to work with Xerox to achieve the environmental leadership driven goals for product design" that Xerox executives had hammered out internally. Among these design goals were the following: "Product, supplies, parts and CRU packaging shall, at a minimum, be 95% recyclable by weight"; "Plastic Parts used in Xerox products shall contain a minimum of 25% post consumer recycled material"; and "95% of parts (by weight) in base product and Customer replaceable Items shall be recyclable at end of life."[44]

All firms that purchase materials or partly finished goods from other firms are inevitably in the business of writing product specifications. Besides these specifications, three other aspects of suppliers' performance might affect their customers' environmental risk: management systems, regulatory compliance status, and actual levels of emissions and discharges. These are considered sequentially below.

The presence of a management system for tracking and reducing environmental impact is obviously a reassuring sign to a customer worried about its own environmental reputation. But from the outside it is difficult to tell whether a particular supplier's management system is delivering the kind of risk reduction the customer might want. Hewlett-Packard, IBM, and other leading firms, working through a trade association called the Computer Industry Quality Council (CIQC), developed a standardized questionnaire that allows them and other electronics companies to determine whether their suppliers' management systems include the basic elements that the leading firms think necessary. These elements include a written environmental policy statement, "written environmental performance objectives/targets and implementation plans to reduce cost or risk," an assigned compliance manager, a system to track and respond to new regulatory requirements, and periodic compliance audits. The companies stop short of

requiring any particular management system or code of conduct, but they at least want to see whether the basic elements are in place so they can work with the suppliers to remedy any omissions.

The questionnaire that HP and IBM developed is published as CIQC Standard 0014. Companies can use it either by itself or as a supplement to other supplier management programs.[45] Hewlett-Packard, for example, distributes to its suppliers a pamphlet that reads: "At minimum, we expect our suppliers to do the following: Develop and adhere to an environmental improvement policy; create an environmental policy implementation plan with well-defined metrics; eliminate ozone-depleting substances (ODS) from manufacturing processes; comply with the HP Supplier Environmental Performance Review Questionnaire (CIQC Standard 0014)."[46]

In addition, some firms also want their suppliers to work toward certification under the environmental management standards of the International Standards Organization (ISO). This standard, called ISO 14001, specifies management systems and procedures for environmental performance, but it does not impose performance or technology-based requirements with respect to the environmental performance itself. Many European electronics manufacturers, and many European operations of U.S.-based firms, require their suppliers to obtain ISO certification. Xerox and some other American firms are encouraging their suppliers worldwide to work toward ISO certification over time. But some American firms have declined to make ISO certification a worldwide requirement either for their own plants or for suppliers, on the grounds that its connection to actual environmental performance is too loose for the certification to be useful.

Firms worried about business interruption and liability risk have an interest in knowing not only about their suppliers' management systems but also about whether their suppliers are in compliance with environmental laws. Requirements that suppliers certify their compliance with existing government rules are widespread.

Some firms, like Xerox, conduct or plan to conduct periodic audits of suppliers to check both their management systems and their compliance status. But other firms, like HP, avoid auditing suppliers' environmental behavior. Such an audit program imposes three types of costs and risks. First, it entails some out-of-pocket costs. Second, the auditing firm's own liability might rise if the audit uncovers environmental problems. Third, the suppliers might perceive the audit as a sig-

nal that only what is required needs to be done; that is, auditing could lead to a compliance mentality that discourages innovation and results in missed chances to improve performance. HP managers think that the incremental benefits of audits do not compensate for these costs, and that environmental audits of operations outside their own firm should be done by the responsible firm or by the government.

Finally, one might imagine that firms like Xerox and HP would want to know the actual emissions and effluent levels of their suppliers' plants. Rather than simply knowing whether a supplier's plant was in compliance on a particular day, they might want to know the levels and how they compare with the standard. In practice, however, few electronics firms require this level of detail from suppliers, presumably because the value of the information is insufficient to offset the suppliers' costs to generate it, the recipient's costs to assemble and analyze it, and the potential increase in liability that the recipient might incur.

Nevertheless, the risk management strategies that HP, Xerox, and other firms are implementing in their supply chains involve generating and transferring large amounts of information. This information, moreover, flows in both directions. The downstream firms require their suppliers to provide information about their own environmental practices; conversely, the downstream firms, which tend to be larger and more environmentally sophisticated, can move information back to their suppliers about how the probabilities and magnitudes of potential problems can be reduced.[47]

The electronics firms have other reasons to understand and influence the environmental behavior of their suppliers. Xerox environmental staff executives, for example, assert that they can help suppliers find private cost savings through increased environmental scrutiny, much as Xerox itself has done. The executives believe that if they can help suppliers identify cost-savings opportunities, they can capture some of those savings through lower prices paid to the suppliers. (If the suppliers are also selling to Xerox's competitors, then these competitors can benefit from Xerox's investments in risk management investments without paying for them. This potential problem of free riders has not been sufficient to deter Xerox from making the investments.)

In this context, managers at leading electronics firms see management of environmental risks in the supply chain as a potential source of competitive advantage. Recall that the initial impetus for outsourcing much of the manufacturing function was cost reduction; the big downstream companies are trying to have their cake and eat it, too,

helping their suppliers reduce their own environmental risk and that of the downstream customers. In the process, the big firms are trying to help their suppliers develop the organizational capability to contribute to discussions on product design and manufacturing, while retaining the cost advantages of a dis-integrated structure.

THE IMPORTANCE OF A WELL-DEFINED OBJECTIVE

One implication of all of these cases is that managers must understand which type of risk they are trying to manage. This chapter has focused on two kinds of risk—the risk of damage to the environment or public health, and the risk of a reduction in the business's cash flows and equity—while noting that a third, the risk of personal criminal liability for executives, is distinct from each of the other two. Damage to human health or the environment does not always have a direct and immediate impact on the company's equity. It may be a trigger for some other event that directly affects shareholder wealth—a lawsuit, a regulation, or loss of markets—but none of these consequences will necessarily follow. Reducing the probability of environmental damage may leave these private risks unaffected, or it may even increase them. Conversely, there may be short-term strategies that reduce the risk of loss of shareholder wealth without affecting the risks to the environment or public health. Similarly, damage to human health or the environment need not trigger exposure to personal criminal liability for executives, and personal liability could conceivably arise even in the absence of risk to the environment.

Champion's Canton mill provides an example of the distinction between reducing risk to the environment and reducing the firm's own risk. The executives responsible for the Canton mill's modernization reduced the risk of damage to the river but did not, at least in the short term, reduce the risk to the company's reputation and public goodwill. Reduction of risk to the physical environment did not convert directly to a reduction of risk to shareholder wealth.

The possibility of personal criminal liability for executives introduces additional complications. In the United States, for example, the Clean Air Act, the Clean Water Act, and the Resource Conservation and Recovery Act explicitly provide for criminal prosecution for violations.[48] Further, under the "responsible corporate officer doctrine" of common law, company executives can be held accountable for criminal acts com-

mitted by employees even if the executives were ignorant of those acts. On the other hand, as one environmental lawyer observed, "the courts have generally not adopted the responsible corporate officer doctrine in its pure form, which would impose automatic liability based solely on an officer's position within the organization."[49]

Considerable uncertainty exists, therefore, about the personal liability to which managers may expose themselves through noncompliance. The main point here is that, just as there is no straightforward connection between risk of damage to the environment and risk of damage to the firm, the risk of personal liability for executives may be different from the risk of liability at the firm level. From an executive's standpoint, the possibility of criminal prosecution increases the incentives to focus on legal compliance even if this means introducing less flexible management systems that might constrain long-term innovation in reducing risk to shareholders and the environment.

A company's environmental risk management policies can be aimed at any or all of these three kinds of risk: personal risk, business risk to the firm, and risk of damage to the environment. As in many other aspects of environmental management, the relationships among these objectives depend to some degree on the time horizon over which the investment decision is analyzed. In the short term, reducing risk to the environment may not mean reducing business risk. The easiest way to reduce business risk in the short run may be to invest in risk-shifting tactics, for example, buying insurance and signaling to regulators that any enforcement actions will be bitterly contested. As the time horizon lengthens, risk-shifting tactics look more expensive, and reducing environmental burden is the only reliable way to reduce (rather than shift) business risk.

Any executive will take all three kinds of risk into account when formulating policies, but some policies are more effective at managing one kind of risk than others, and some reduce risk in the short run while increasing it in the longer term. There is no simple recipe for making the trade-offs, but it is necessary to consider them explicitly.

To say that executives should be clear about their risk management objectives and to say that they should be able to quantify the benefits of their risk management strategies are two different things. As we have seen repeatedly in this chapter, it can be extremely difficult to quantify the benefits of risk reduction. It can be equally difficult to quantify the benefits of risk shifting, or of additional information about

risk. The reasons for these difficulties are numerous: the benefits are uncertain, it is hard to discern the marginal impact of a particular action, the benefits often are expected to occur well into the future, and the benefits often relate to real but intangible values like reputation and goodwill. Further, the fear of increasing liability can constrain managers from even trying to quantify these benefits. Nevertheless, a more analytic and systematic approach to environmental risk management can create considerable value for firms. It is impossible to quantify everything, but it is critical to figure out which risks are important, and to assess the benefits of risk management strategies as accurately as organizational capabilities and legal constraints allow.

TOOLS AVAILABLE FOR RISK MANAGEMENT IN BUSINESS

Recall that governments use command-and-control regulation, subsidies, and price-based incentives to reduce the likelihood and severity of environmental degradation or human health problems. Federal grants to states and municipalities to build wastewater treatment plants are an example of subsidies. Price-based incentives include tradable pollution permits that make the cost of pollution directly visible to firms and thus encourage the firms to reduce their loadings. For the most part, however, governments rely heavily on command-and-control regulation, even though this approach can impose unnecessary inflexibility and cost on the economy compared with price-based systems. The reasons for this behavior include the regulators' own risk aversion; risk aversion on the part of some of the executives whose companies they regulate; and a philosophical distaste on the part of some environmentalists and legislators for solutions that treat pollution as an economic rather than a moral issue.[50]

Company executives, too, use command and command-and-control regulations, subsidies, and price-based mechanisms to manage risk. We saw regulations in the case of the electronics firms, and both regulations and subsidies in the Chevron example. As for examples of price-based mechanisms, companies routinely manage many financial risks by hedging through forward contracts or insure against them by buying options; they manage some kinds of liability risks through insurance contracts.[51] They are able to use these contractual tools because they and the other parties to the contracts are comfortable that the

probabilities of the risky events are relatively well understood and that the past is a reasonably reliable guide to the future. If executives are comfortable with their probability assessments, they can even incorporate them into price-based incentives like transfer prices or in-house insurance premiums.

But with many environmental risks, neither the firms nor potential insurers have any assurance that the future will look like the past, since this will depend on the resolution of scientific and legal uncertainties. In managing this kind of uncertainty, companies typically make less use of price-based mechanisms. They may rely more heavily on command-and-control regulation, as government officials would be likely to do. But unlike the government in its regulation of firms, the firms can also use incentive pay systems and promotions to shape managerial decisions within the organization. Negotiated targets for managers, performance reviews, the management promotion system, and other tools can shape managers' incentives and hence reduce or shift business risk. These additional tools give the firm powerful risk management capabilities.

Executives' decisions about which risk management tools to use will thus depend on the nature of the risk and on the quality of the information available to them.[52] For example, in making choices among a variety of investment opportunities, all of which reduce the probability or severity of relatively small operating risks at a refinery, Chevron executives are trying to make more use of price-based systems that balance costs and benefits. Where the benefits are extremely difficult to assess and the exposure (if not the probability) of the risk is large, as in the case of spills from oil tankers, the executives rely more heavily on internal command-and-control regulation. And for a broad range of decisions in the middle of this spectrum, the same executives may use negotiated targets and reviews. Executives need to consider the entire kit of tools for managing risk to the firm, whether by altering managers' incentives or shifting risk to external parties.

RELATIONSHIPS AMONG THE RISK MANAGEMENT TOOLS

Recall that four elements influence the management of business risk: the probability of an event, the event's magnitude, the share of the total costs for which the firm is responsible, and the quality of the informa-

tion about the risk. Actions taken to affect any one of these elements can have implications for one or more of the others, and these implications need to be considered before the company locks itself in to a particular approach.

For example, bankers and other creditors may legitimately worry that they can incur liability for hazardous wastes if they foreclose on an industrial property and then play an active role in waste management at the site. Suppose a secured lender plays an active role in hazardous waste management at an industrial facility while the facility is on the bank's balance sheet following financial distress of the original owner. That secured lender can incur financial liability for environmental damage under the provisions of the Superfund law.[53] Actions taken to reduce the risk of environmental damage can increase the risk of private damage.

Similarly, companies that have to manage environmental risks through the supply chain may worry that by controlling the behavior of their suppliers too closely, they can increase their own liability. As we have seen, manufacturers like Xerox and HP try to influence the behavior of their suppliers. This presumably improves the environmental behavior of those suppliers and therefore may reduce the overall expected costs of environmental problems at the suppliers' plants. At the same time, however, these attempts at control may increase the fraction of the total damages for which Xerox or HP might be liable should an accident occur at a supplier's facility. In this case, however, the risks created by the exertion of increased control appear to be manageable compared with the risks involved in eschewing any role in influencing the suppliers' risk management processes, especially given the opportunities for value creation that exist if the downstream firms play a more active role.

The interdependence of the four risk elements is especially important for managers when they are deciding whether to invest in more information about environmental risks. The act of generating more information about the risks can itself increase the likelihood that the firm will be made responsible for any costs that arise. Recall, for example, that Xerox and HP do not ask for explicit information about their suppliers' environmental performance. It is impossible to make definitive statements about motive, but it is certainly plausible that executives in these and similarly positioned firms are worried that such information might increase their own liability.

The possibility that a firm can increase its liability simply by investing in more information about an environmental risk makes investments in such information different from investments in other sorts of information. Purchasing other kinds of information may be costly, but the costs tend to be confined to the out-of-pocket expenses involved in acquiring the information: consultants, data, staff time for analysis, and so on. By contrast, investment in information about environmental risks can change the risks themselves. Executives might fear that if they obtain information about a contingent environmental liability, they may also incur an obligation to disclose that liability. In addition, they might worry that estimates of environmental risk that a company generates internally might be discovered in some future lawsuit and hence create additional risk for the firm. The needs of the company to generate information to help it make sensible decisions and the needs of the company not to create documents that would increase its own liabilities may seem to be at odds.

Audits of a company's own facilities present a striking example. An attorney at the large law firm Kirkland & Ellis wrote about "considerable concern that an environmental compliance audit would aid prosecutors by providing a 'road map' of the company's compliance status."[54] Frank Friedman, who has held senior environmental positions in several oil and chemical companies, said, "In today's regulatory climate a well-run auditing program [to uncover environmental problems at a firm's own facilities] reduces legal exposure—with an important caveat. A company should not conduct auditing or similar programs designed to insure that problems are discovered unless it is prepared to fix them."[55] This might not seem very useful advice: since it is only after the audits that the costs of fixing any problems are known, it is impossible to be certain in advance that the company will be able to bear those costs.

Fortunately, government officials, recognizing that the regulatory and legal apparatus creates disincentives to invest in information that might be socially beneficial, have been trying to tilt the incentives back in the other direction. A 1991 report by the Department of Justice announced that government prosecutors would consider the existence of preventive measures and compliance programs, internal disciplinary action, and other factors in determining whether to bring criminal prosecutions for environmental violations. In doing so, the department intended "that such prosecutions do not create a disincentive to or

undermine the goal of encouraging critical self-auditing, self-policing and voluntary disclosure."[56] At the same time, efforts to make the generation of information less risky for firms and managers have made a failure to generate information risky as well. Environmental and criminal lawyers at the large Washington, D.C., law firm of Arnold & Porter wrote, "Under several federal environmental statutes, the barest degree of knowledge or intent can sustain a prosecution, and 'responsible corporate officers' who should have, but did not know about and prevent an incident can be convicted."[57]

Given this state of affairs, managers need to recognize not only the risks of buying more information but also the risks of not acquiring the information. Further, they need to have plans in place both to manage those risks and to make use of any information they obtain. The decision about whether to invest in more information depends on the costs and benefits: the benefits are obviously greater if the managers intend to use the information once they acquire it.

As of 1999, the National Association of Manufacturers and an industry consortium called the Corporate Environmental Enforcement Counsel were lobbying in Washington to make it easier to protect information developed under voluntary audit practices, so as to reduce the disincentive that liability concerns create for the active management of environmental risk. Nearly half of the states have passed legislation "offering qualified protections for audit reports and/or voluntary disclosures." The companies are proposing that federal legislation offer similar protection as long as violations are "promptly corrected and disclosed to the appropriate governmental agency." The EPA opposes these proposals.

While managers need to protect themselves against the undesirable side effects that information can create, it is important not to lose sight of the basic fact that the information—and the processes by which it is generated—can be of great value to the firm. As the cases on Chevron and the electronics firms showed, improved information about environmental risks can put managers in a better position to reduce those risks in sensible and cost-effective ways. Indirect benefits exist as well. Alberta-Pacific, by conducting its forestry and biology research in cooperation with local governments and universities, not only bought information to contribute to better risk management but also strengthened its relationships with those organizations and thus reduced the risk of poor community relations. Although the preceding paragraphs have

focused on possible conflicts between the objectives of obtaining better information and reducing short-term business risk, it is worth remembering that these two objectives can also be complementary.

RELATIONSHIPS BETWEEN
RISK MANAGEMENT AND VALUE CREATION

The successful risk management strategies observed in this chapter have implications for value creation as well.

Alberta-Pacific's risk management strategy bears some superficial similarity to the value creation strategy adopted by DuPont's Freon Products Division, examined in chapter 3. Both DuPont and Alberta-Pacific demonstrated the feasibility of managing operations in such a way as to reduce environmental impact, and in both cases regulators took notice. Alberta-Pacific's policies make little sense as a device for raising competitors' costs though regulation, however, since the regulators could not possibly control the behavior of all industry competitors. Alberta-Pacific's managers had no realistic expectation that mills elsewhere in Canada, much less mills in Brazil or Indonesia, would be forced by regulators or market pressures to adopt similar practices. In Alberta, forest products companies have been pressured by the provincial government and local environmental groups to implement forest management practices similar to Alberta-Pacific's. But this has not enabled Alberta-Pacific to raise its prices, which are set in a global market for wood pulp.

To see the value creation element in Alberta-Pacific's risk management, we need to look more deeply at the company's strategy. Alberta-Pacific's successful management of political risk supports its overall strategy of managing the forests it controls for the long term, using forest practices that lower long-term costs at the expense of some short-term fiber extraction. Given a choice between "cut and run" forestry and practices that involve longer rotation times and lower out-of-pocket costs for planting, thinning, and other silvicultural practices, Alberta-Pacific opted for the latter. That choice only makes sense if supported by strategies that reduce the risk that government will later curtail the company's ability to manage flexibly. The risk management supports an overall strategy of cost minimization.

The risk management strategy implemented by Xerox and the

other electronics firms has more immediate competitive implications. Here the appropriate comparison is with the Responsible Care and Sustainable Forestry Initiative programs, also discussed in chapter 3. In all of these cases, de facto industry standards altered the business landscape for competitors or suppliers. As is apparent in those earlier cases, some care is required to make sure that these environmental management tactics do not give rise to antitrust violations. It would be illegal for a group of electronics companies collectively to refuse to buy chips from a particular supplier because of that supplier's environmental record, just as it would be illegal for forest products companies collectively to refuse to hire logging firms that did not agree to some code of environmental conduct. On the other hand, the electronics companies, like their counterparts in chemicals and forestry, appear successfully to have managed this issue.

More systematic and analytical risk management policies can also contribute to shareholder value by reducing the costs of inflexibility within the firm. If executives rely on command-and-control regulations to motivate their employees' risk management, one of the costs of this risk reduction is a loss of flexibility and perhaps a loss of initiative. The employees have lost some of their ability to seize opportunities to behave more efficiently. New approaches to risk management, like those practiced within Chevron, can give back this flexibility while retaining the appropriate incentives for managing risk. These approaches, which relate closely both to information flows within the firm and to incentive design, are discussed in greater depth in the next chapter.

The distinction between "value creation" and "risk management" thus turns out to be blurrier than it seems at first glance. Risk management is usually thought to be another cost, at odds with the spirit of value creation. This is the right way to think about it if the only sort of risk management available is the purchase of an insurance policy against environmental impairment liability. As we have seen, however, managers have a much larger toolbox with which to work on risk management problems, and some of the tools, if properly handled, can help to create value as well.

THREE MAIN conclusions emerge from this chapter. First, executives have at their disposal a wide variety of tools with which to manage risk

and uncertainty. Second, if these tools are used properly, the management of risk and uncertainty can serve as a source of competitive advantage for the firm. And third, in order fully to realize that advantage, the management of environmental risk and uncertainty must be integrated into the firm's overall strategy.

The companies examined in this chapter, like others confronting environmental risk and uncertainty, make use of internal command-and-control regulation and a wide variety of other devices to alter managers' incentives and bring about desirable levels of risk reduction. For any given problem, they manage the probability that an undesirable event will occur, the magnitude of the damage if it does occur, and the fraction of that total damage for which they will be responsible. They also make significant investments in information that enable them to assess more accurately the investments they can make in reducing risk.

To see that managing risk and uncertainty more effectively than competitors is a long-run strategy for competitive advantage, we only need to observe that environmental risk imposes costs on the firm. They may not be routine costs that arise every day; depending on the particular risk, months or years may elapse before the costs make themselves felt. But in the long run, on average, a company that manages contingent costs more effectively than its competitors will see the results on its balance sheet.

Because the firm's competitors may be shaving short-term costs at the expense of greater longer-term risk, however, a company trying to take a longer-term view may face competitive difficulties in the short run. For this reason, longer-term risk management strategies that also deliver short-term benefits are highly desirable. The companies described in this chapter tried to capture some of those benefits in the form of improved product quality, community relations, and customer goodwill. To capture those benefits, they integrated their risk management strategies with their basic business strategies.

It is desirable in any case to integrate environmental risk management with the management of other forms of risk and to consider both in the context of the firm's basic strategy. As we have seen, companies commonly create walls between the executives responsible for environmental risk management and the management of other business risks like currency risk and the risk of business interruption. The common rationales are that environmental risk management requires so much specialized technical and scientific skill that it must be given

over to specialists, or that too little is known about the true nature of environmental risk for it to be managed like other business risks. General managers ought to be suspicious of the first of these arguments, which is a recipe for internal bureaucracy. As for the second argument, firms can begin managing environmental risk in the same ways that other risks are managed as their understanding of the environmental risk improves. Firms at the forefront of this process will have an advantage in controlling costs because they will be better able to identify and invest in those kinds of risk management that actually deliver value to shareholders.

Integrating Environment and Business Practice

THIS CHAPTER has two main purposes. First, its case histories integrate the economic and strategic ideas emphasized in earlier chapters with administrative and organizational considerations to explore in detail the ways in which environmental policies are developed and implemented in large, decentralized firms. Second, the cases emphasize environmental controversies that remain unresolved and that are likely to increase in importance in the coming years—controversies about which executives cannot afford to be uninformed.

New environmental strategies, employed both by the firms profiled here and more generally, are heavily affected by three interrelated developments within and outside the firm. First, firms have begun to develop information systems that evaluate both the environmental costs of various business processes and the benefits to firms of their environmental investments. Second, firms are developing internal, structural incentives that more closely align managerial and company interests. Third, environmental institutions—the "rules of the game"—both within and outside the firm are evolving in ways that contribute to the convergence of private and social costs. Changes in information, incentives, and institutions appear repeatedly in the cases, and understanding them will help us to make sense of the complicated problems of strategy design and business administration that concern about the environment presents to firms.

The case histories in this chapter show the relationships among these three developments, their relationships with the basic economic

circumstances of the firms in question, and their effects on the environment and on the firms' performance. These developments will be critical in coming decades if companies are to continue to make progress toward reconciling social demands for environmental quality with traditional imperatives of shareholder value creation.

In addition, these cases shed light on controversies that are still far from resolved and that are likely to increase in importance in the first decades of the new century. These include global climate change, the preservation of biodiversity, and the incorporation of environmental considerations into the development strategies of third world countries. Regardless of one's views about the scientific aspects of any of these questions, they seem likely to play significant roles in political and diplomatic debates—and therefore in firms' planning and operational decisions—for some time to come.

Before turning to the case histories, this chapter examines each of the three developments briefly. Then, the case histories show how these developments have affected firms in real-world situations. The chapter ends with a more detailed discussion of the three developments that draws upon the experiences of these and other firms.

INFORMATION

Firms invest in various types of information for a number of users: financial accounting data for shareholders, tax accounts for government authorities, management accounting data for internal decision makers. In this chapter, we focus on the development and use of supplemental information, beyond what is collected by traditional accounting systems, that enables firms to improve their assessment of alternative environmental policies. As the environment has become a more significant managerial issue, firms have sought to improve their ability to collect, manage, and use information of this sort.

To design and implement environmental policy, managers may want to improve their understanding of the indirect costs that arise from environmental pressure. They might, for example, want to track waste disposal costs back to individual products rather than aggregating them all at the facility level. Managers may also want to do a similar analysis for contingent costs like those arising from accidents or lawsuits, so that they can determine the risks their firms incur. Look-

ing beyond the traditional boundaries of the firm, managers may wish to improve their understanding of the environmental impacts of their products through the entire life cycle of materials sourcing, production, use, and disposal. They can develop and use these kinds of information at almost any level of sophistication and cost, from calculations literally scrawled on the backs of envelopes through multiyear, multimillion-dollar reporting exercises. Further, they can express the information on environmental impacts in dollar terms, or alternatively leave the financial implications implicit or unquantified.

Beyond these measurements and estimates, managers also require information that is inevitably less amenable to quantitative measurements and statistical analysis. Firms' environmental policies must take into account not only physical and economic conditions but also social concerns and expectations. Information about the perspectives of various interested parties—customers, policy makers, environmental advocates, employees—can be as important in designing durable environmental policies for the firm as more concrete information about materials flows and costs.

Managers possess a great deal of flexibility in deciding what information to generate and use, so it makes sense to think about the costs and benefits of any information strategy before setting out. Improved environmental information can be costly, as discussed at length in the previous chapter. At the same time, better information often confers considerable benefits. It can help in identifying regulatory risks and market opportunities, and hence in product development and the selection of product attributes. For example, the decision of Ciba Specialty Chemicals to develop low-salt textile dyes, discussed in chapter 2, was motivated by new information that identified an opportunity to lower the environmental costs of the dye maker's customers. Better environmental information will be especially useful if environmentally preferable products and processes increase in economic attractiveness in the future because of changes in consumer behavior, regulation, or both.

INCENTIVE DESIGN

For a long time, social philosophers have tried to think systematically about the incentives that societies and organizations can use to encourage certain behavior among their members. At an abstract level, one

can distinguish three categories of incentives, which can be labeled economic, hierarchical, and cultural. Economic incentives are based on considerations of material self-interest; hierarchical incentives on power and physical force; and cultural incentives on status, organizational culture, and other factors, less readily quantifiable but nevertheless important.[1] Although these three categories are useful, the boundaries between them are blurrier in practice than in theory. For example, if a company rewards proactive behavior in environmental matters by promoting managers who display that behavior, it is using all three kinds of incentives. Economic rewards for good performance are combined with the threat that poor environmental performance can impede a manager's career progress within the hierarchy, and a policy of rewarding proactive behavior with promotions will affect the corporate culture as well.

In practice, any given society or organization is almost certain to use all three kinds of incentives to some extent. The relative importance of each depends on the purpose of the organization, and on the information and technologies at its disposal. Modern-day churches and volunteer organizations—including many environmental groups—tend to use cultural incentives, associating the "right" activities with a sense of individual self-worth and status within the community. Military organizations make heavy use of incentives based on hierarchy and the threat of force, but successful militaries rely even more heavily on cultural incentives, inculcating in their soldiers an overriding sense of identity with the organization. As we have already seen, all three kinds of incentives are used in firms, but their relative importance depends on the nature of the business. A business in an industry where performance is relatively easy to measure—say, sales and distribution—may rely more heavily on bonuses, awards, and other economic incentives. Where output is harder to measure or the returns to individual activity are riskier, as in scientific research, economic incentives may be more difficult to use, and the firm may rely more heavily on cultural and status-based incentives.

As we saw in chapter 6, companies tend to make relatively little direct use of price mechanisms in setting up systems to reward environmental performance. Some make heavy use of hierarchical incentives, specifying procedures that must be followed and then penalizing those who don't comply. Others have relied very heavily on cultural incentives, although this can prove difficult if these are not aligned with the eco-

nomic incentive pay systems that dominate managerial incentive design outside the environmental arena. Environmental pressure from government and other groups has encouraged firms to experiment with new incentives designed to foster improved environmental performance. One of the questions for executives is whether increasing the use of economic incentives, for example by tying bonuses more closely to environmental performance, would be effective or counterproductive.

ENVIRONMENTAL INSTITUTIONS

Institutions are the rules of the game under which economic activity is conducted. In the vocabulary of Nobel laureate Douglass North, they are the "humanly devised constraints that shape human interaction": they include the general structure of property rights, the scope and limits of government activity, and so on.[2] Dissatisfaction with some of the existing arrangements in recent decades has led to institutional innovation in the private sector and in the governmental community. Firms and governments have looked for ways to ensure the desired levels of environmental quality without undermining the economy's ability to generate traditional private goods and services.

Some of the approaches to environmental management discussed in earlier chapters can be considered examples of institutional innovation. For instance, the product takeback initiatives in the electronics industry, discussed in chapter 5, represent a realignment of private property rights among producers and consumers of the equipment, with the producers retaining environmental responsibilities that formerly passed to their customers along with title to the products.

Governmental actors have also made attempts to redefine institutions. Like product takeback schemes, systems of tradable pollution permits represent a change in property rights regimes: most pollution permits cannot be bought and sold, and thus they lack one of the central features of private property rights. A system of tradable permits, like the one established for sulfur dioxide in the United States in 1990, can result in far cheaper reductions in pollution than would otherwise have been possible, because the tradability of the permits forces firms to confront a cost for each unit of the pollution that they emit. This provides firms with an incentive to reduce pollution continually, unlike the incentives established by command-and-control regulations. In

other words, it motivates the integration of environmental and traditional business objectives.

Beyond the formal institutions on which economists tend to focus, informal institutions play significant roles in shaping companies' environmental policies. Social expectations about corporate performance, whether in the environmental arena or more generally, matter to firms in part because they eventually affect formal institutions like the regulatory apparatus and the court system. But informal expectations can affect corporate behavior more directly for the simple reason that companies are cultural and social as well as economic entities.

Each of the three developments discussed here—in information, incentives, and institutions—affects both of the others. The information that managers have at their disposal determines the kinds of incentives a business can use internally; more broadly, it affects the kinds of institutions that society will find feasible. Improved information and incentive systems within firms facilitate businesses' ability to design policies that deliver more environmental shareholder value, while tradable pollution rights and other institutional innovations will bring about more situations in which these new systems can be successfully implemented.

THREE HISTORIES

The first of these histories describes the efforts of Monsanto Company, after a long and checkered environmental history, to integrate environmental considerations into business planning and to contribute actively to "sustainable development." The second discusses Chevron Corporation's environmental management initiatives in a decentralized empire stretching from oil fields in Kazakhstan to gas pumps in Santa Monica. The third describes Georgia-Pacific Corporation's efforts in the forest products industry to change both internal environmental management practices and the firm's environmental image in the public arena.

MONSANTO COMPANY

We have seen Monsanto Company in previous chapters. Chapter 2 analyzed the firm's repositioning of Roundup herbicide as a complement to no-till agriculture, providing both increased social benefits and

an improved market position. Chapter 5 investigated the company's efforts to transform the system by which crops are protected from insects, substituting biotechnological know-how for the traditional synthesis of chemical pesticides. The present case history places these individual initiatives in the context of Monsanto's overall strategy and assesses its ongoing efforts to contribute to the goal, emphasized repeatedly in Monsanto's internal and external communications, of "sustainable development."[3] (Table 7-1 shows Monsanto's financial data.)

An overview of the company's history. John F. Queeney established Monsanto as a manufacturer of saccharin in 1901, giving the company his wife's maiden name. The company subsequently expanded its product line opportunistically to exploit scientific synergies and to invade potentially lucrative new markets. As a result, by the end of the 1940s the company's product mix extended from vanillin and aspirin to polystyrene and DDT. [4]

During the 1960s and 1970s, Monsanto acquired an environmental reputation similar to that of the other large chemical companies. Controversies arose about pollution near its manufacturing facilities and about the effects of its products on the environment after they were sold. In addition to DDT, Monsanto manufactured 2,4,5-T, a constituent of the Agent Orange defoliant used by the American military in Southeast Asia. Like DDT, this herbicide was mentioned by name in Rachel Carson's *Silent Spring;* also like DDT, it was later banned by the U.S. Environmental Protection Agency (EPA).[5] Monsanto also manufactured polychlorinated biphenyls (PCBs), widely used in electrical equipment because of their insulating properties. Monsanto stopped producing PCBs in 1977, two years before the EPA banned most uses of the compounds.[6]

The public reputation of the chemical companies was largely responsible for passage of the major environmental statutes of the Ford and Carter eras: the Toxic Substances Control Act of 1976, the Resource Conservation and Recovery Act of the same year, and the Superfund law of 1980. Like other large chemical firms, Monsanto was named a potentially responsible party (PRP) at dozens of Superfund sites; under the joint and several liability provisions of the law, it was theoretically accountable for all cleanup costs at each of these locations. These liability provisions reflected an unusual degree of mistrust of the chemical

Year	1998	1997	1996	1995	1994	1993
Revenues ($m)	8,648	7,514	6,348	5,410	4,679	4,304
Profits after taxes ($m)	-250	470	385	739	622	494
Total assets ($m)	16,724	10,774	11,237	10,731	9,103	8,788
Book value equity ($m)	4,986	4,104	3,690	3,732	2,948	2,855
Market value equity ($m)	29,878	24,990	22,703	14,088	7,910	8,555
Long-term debt ($m)	6,259	1,979	1,608	1,667	1,405	1,502
Number of employees	31,800	21,900	28,000	28,500	29,400	30,000
LTD/LTD+ book equity	55.7%	32.5%	30.4%	30.9%	32.3%	34.5%
Return on sales	-2.9%	6.3%	6.1%	13.7%	13.3%	11.5%
Return on beginning assets	-2.3%	4.2%	3.6%	8.1%	7.1%	5.4%
Return on beginning book equity	-6.1%	12.7%	10.3%	25.1%	21.8%	16.4%
Market/book equity	6.0	6.1	6.2	3.8	2.7	3.0

Segment data, 1998	Agricultural products	Nutrition and consumer	Pharma- ceutical	Corporate and other
Assets ($m)	10,278	2,477	2,778	1,191
Revenues ($m)	4,032	1,533	2,894	189
EBIT($m)	737	278	309	-195
EBITDA ($m)	1,092	405	451	-183
Capital expenditures ($m)	468	130	236	145
% of company net sales	47%	18%	33%	2%
EBIT/revenues	18%	18%	11%	N/A
EBIT/beginning assets	17%	11%	12%	N/A
EBITDA/revenues	27%	26%	16%	N/A
EDITDA/beginning assets	25%	15%	17%	N/A

Table 7-1. Monsanto Company Financial Data

Source: Adapted from Monsanto Company 1997 and 1998 Annual Reports.

firms. Over time, the firms' reputations continued to suffer. Public confidence in the industry bottomed out after the 1984 catastrophe at a Union Carbide subsidiary's facility in Bhopal, India, in which more than 2,000 people were killed. This event was the catalyst for the Responsible Care program (discussed in chapter 3) and for unilateral efforts at environmental risk reduction throughout the industry.

The Bhopal disaster also triggered the inclusion, in the 1986 reauthorization of the Superfund law, of provisions requiring firms to disclose their releases of a long list of chemical substances to air, water, and land. Title III of the Superfund Amendment and Reauthorization Act (SARA), called the Emergency Planning and Community Right-to-Know Act (EPCRA), covered 600 substances and applied to all firms with ten or more full-time employees in a broad range of industrial categories.[7] The EPA began compiling this information in an annual Toxics Release Inventory (TRI), which it released to the public. The TRI itself proved to be a further stimulus for change within Monsanto and other firms.

The first TRI data covered the 1987 calendar year. Monsanto CEO Richard Mahoney reportedly said on seeing the data for his firm, "The air emission numbers aren't acceptable. They're not acceptable to me and they won't be acceptable to the public." Mahoney announced that Monsanto would reduce toxic air emissions to 10 percent of their 1987 levels by the end of 1992.[8]

Information compiled in response to the external reporting requirements altered incentives within the firm as well. Mahoney, not previously known as an environmental advocate, directed the preparation of a statement of environmental philosophy called "The Monsanto Pledge." Mahoney wrote to employees, shareholders, and other interested groups:

> The Pledge recognizes that outstanding environmental performance isn't a cost of doing business, but is integral to our business success. It assumes that compliance with the law and our own worldwide guidelines is basic, wherever we do business. But the environmentalism embodied in the Pledge is far more than compliance. We believe: [1] It is the right thing to do. [2] It will help us take a more comprehensive and cost-effective approach to solving environmental problems. . . . [3] It is good business—good for all of our stake holders, including our customers, employees, shareholders and others. Improved environmental performance will result in greater manufacturing efficiencies and higher

product quality. As we eliminate waste from our operations, we will also eliminate the cost of treating or disposing of that waste.[9]

Mahoney's emphasis on environmental performance complemented his overall strategic objective: to move the company from commodity chemicals into knowledge-intensive products with applications in health care and nutrition. In 1985, Monsanto bought G. D. Searle and Company, a pharmaceuticals firm. Partly as a result of this acquisition, Monsanto's research and development expenditures, which had accounted for just 3 percent of sales before Mahoney became CEO, rose to 7 to 8 percent during his tenure.[10] The expansion of markets for Roundup glyphosate herbicide also occurred under Mahoney's direction. As discussed in chapter 2, Monsanto expanded these markets through cost and price reductions and through the active promotion of conservation tillage; Roundup was the cash cow that funded Monsanto's new ventures in pharmaceuticals, nutrition, and biotechnology.

Robert Shapiro assumed the CEO job upon Mahoney's retirement in March 1995. This was a transition of some symbolic import. Mahoney, a chemist trained at the University of Massachusetts, began his career at Monsanto's chemicals manufacturing complex in Springfield, Massachusetts.[11] Shapiro, a graduate of Harvard College and Columbia Law School, was vice president and general counsel of Searle when Monsanto bought that company in 1985. The executive transition reflected Monsanto's change from a chemicals business to what Shapiro called a "life sciences company."[12]

In 1997, Shapiro split the company into two parts. Monsanto spun off its traditional chemicals businesses, which make products as diverse as carpet fiber, solvents, and a plastic interlayer for glass that prevents the glass from shattering. The spin-off created a $3 billion firm called Solutia. Monsanto became a $6 billion company encompassing pharmaceuticals, NutraSweet aspartame sweetener, the biotechnology businesses, and agricultural chemicals like Roundup.

Robert Shapiro's approach to environmental management. Shapiro and his team aggressively repositioned Monsanto as a champion of "sustainability," a firm that would use technological tools to contribute to the solution of problems involving global food supply and soil depletion. Business executives do not often invoke Malthus, but in an interview with *Harvard Business Review* Shapiro told editor Joan Magretta:

As many as 800 million people are so severely malnourished that they can neither work nor participate in family life. That's where we are today. And, as far as I know, no demographer questions that the world population will just about double by sometime around 2030. Without radical change, the kind of world implied by those numbers is unthinkable. It's a world of mass migrations and environmental degradation on an unimaginable scale. At the very best, it means the preservation of a few islands of privilege and prosperity in a sea of misery and violence. . . . The whole system has to change; there's a huge opportunity for reinvention.[13]

This philosophy informs Monsanto's decisions to pursue biotechnology as a way of increasing agricultural yields through improved pest management, more productive strains of crops, and related innovations like Posilac bovine somatotropin (BST) to increase cows' production of milk, all of which were discussed in chapter 5.

Shapiro's aggressive environmental policies and emphasis on sustainability complement broader cultural changes within Monsanto. Its headquarters in suburban St. Louis looks like the headquarters of a large firm in Silicon Valley: a set of low-lying, unassuming buildings on a parklike campus. Since his accession, Shapiro and his team have tried even harder to emphasize their similarities to Silicon Valley: their goal is to manage the biotechnology revolution as their California counterparts rode the revolution in electrical engineering. As the company moved from its traditional base in commodity chemicals toward pharmaceuticals, agricultural biotechnology, and other businesses based on cutting-edge science, it adopted many of the cultural innovations of the electronics and software companies: casual dress, offices without doors, and even organization charts that show interlocking hexagons rather than hierarchical arrangements of boxes.[14]

Day-to-day environmental management within Monsanto is conducted through a matrix organization. An environmental specialist at a manufacturing site reports both to the site manager and to a "foundation team," analogous to an environmental, health, and safety staff office at the corporate level. This foundation team is responsible for compliance audits, remediation strategies, and information management.

In designing incentives for management, Monsanto incorporates environmental considerations both into the formal compensation system and into the process by which managers are evaluated for possible promotion. At the formal level, managers hold discussions each year with

their supervisors or team leaders to negotiate their objectives for the year. The company bases managers' compensation in part on the achievement of these objectives. Depending on the importance of the environment in a manager's job, one or several of the objectives for a particular year might be environmentally related. For example, general managers of manufacturing facilities would be evaluated on the basis of permit exceedances, community complaints, and other environmental criteria. In addition, of course, informal signals about the importance of environmental considerations play a role in shaping managerial behavior.

Management of environmental information at Monsanto. New systems for the collection and analysis of information support Monsanto's environmental emphasis. Like all companies, Monsanto analyzes the direct costs of each product or production process. In addition, the company has invested substantial resources in the organizational capability to undertake life-cycle analyses. It has used this tool to assess the impacts of BST and to examine the impacts of biotechnologically engineered seeds containing genetic information that allows plants to protect themselves against insects. Monsanto managers discuss their efforts in this arena as follows:

> To identify the best opportunities for making its products more sustainable, a company must understand what is involved in the manufacture, use, recycle or disposal of its products. This means studying quantities of materials, energy and other "inputs" used to make products as well as the nature and quantity of wastes that results. The products made and resulting wastes or usable byproducts are called "outputs."
>
> Equally important is to understand both the value of using the products and the environmental and other effects that can result. Altogether, this sort of evaluation can be loosely called a "life-cycle assessment."[15]

In other words, Monsanto's life-cycle analysis has two components. The first is an inventory of materials and energy flows. The second is an improved understanding of the products' value in use and of the externalities, positive and negative, that arise from the products' manufacture, use, and ultimate disposal. While some product changes may result in superior economic and environmental performance along every possible dimension, more commonly a new product or process will improve performance along some dimensions while increasing

some other costs, environmental impacts, or risks. For example, biotechnologically engineered seeds result in "fewer inputs, less labor, less manufacturing of inputs, reduced insecticides, reduced fuel use," and so on. But they cost more to produce than conventional seeds and also may result in increased risk of pests rapidly developing resistance to the natural toxins on which the biotechnology draws.[16]

To reach an improved understanding of these various impacts, at least some implicit qualitative weighting system is necessary. The company needs qualitative or quantitative tools for comparing the total cost implications of different ways of delivering a given amount of value to society. In principle, it would be possible to apply a full-blown quantitative analysis, using numerical conversion factors to reduce all private and social costs to a single value. In practice, this degree of quantification and aggregation may not be necessary. At Monsanto as elsewhere, the tools tend to be qualitative. The company examines the important inputs and outputs of production processes to obtain at least rough calculations of materials and energy balances. If each of the flows of energy and materials was assigned a monetary social cost, this exercise would look like social cost accounting, but Monsanto has not taken this next step on anything but an experimental basis.

"Sustainable development" and the life sciences: institutional factors. In 1997, Monsanto established a new "business sector focused on creating new businesses in sustainable development." The idea behind this new unit is that the environmental problems Shapiro discussed in the *Harvard Business Review* will create huge opportunities for alert companies. "The growing disconnections between how the world operates today—the quantities of resources consumed and the wastes generated—and the ability of ecosystems to continue absorbing all this will create major opportunities for companies to develop more sustainable ways of doing things," said Jan Novak, one of the leaders of the new Monsanto initiative.[17]

In other words, Monsanto managers expect that environmental change will lead to changes in the prices of various goods and services, notably those relating to agriculture and food. They expect that agricultural land will rise in value, and this will create incentives to shift to production methods that require less land and increased amounts of other inputs. Not coincidentally, Monsanto specializes in the production of these inputs.

Monsanto's spin-off of Solutia was one of the initial moves in a larger trend toward the creation of stand-alone "life sciences" companies. Most of the major players in the biotechnology industry, including not only Monsanto but also DuPont and Hoechst, had their roots in the chemical industry. The same is true of Swiss firms Ciba-Geigy and Sandoz, both of which began in chemicals and branched out into agricultural chemicals and pharmaceuticals. Shortly after Monsanto announced the Solutia spin-off, Ciba-Geigy and Sandoz announced that they were merging; Sandoz spun off its chemicals businesses just before the merger, and Ciba-Geigy did the same immediately afterward. This 1997 reorganization created a newly named company, Novartis, with interests in crop protection, nutrition, and pharmaceuticals—the same mix of activities as Monsanto minus Solutia. Later in 1997, Hoechst announced that it would sell its chemicals businesses by 2000 in order to focus on life sciences.[18]

Reflecting the convergence among the firms in the industry, Monsanto agreed in June 1998 to merge with American Home Products (AHP), which makes such nonprescription staples as Advil and Chap Stick, as well as Premarin, an osteoporosis medication. AHP, which also manufactures pesticides and herbicides and has made investments in biotechnology, earned $2 billion in post-tax profits in 1997 on $14.2 billion in sales. The Monsanto-AHP merger was intended to capture synergies in research and development. Access to AHP's distribution channels was supposed to help Monsanto's health care products. And Monsanto hoped that the cash generated by AHP's existing stable of products would enable the joint firm to compete with the deep pockets of DuPont, Hoechst, and Novartis.[19] In October 1998, however, the deal fell through, reportedly over personal clashes between Shapiro and AHP CEO John Stafford and over difficulties in reconciling very different corporate cultures. The collapse of the deal left observers wondering whether Monsanto would try to merge with another large firm.[20]

Institutional factors are critical to the success of Monsanto's strategy, both in the developed countries and in the developing world. As described in chapters 2 and 5, the markets in which Monsanto operates are subject to pervasive government regulation, as are the markets of its customers (whether these customers are doctors prescribing medication or farmers growing and selling cotton). Monsanto's own operations are watched in the United States by the Food and Drug

Administration, the EPA, and the Department of Agriculture, and by similar agencies in other nations. Governments in both rich and poor nations subsidize agriculture, and restrict international trade in food more tightly than trade in most other commodities. For this reason, strategies at Monsanto need to take into account the likely evolution of regulatory policy in the various nations where the firm does business, and Monsanto, like its competitors, actively tries to shape those policies as well.

For example, considerable controversy exists about the true social costs and benefits of biotechnological solutions to agricultural productivity problems. Total plantings of genetically engineered crops have increased rapidly, from 7 million acres in 1996 to 32 million in 1997, but the crops remain controversial.[21] When Monsanto first started shipping U.S.-grown Roundup Ready soybeans to Europe in 1996, Greenpeace and other consumer and environmental groups protested vehemently.[22] Concerns focus on the risks that genetically engineered crops could impose on wild plants and animals, including the possibility that beneficial insects might be adversely affected or that herbicide-resistant genes could "escape" into other plant species. In 1998, European regulators reaffirmed their decision to allow the import of selected genetically modified crops into the countries of the European Union, but so far no such crops have been grown in Europe except on an experimental basis.[23]

European controversies over agricultural biotechnology continue. In February 1999, for example, Monsanto received significant negative press attention in Britain after a scientist claimed to find immune system damage and brain shrinkage among rats that were fed genetically modified potatoes. The potatoes were created for the particular experiment and were not available to the public, but an outspoken group of scientists used the occasion to call for a five-year moratorium on the sale of genetically modified foods.[24]

The Union of Concerned Scientists (UCS), an organization based in Cambridge, Massachusetts, articulates some of the environmental community's concerns about agricultural biotechnology: "In general, of the risks currently associated with genetically engineered organisms, some appear to be unique to such organisms (for example, added allergens in foods) and some overlap those posed by non-engineered organisms (for example, creation of new weeds). Because genetic engineering is a radically new technology, unknown risks may be possible. . . . It is

hard to believe that any current list is complete." The UCS further argues, "Although industry has touted both kinds of crops [i.e., insect-resistant and herbicide-tolerant plants] as having major environmental benefits, . . . these genetically engineered crops have not put us on a fundamentally different pathway in agriculture and have produced only minor reductions and substations in pesticide use in an agriculture that continues to be pesticide-dependent."[25]

Monsanto executives think they have a compelling case for their technology, not just from a profitability standpoint but also from a social cost perspective. "We need to remember as well that the question of risk occurs in a context of other key factors," they have asserted. "Given future population growth, the risk of not continuing to pursue high-yield agriculture, including biotechnology, is very real and grave. It might mean the destruction of millions of acres of undeveloped land, with disastrous biodiversity consequences, to feed our new fellow human beings."[26] Nevertheless, Monsanto managers assert that they are trying to engage their adversaries in a dialogue on the issues raised by agricultural biotechnology, not only to try to persuade skeptics that its costs exceed its benefits but also to develop a deeper understanding of their critics' perspectives and attitudes.[27]

In their 1995 annual report to shareholders, Shapiro and the other Monsanto executives announced in large type that "we've drastically reduced waste and pollution . . . but we haven't yet learned how to operate in an environmentally sustainable manner. We want to help the world find solutions."[28] Monsanto, like the agricultural biotechnology industry more broadly, faces considerable scientific and regulatory uncertainty as it endeavors to realize its vision of a transformed agricultural sector.

CHEVRON CORPORATION

We examined Chevron Corporation's risk management systems in chapter 6. Here we consider more broadly the evolution of the company's environmental policy and management systems, its attempts to capture the environmental value that it is creating or maintaining in its operations, and its confrontation with the new business challenges presented by global climate change.

An overview of the firm and its history. Chevron traces its roots back to the dawn of the industrial history of the state of California.

Now it is one of the world's hundred largest firms, integrated from oil wells and gas fields on every continent but Antarctica through thousands of retail gasoline stations. In 1998, it turned assets of $35 billion into revenues of $30 billion and earned over $1.3 billion in net income. (Financial data in Table 7-2.)

The first significant oil discoveries in California took place in the 1860s and 1870s, in Santa Clara County (now the site of Silicon Valley) and in Ventura County northwest of Los Angeles. The early history of the California oil fields, like the histories of many deposits in the United States and elsewhere, entailed wildly optimistic projections of the amount and quality of oil available, followed by a rush of investment and then despair. In this case some of the projections came from the eminent Yale chemist Benjamin Silliman Jr., after whom one of Yale's residential colleges is named. Silliman was apparently taken in by salted oil samples (i.e., samples spiked with oil from elsewhere so that they would appear more valuable) provided by California oil entrepreneurs, one of whom was his brother-in-law. He had to resign his Yale professorship because of his role in what was seen as a "swindle."[29]

In 1879, entrepreneurs Charles Felton and Lloyd Tevis established the Pacific Coast Oil Company, the first integrated oil operation in California. At about the same time, John D. Rockefeller's Standard Oil Company set up a marketing office in San Francisco to sell products brought in from the eastern United States. Standard Oil (New Jersey) bought Pacific Coast Oil in 1900. When the Supreme Court, in a landmark antitrust decision, dissolved Standard Oil in 1911, Standard's operations in California became an autonomous entity. Over the ensuing decade it expanded its share of California oil production and integrated downstream into service stations. It was renamed Standard Oil Company of California in 1926.[30]

In the 1930s, the company discovered huge quantities of oil under Bahrain and Saudi Arabia. The formation of a joint venture with Texaco, called Caltex, enabled Standard of California to process and sell this oil through Texaco's existing refineries and distribution channels in Europe, Africa, and Asia. Standard of California changed its name to Chevron in the early 1980s. In 1984, it acquired Gulf Oil Limited Partnership for $13.2 billion in the largest corporate acquisition to that point in history.[31]

Like the manufacturers of agricultural chemicals and pharmaceuticals discussed in the Monsanto case history, and like Georgia-Pacific

Year	1998	1997	1996	1995	1994	1993
Revenues ($m)	30,557	41,963	43,893	37,082	35,854	37,082
Profits after taxes ($m)	1,339	3,256	2,607	930	1,693	1,265
Total assets ($m)	36,540	35,473	34,854	34,330	34,407	34,736
Book value equity ($m)	17,034	17,472	15,623	14,355	14,596	13,997
Market value equity ($m)	54,161	50,507	42,451	34,166	29,084	28,380
Long-term debt ($m)	4,393	4,431	3,988	4,521	4,128	4,082
Number of employees	39,191	39,362	40,820	43,019	45,758	47,576
LTD/LTD+ book equity	20.5%	20.2%	20.3%	24.0%	22.0%	22.6%
Return on sales	4.4%	7.8%	5.9%	2.5%	4.7%	3.4%
Return on beginning assets	3.8%	9.3%	7.6%	2.7%	4.9%	3.7%
Return on beginning book equity	7.7%	20.8%	18.2%	6.4%	12.1%	9.2%
Market/book equity	3.2	2.9	2.7	2.4	2.0	2.0

Segment Data, 1998

	Exploration and production	Refining, marketing, and trans- portation	Chemicals	All other
Segment sales and other operating revenues ($m)	7,662	21,070	3,216	456
Assets ($m)	16,820	11,643	3,873	4,204
Segment earnings ($m)	1,072	600	122	-455[*]
Earnings/sales	14.0%	2.8%	3.8%	N/A
Earnings/beginning assets	6.8%	5.0%	3.5%	N/A

*Includes interest expenses and other corporate expenses.

Table 7-2. Chevron Corporation Financial Data

Source: Adapted from Chevron Corporation 1997 and 1998 Annual Reports.

and its forest products competitors, Chevron and all other energy companies operate in markets that are pervasively affected by government intervention. In the oil markets this intervention occurs for several reasons, some of which are related to the environment. Economies of scale push the oil industry's structure toward a small number of firms, at least some of which enjoy some market power. As in any industry based on natural resources, governments are interested in the distribution of the resource rents and intervene in markets to influence that distribution, whether through direct ownership of the resources or through concessionary arrangements with private entities. Oil is intimately tied to national security considerations, providing governments with a further rationale to intervene in markets: at least some government officials regard oil as too important to leave to market forces. And because oil is so widely used, it is a natural target for tax authorities.

Further, oil companies like Chevron encounter problems of public goods and environmental externalities—and hence legitimate reasons for government intervention—at every stage of their value chains. Crude oil must be produced where it is found, often in locations of great ecological or aesthetic value: rain forests, the Rocky Mountains, the continental shelf. Transportation, whether by pipeline or tanker, carries the risk of accidental spills. Refining is a traditionally pollution-intensive business, although continuous innovation has reduced its environmental impacts. Leaks from underground steel storage tanks have proven problematic at the distribution stage. When they use the product, the oil companies' customers generate further externalities, in the form of smog, particulate matter, and carbon dioxide. Finally, the related businesses of diversified oil companies—natural gas production and transportation, coal mining, and petrochemicals—are traditionally pollution-intensive as well.

During the 1960s and 1970s, the oil industry's public reputation suffered badly. The companies were widely blamed for increases in gasoline prices engineered by the Organization of Petroleum Exporting Countries (OPEC) in 1973 and again in 1979. In 1979, Standard Oil of California's CEO spoke bitterly about "an unprecedented barrage of hostility and criticism from many parts of government, the news media and the public" and the "tide of rhetoric and demagoguery that has been washing over our industry."[32] Although the public directed its ire largely at gasoline price hikes, the industry's environmental performance did not help. A 1969 oil spill at a platform operated by Union Oil

off the coast of Santa Barbara, California, is cited by some environmental historians as equal in importance to the publication of *Silent Spring* as a catalyst for environmental concern in the United States.[33] And the controversy over the development of oil fields on government-owned lands in Alaska during the Nixon administration was a donnybrook between preservationists and the oil companies, won by the latter.

In the 1960s, Chevron and other oil companies began investing significantly in environmental controls, both at oil production sites and at refineries and downstream facilities. In contrast to some other firms, where an identifiable event like the accession of a new CEO or a serious environmental accident triggered a sharp change in executive attitudes toward environmental management, environmental policy making within Chevron has evolved gradually. Expenditures and management attention have increased over time at a relatively steady rate.

Chevron's explicit strategy involves "emphasizing the value of the Chevron brand name, focusing on reducing costs and maintaining incident-free operations."[34] Accordingly, in the environmental arena Chevron maintains an extensive internal regulatory system to prevent accidental releases and legal noncompliance, voluntarily undertakes to provide environmental goods to enhance the company's reputation, and participates actively in private organizations intended to reduce the environmental risks of the oil industry as a whole.

Environmental management systems. Chevron's internal environmental management system is based philosophically on a document called "The Chevron Way," which sets out the company's approach to its businesses, including a statement of environmental principles: "We are committed to protecting the safety and health of people and the environment. We will conduct our business in a socially responsible and ethical manner. Our goal is to be the industry leader in safety and health performance, and to be recognized worldwide for environmental excellence."[35] An explicit environmental policy statement, Chevron Policy 530, issued in 1989, reinforces these principles: "The goal is to be a leader within industry by emphasizing innovation and encouraging creative solutions, both of which will improve our competitive position."[36]

To manage the environmental effects of operations, the company relies heavily on a system of internal regulations, discussed in chapter 6. Managers identified ten "key elements" that are critical to the success-

ful implementation of Policy 530: compliance assurance, community awareness and outreach, emergency preparedness and response, energy conservation, legislative and regulatory advocacy, pollution prevention, product stewardship, property transfer, safe operations, and transportation and distribution. For each of these, several management practices are considered especially important. For example, the pollution prevention element of Policy 530 encompasses a dozen management practices, including, for example, "Develop and maintain a comprehensive inventory of all wastes generated and all releases into the air, water and ground. . . . Prioritize wastes and releases for a reduction effort; if appropriate, identify and prioritize products targeted for pollution prevention efforts. . . . Measure progress in pollution prevention efforts, at least annually."[37] Environmental managers at Chevron headquarters have identified a total of 102 such management practices, each of which relates to one of the ten key elements. Each of these 102 practices is to be implemented by each Chevron business unit worldwide; Chevron reported in early 1998 that "nearly all Chevron operations met their 'Protecting People and the Environment' program goals, fully implementing 102 management practices worldwide by year-end 1997."[38]

The regulatory structure of objectives, key elements, and management practices is quite similar to that of the Responsible Care program undertaken by the chemical manufacturers, described in chapter 3. The resemblance is not coincidental; Chevron's chemicals subsidiary was one of the leaders of the Responsible Care initiative, and when Chevron began setting up its own internal program and looked for models, it was natural to consider the work that Chevron Chemical had done in collaboration with the other chemical firms.

In designing incentives for managers, Chevron makes use all of the tools discussed in chapter 6. Policy 530 and its implementation guides are less a rigid set of command-and-control regulations than a framework within which negotiations between managers and their superiors can take place, with priorities, timetables, and targets determined by the particular circumstances of the business. Because management evaluation and promotion systems already rely heavily on executive judgment and other intangibles, they are logical vehicles for managing environmental performance decisions, where precise information about costs and benefits is often unavailable. At the same time, Chevron does use explicit command-and-control regulation where the stakes are especially high, as in managing the risk of spills from oil tankers.

Chevron operates in dozens of countries, some of which have lax environmental standards or governments with very little enforcement capability. For this reason, the applicability of Policy 530 and all of its management practices across all Chevron sites is a decision of great importance. Like most firms, Chevron does not assert that it will apply the same technological standards at all of its worldwide operations, or that emissions from a facility in Kazakhstan will be exactly the same as emissions at a facility of comparable size in California. On the other hand, Policy 530 does require that any Chevron operation comply with all applicable legal requirements and with all of the company's internal policies. The stricter of the two sets of standards determines the required performance.

Collecting and analyzing environmental information. Until the mid-1990s, according to Chevron managers, environmental decision making was often "more judgmental than analytical." For example, in the early 1980s the company decided to replace old underground steel tanks at service stations with double-walled fiberglass tanks in advance of any regulatory requirement to do so. The costs to Chevron of a leaking tank were estimated at $250,000, while it cost $25,000 to $50,000 to take preventive measures.[39] It would have been easy to calculate a break-even probability for leakage above which it would save expected costs to change the tank. It would have been possible, too, to adjust the $250,000 figure to reflect the risk of legal liability or damage to the company's reputation and to adjust the break-even probability to reflect these costs. There was some risk, too, in installing the fiberglass tanks in advance of regulation, since it was possible that regulators might later require some other technology; this risk, too, could be incorporated into a decision analysis. In the event, though, these analytical procedures were not undertaken in any formal way: instead, the decision to replace all the tanks was based on managerial judgment. As we saw in chapter 6, Chevron is now applying quantitative decision-making tools to set priorities among environmental investments. The tools could be extended so that they would be useful not only for comparative priority setting but also for cost-benefit analysis that would help to determine the appropriate level of investment; so far, the company has not used them for this purpose.

Chevron's corporate audit program, initiated in the early 1980s, is intended to improve both information management and incentive

design within the firm. Like many companies, Chevron has an in-house auditing program to evaluate the compliance status of its facilities. In Chevron's case, the audits cover compliance both with applicable government regulations and with the implementation guides under Policy 530. The company conducts twenty to twenty-five audits per year, each lasting one or two weeks.

Information about compliance status is factored into management evaluation and promotion decisions, so the existence of the audit program reinforces employees' incentives to manage environmental problems in a manner consistent with the vision of the company. Moreover, each audit team consists not of full-time auditors but of professionals recruited for that particular audit from other facilities or operating companies. Hence the audits also serve as mechanisms for informal information exchange among the members of the team and between team members and facility staff.

Many of Chevron's initiatives in the environmental arena go beyond the company-wide baselines established under Policy 530. For particular business units, it may make sense to be considerably more aggressive in providing public goods than the language of Policy 530 and its implementing rules would suggest. This may be especially true in exploration and production activities, which often take the company into areas that are unusually sensitive for aesthetic or ecological reasons: the California continental shelf, for example, or the Rocky Mountains.

Decisions about special efforts to reduce ecological damage are undertaken at the ground level rather than through any formal top-down management directive. If exploration managers decide, for example, that the investment of extra money to reduce the aesthetic impacts of a test well is warranted, they can undertake this investment on their own initiative. In the view of many Chevron executives, such measures tend to be relatively inexpensive compared with the amount of conflict and delay that can thereby be avoided.

Relations with customers, regulators, and employees. In the mid-1980s, Chevron began calling attention to some of these initiatives by airing corporate image advertisements in a campaign called "People Do." The company had long advertised its products and had experimented with corporate advertising in the 1970s in a campaign that "featured an animated dinosaur and focused on a much-needed conservation theme."[40] The People Do campaign, by contrast, was neither about

Chevron's products nor about the need for energy conservation. Featuring beautiful pictures of birds, bears, and marine creatures coexisting peaceably with Chevron oil wells and refineries, it was aimed at creating an image of Chevron as a company that can be trusted to work on sensitive projects in an environmentally responsible manner.

For example, one 1984 television ad showed clean water "pouring into something we cannot see as a shape . . . gradually our TV set seems to fill up with water. . . . A stickleback fish swims into view. Another comes in. Then a third. Then a fourth. Pull back to see tank in lab. Worker peeks through to see that fish are doing okay." Meanwhile, a voice-over says that the water "came from an oil refinery where it was used to help turn crude oil into gasoline. . . . Before it goes back into the bay where it came from, the traces of the work it has done have to be removed. Who makes sure of that? Our final inspectors . . . Oscar . . . Fred . . . Susie . . . Miranda. After all, they have to live in it." The ad ends with the Chevron hallmark and the voice-over: "Do people really go to all that trouble to make sure that you don't hurt the fish? Some people do." [41]

Later, Chevron expanded the campaign to print, placing ads in *Time, Newsweek, Harper's,* and the outdoorsperson's magazine *Outside.* For example, one ad called attention to Chevron's tactics in exploring for oil in northwestern Montana: "A number of steps were taken to protect the grizzlies and their habitat: leaving the area to the bears in the spring by working only in the winter; exploring at an elevation far below grizzly dens; restricting human access; prohibiting off-road driving; installing a less obtrusive drill pad and revegetating the area." Another ad calls attention to Chevron's policy of applying bioremediation technology to break down oily wastes at old oil and gas wells and using the resultant compost to revegetate the sites for wildlife habitat. The print ads are less emotive than the television ads, but they, too, contain color photographs of whales, grizzly bears, and pronghorn antelope. [42]

With these advertisements, Chevron is trying to reach several groups: residents of the communities in which it does business; decision makers and opinion leaders within and outside of Chevron's market areas; customers, employees, and people who might someday work for the company. In each case, the benefits of corporate image advertising about environmental performance are difficult to quantify, but since the company spends about $8 million a year on People Do advertising, it is clear that Chevron executives believe the benefits to be sig-

nificant.[43] For example, they believe that a reputation for trustworthiness and probity helps them obtain regulatory clearance for new projects or expansions over firms that do not possess such a reputation. Hence the television and print ads in areas where Chevron owns wells and refineries, and the print ads aimed at officials in Washington and Sacramento.

The effect of corporate image advertising on gasoline customers' behavior is also difficult to analyze. It is possible to measure the effects of the People Do campaign on potential customers' perceptions of Chevron, just as one would measure the effects of any ad campaign on customer perceptions of a product or company. But the next step in the chain, from changed attitudes and beliefs to changed behavior and hence to the financial performance of the company, is so difficult to define that Chevron executives do not try to analyze it quantitatively. Price, convenience, and perceived product quality remain the primary criteria on which retail buyers of gasoline base their purchase decisions. Chevron executives think that if all these factors are roughly constant, customers will prefer to buy fuel from a firm they regard as trustworthy from an environmental standpoint, although this effect is difficult to pin down statistically.

Chevron executives also think that a reputation for environmental probity helps in employee relations and perhaps even in recruiting. As with customers, it is possible to measure the effect of environmental initiatives or advertising on employees' ideas and attitudes about the company. It seems plausible that there is a connection between these ideas and attitudes and the employees' enthusiasm about their work and their commitment to the company, although Chevron managers do not try to analyze this second link in any quantitative fashion. But by calling favorable attention to managerial and employee initiatives like the bioremediation and composting for old oil and gas wells, the People Do campaign creates internal incentives for others within Chevron to look for similar opportunities.

Environment and shareholder value. In its messages to both internal and external audiences, Chevron executives repeatedly assert that what's good for the environment is good for business. As we have seen, however, it is difficult to quantify this relationship. In a speech, Vice Chairman of the Board James N. Sullivan cited an academic estimate of the value of Chevron's reputation: it came to $10 billion. But

Sullivan immediately went on to say, "I'm not sure $10 billion is right— might be more or less."[44] The uncertainty about the reputational value is significant, and the uncertainties about the effects of different policies on that value even greater. So, despite Chevron's progress in increasing the use of analytical tools to assess the costs and benefits of various environmental investments, the company's overall position with respect to the environment is bound to be determined in part by executive judgment and personal and cultural values.

Environmental incentives for Chevron managers are still based largely on the firm's command-and-control structure. Executives at Chevron are considering a plan in which the costs of corporate-level risk management programs like environmental liability insurance or rapid-response teams are allocated on some experience-weighted basis. Traditionally, costs of this sort are bundled into a corporate overhead account, so managers in the operating companies do not see them labeled as costs of environmental risk management and do not have the opportunity to reduce their share of these costs by improving their environmental performance. The prevailing view has been that the costs are small enough that it may not make sense to invest much effort in tracking them.

Chevron executives wonder as well whether they should invest more in developing information about environmental costs. As noted in chapter 6, information systems used in the refineries allow managers to compute the benefits and costs of various environmental investments, but such tools are not universally used within the firm. If it attempted to use such tools more widely, the company would face some very difficult questions about the values generated by environmental investments: for example, the relative value of ecosystem damage in the United States as opposed to ecosystem damage in Kazakhstan.

The international nature of Chevron's business creates dilemmas whether or not the company chooses to be explicit about quantifying environmental values. As discussed earlier, Chevron, like many other companies based in the industrialized world but doing business in developing countries, applies standards that may be tighter than those imposed by the host government. At the same time, these standards may be less stringent than the ones imposed by regulatory authorities in the United States or other rich countries. Environmentalists might ask why the company does not apply exactly the same standards all over the world; meanwhile, diversified shareholders might raise ques-

tions about the advisability of making any investments beyond what is required by local law.

As we have seen, Chevron's attitude in walking this tightrope is influenced by its executives' ideas about the nature of competition in the oil industry. First, the Chevron executives know that the assets that they or their competitors put in place are potentially useful for several decades. Second, the executives believe that over time periods of this length, environmental attitudes in developing countries will tend to shift toward more concern, not less, as the countries become richer. Third, Chevron executives see an oil company's reputation as critical in enabling it to continue doing business: other firms and governments prefer to do business with a company that has a reputation for responsibility and probity. Hence, the executives believe that in the global petroleum exploration and production business, it makes economic sense to invest substantially in enhancing their environmental reputation. In other industries this case might be easier, harder, or perhaps even impossible to make.

Global climate change. Questions about information, incentive design, and companies' contribution to environmental institutions all come together in the issue of global climate change. It now seems very likely that human activities, especially the burning of fossil fuels, will lead to measurable changes in global average temperatures over the lifetimes of the current population by raising the atmospheric concentrations of carbon dioxide and other gases. It also seems clear that these changes would impose economic costs on society. It remains far less clear how large these costs will be, or how much it would cost to slow the process that leads to global warming.

The major oil companies are divided on the subject of global warming. Chief executive John Browne of British Petroleum (BP), in speeches in Berlin and at Stanford in 1997, said:

> The time to consider the policy dimensions of climate change is not when the link between greenhouse gases and climate change is conclusively proven, but when the possibility cannot be discounted and is taken seriously by the society of which we are part. We in BP have reached that point. . . .
>
> We have a responsibility to act, and I hope that through our actions we can contribute to the much wider process which is desirable and necessary. BP accepts that responsibility and we're therefore taking

some specific steps: [1] To control our own emissions [2] To fund continuing scientific research [3] To take initiatives for joint implementation [4] To develop alternative fuels for the long term [5] And to
contribute to the public policy debate in search of the wider global
answers to the problem.[45]

There is now an effective consensus that there is a discernible human
influence on the climate and a link between the concentration of carbon dioxide and the increase in temperature. . . . Even though there is
no certainty in the science, it is clear that climate change is a serious
concern which merits precautionary action.[46]

Representatives of the world's national governments, meeting in
Kyoto in late 1997, inked a treaty under which industrial nations would
cut their carbon dioxide levels by 6 to 8 percent from 1990 baselines by
about the year 2010. Ratification of the Kyoto Protocol was not guaranteed, and national governments remained uncertain about how to
establish accounting mechanisms under which individual firms could
get credit for emissions reductions. Despite these uncertainties, however, BP announced in 1998 that it was undertaking voluntary cutbacks
of carbon dioxide emissions from its own operations, with a plan to
reduce those emissions by 10 percent from a 1990 baseline by 2010.
British Petroleum further announced that it was working with the
Environmental Defense Fund, a prominent American environmental
group that had long been a champion of market-based pollution control mechanisms, to develop an intrafirm system of tradable emissions
rights for carbon dioxide.[47]

Meanwhile, just two weeks after Browne's speech in Berlin,
Exxon CEO Lee Raymond exhorted delegates to the World Petroleum
Congress in Beijing not to succumb to "energy rationing administered
by a vast international bureaucracy responsible to no one" or to "pun-
ishing, high energy taxes." Raymond argued that to cut human-caused
greenhouse gas emissions "on the premise that it will affect climate
defies common sense and lacks foundation in our current understanding of the climate system. . . . It would be tragic indeed if the people
of this region were deprived of the opportunity for continued prosperity by misguided restrictions and regulation. It is up to all of us—the
petroleum industry, the governments of this great region, and the international community—to ensure that this does not happen."[48]

Chevron executives' views on climate change fall somewhere
between those of Browne and Raymond. For them, as for other energy
company executives, global climate change presents an extraordinarily

difficult set of problems. Environmental institutions to manage the issue do not yet exist. Information on costs and benefits remains highly uncertain. The implications of this institutional and informational vacuum for incentive design are also unclear.

Because of these uncertainties and complexities, in combination with the large potential costs, global climate change seems certain to be a significant issue for Chevron over the coming decades. Mark Keller, the chemical engineer and twenty-five-year Chevron veteran who runs the company's environmental organization, argues that "climate change is a subset of a much larger question of sustainable development, involving social as well as economic and environmental factors. It would be myopic to see global climate change as an acid test for environmental management."[49] At the same time, Chevron and its competitors face a significant challenge in integrating the possibility of climate change, and the possibility of regulations triggered by fear about climate change, into their decision-making process as they have integrated other environmental considerations.

GEORGIA-PACIFIC CORPORATION

The forest products industry's record on environmental matters has been consistently controversial. Public goods and environmental externalities are important at every stage of the industry's value system. Timberlands are bundles of public goods (erosion control, habitat for wildlife, and so on) and private goods (the raw material for paper and plywood). A firm cannot capture the private value—the commodity value of the wood—without impinging to some degree on the public goods. At the same time, the firm cannot produce the raw material for paper and plywood without also creating wildlife habitat, erosion control, and other public goods for which it is generally not compensated. Further down the vertical chain, the factories that make pulp and paper have historically been significant water and air polluters (recall the case examples on Champion International and Alberta-Pacific in chapter 6). Even after the companies sell their products, externalities remain important: government-sponsored recycling programs, initiated in response to perceived shortages of raw materials and landfill space, have significantly affected the industry's economics over the past decade.

At the same time, government ownership of timberlands is common, not just in the United States but all over the world. At the turn

of the last century, fears that wood prices did not reflect future scarcity and that "timber famine" would constrain future economic growth led to the establishment of the national forest system in the United States and similar measures in other countries. The industry now has enormous value at stake in global debates about biodiversity, since much of the world's biota lives in forests. The industry has perhaps an even greater stake in debates on climate change, since forests remove carbon from the air while they grow, and loss of forests contributes to atmospheric carbon dioxide levels. Government intervention in the industry's marketplaces, and social concern about its environmental effects, are thus pervasive and likely to remain so.

In these respects—the importance of environmental considerations, and the pervasiveness of government intervention—the forest products industry resembles the industries in which Monsanto and Chevron compete. There is one critical distinction, however. Competition in the markets for forest products is global, with pulp manufacturers from Georgia, Finland, and Indonesia chasing the same customers. But the firms themselves are not global in the way that Monsanto, Chevron, and their competitors are. Forest products firms tend to serve world markets from a well-defined base in one part of the world or another. Few European firms own timberlands or mills in North America or Asia, and few American or Canadian firms own those assets outside North America. Countries with timber bases have tended to want to nurture national champions rather than inviting in equity participants from outside. They have been able to pursue this strategy because the technical expertise to grow trees and make products from them is more widely available in the marketplace than expertise in petroleum engineering or biotechnology. The result is a fragmented industry in which no firm can integrate the interests of timber producers in North America, Europe, and the tropics.

The company's early history. Georgia-Pacific was founded in 1927 in Augusta, Georgia.[50] Initially a lumber wholesaler, it soon began manufacturing lumber as well, first in the South, and, following the Second World War, also in the Pacific Northwest. In the early 1950s, it moved its headquarters to Portland, Oregon, simultaneously moving into the manufacture of plywood and purchasing substantial tracts of timberland. It added pulp and paper to its product portfolio in 1957, building a mill on the Oregon coast as a way of exploiting the "residuals"—sawdust and scraps from

plywood and lumber manufacture—generated in its other operations. In 1963, the company developed new technology that enabled the first production of plywood out of southern pine, and within three years it made pine plywood at five locations in the American South.

By the mid-1960s, Georgia-Pacific's aggressive strategy of growth by acquisitions had attracted the attention of regulators at the Federal Trade Commission. A 1971 settlement with the FTC created the Louisiana-Pacific Corporation, which took control of many of Georgia-Pacific's western assets.[51] In 1982, Georgia-Pacific moved its headquarters back to Atlanta. Its motives, according to CEO Marshall Hahn, were "to be closer to the bulk of our operations and to be at the new center of industry growth." Hahn cited uncertainty about government environmental policy as a contributing factor in his company's move back to the South. "In the Pacific Northwest," he said in 1990, "where the federal government owns most of the timber inventory, changing government policies are creating tremendous uncertainty about raw material supply and prices. The South's commercial timberlands, however, generally are in the hands of private landowners." The company continued to grow by acquisition, and its 1989 purchase of paper producer Great Northern Nekoosa (GNN) was the largest merger in the industry to that time.[52]

Environmental changes. Like Georgia-Pacific, the American forest products industry has been footloose, moving from the Northeast to the Great Lake states and then to the South and the West as timber stocks in each area were depleted. During the nineteenth and early twentieth centuries, the industry pursued practices that offend the sensibilities of the late twentieth century. Firms harvested timber with little regard for regrowth, much less for wildlife habitat or aesthetic values. Pollution from mills was left completely uncontrolled (as we saw in the previous chapter's case example on Champion) until federal air and water pollution statutes were enacted in the 1960s and 1970s.

Besides those new pollution control laws, a series of related external events forced Georgia-Pacific and other forest products firms to reassess their environmental practices. The preceding quote from Marshall Hahn's 1990 speech refers to one such change: the impact of environmental concerns on forestry, particularly in the western United States. As of about 1960, the West was the one part of the contiguous United States in which significant areas remained that had never been

harvested. Clear-cutting, long a standard industry practice, became controversial in the mid-1960s for both aesthetic and ecological reasons. Concern about depletion of "old growth" timber intensified after the 1973 passage of the Endangered Species Act and the discovery that some species, like the northern spotted owl, appeared to require significant areas with older trees in order to survive. The federal agencies that control much of the Pacific Northwest timber base essentially got out of the business of selling timber in the early 1990s in order to satisfy the demands of environmental groups.

In its immediate economic consequences, the owl had a greater effect on small mills that did not own their own timberlands than it did on large integrated firms like Georgia-Pacific and Weyerhaeuser. In fact, the integrated firms were beneficiaries of the higher log prices that resulted from the diminished supply from federal lands. At the same time, however, the owl case raised the possibility that traditional private property rights might be curtailed in order to maintain public goods like the existence of endangered species. The endangered species law clearly required the federal government to restrict timber harvests on its own lands if this was necessary to protect the owl, but it also appeared to grant the government the power to restrict harvests on private land. One integrated firm with extensive holdings of potential owl habitat near Mount Rainier National Park in Washington State estimated that every owl nest found on its property could tie up a million dollars' worth of timber.[53]

During the same period, class action lawsuits against a number of major paper companies, like the $6.5 billion suit against Champion discussed in chapter 6, dramatized the contingent costs to firms of pollution from mills. The suits were primarily aimed at dioxins, a class of compounds that have been implicated in Love Canal and other dramatic environmental crises and that are produced in trace amounts in the pulpmaking process. The suits were often settled out of court for a small fraction of the amounts initially demanded, and even when companies lost in court the awards tended to be small relative to the firms' net worth. For example, juries found against Georgia-Pacific in 1991 and in 1992 in suits relating to pollution along the Leaf River in Mississippi. But the awards were just $1 million and $3 million, respectively, and even these decisions were later reversed.[54] Despite the relatively small amounts paid out, such lawsuits highlighted the contingent liabilities inherent in traditional methods of pulp manufacture.

Georgia-Pacific, like the other large forest products firms, persisted in policies that externalized social costs for some time after social expectations of companies began changing. During the 1960s and 1970s, for example, Georgia-Pacific acquired a reputation for "cut and get out" timber policies in the Pacific Northwest.[55] The trade journal *Pulp and Paper* wrote in 1994 that "the company is emerging from the GNN takeover as one of the major world players in both the building products and pulp and paper sectors. But with that status has come a reputation among some in the industry (particularly former GNN employees), environmentalists, and the public that the company has been too financially aggressive and is insensitive to environmental and community issues."[56]

After assuming the CEO job in 1993, A. D. "Pete" Correll made three significant statements in an attempt to change this company culture. In February 1993, he hired Lee Thomas to oversee governmental and environmental affairs. Thomas had gained a reputation as a tough and honest regulator during his tenure as administrator of the U.S. EPA during Ronald Reagan's second term. In April 1993, Correll and Interior Secretary Bruce Babbitt announced that Georgia-Pacific was undertaking a voluntary effort to maintain habitat for the red-cockaded woodpecker on its southern timberlands. This represented a departure from the company's earlier confrontational approaches to endangered species protection.

Both Thomas's hiring and the woodpecker deal were aimed at external as well as internal constituencies: Georgia-Pacific was interested in showing environmental critics, and not just its own employees, that management philosophies were changing. According to Jim Bostic, senior vice president for Environment, Government Affairs, and Communications, Correll aimed his third initiative primarily at the internal audience. Previously, the company had been more tolerant of regulatory noncompliance than of production losses and forgone revenue. For example, toward the end of a given month a mill manager could generally tell whether his or her mill was likely to exceed the permitted levels of water pollution, which were based on monthly averages. Given the internal incentives that existed at the time, it was in the manager's interest to keep running the plant at full tilt and to worry about the environmental fines later. Correll and his team announced that such noncompliance would not be tolerated, and they ordered a number of mills to shut down for several days to pull down their monthly average

pollutant loadings below the permitted level.[57] This created an enormous business interruption risk for mill managers who did not pay attention to their pollution levels, a risk much larger than the cost to the company of the environmental fines. It was a dramatic and effective way of communicating the new priorities to managers.

In retrospect, at least some company executives see the events of the early 1990s as a case of overshooting. In this view, the company's aggressively results-oriented culture—"Put me in and give me the ball; I know I can do it"—amplifies messages sent from the top. When Correll sent signals that the environment was a new and important goal, he was heard immediately. In the more balanced situation that has since emerged, managers realize that it is possible, from the shareholder's viewpoint, to spend too much money on environmental risk management and on proactive environmental investments. An objective that takes this reality into account, according to Executive Vice President John F. Rasor, is "proactive behavior within a fiduciarily responsible context."[58] (Table 7-3 shows Georgia-Pacific's financials.)

Environmental management: structure and objectives. Georgia-Pacific's environmental management is organized in a manner typical for large forest products firms. A staff office headed by Vice President for Environmental Affairs Susan Moore, a former EPA official who joined the company at Thomas's request, is responsible for establishing environmental policies for the company and monitoring the behavior of the various business units with respect to those policies. Moore's office conducts periodic audits of facilities and woodlands to track compliance with government regulations and Georgia-Pacific's own internal standards.

Environmental considerations are incorporated into the formal management incentive system in the same ways as they are at Monsanto and Chevron. About a third of a manager's bonus depends on his or her performance relative to targets that are negotiated at the beginning of each year between manager and supervisor; some of these targets might relate to environmental performance, depending on the manager's particular responsibilities. (The other two-thirds of the bonus is based on profitability numbers at the business unit and corporate levels.) Ordinarily, then, environmental performance accounts for a small fraction of the bonus. At the same time, as at the other companies studied in this chapter, environmental performance influences managers'

Year	1998	1997	1996	1995	1994	1993
Revenues ($m)	13,336	13,094	13,024	14,313	12,738	12,287
Profits after taxes ($m)	274	69	156	1,018	310	-34
Total assets ($m)	12,700	12,950	12,818	12,335	10,864	10,545
Book value equity ($m)	3,124	3,470	3,511	3,519	2,620	2,402
Market value equity ($m)	7,139	7,702	6,581	6,266	6,471	6,208
Long-term debt ($m)	4,125	3,713	4,371	4,704	3,904	4,157
LTD/LTD+ book equity	56.9%	51.7%	55.5%	57.2%	59.8%	63.4%
Return on sales	2.1%	0.5%	1.2%	7.1%	2.4%	-0.3%
Return on beginning assets	2.1%	0.5%	1.3%	9.4%	2.9%	-0.3%
Return on beginning book equity	7.9%	2.0%	4.4%	38.9%	12.9%	-1.4%
Market/book equity	2.3	2.2	1.9	1.8	2.5	2.6

Note: On December 16, 1997, the Georgia-Pacific Corporation split its business into two companies, Georgia-Pacific Group and The Timber Company. These two companies' stocks trade separately on the New York Stock Exchange. The Market Value Equity numbers shown above for 1997 and 1998 were calculated by multiplying the number of outstanding stock shares for each company by their respective prices and adding these results together.

Segment data, 1998

	Building products	Distri-bution	Timber	Container-board and packaging	Pulp and paper	Corporate and all other
Net sales to unaffiliated customers ($m)	3,337	4,325	125	2,044	3,515	-10
Operating profits ($m)	603	1	364	106	133	-273
% of company net sales	25%	32%	1%	15%	26%	0%
Operating profits/revenues	18%	0%	291%	5%	4%	N/A

Note: Inter-segment sales are significant, especially for the timber segment.

Table 7-3. Georgia-Pacific Corporation Financial Data

Source: Adapted from Georgia-Pacific Corporation 1997 and 1998 Annual Reports.

reputations and ultimately their chances of promotion. This combination of formal and informal procedures allows the emphasis on environmental measures with the incentive system to vary across business units and across time as internal and external requirements change.

Most of Georgia-Pacific's environmental initiatives have been aimed at reducing regulatory and public relations risk, and on ensuring that the company maintains its ability to operate. The company has not tried to differentiate products along environmental lines. Nor has it attempted explicitly to redefine its markets in such a way as to create synergies between environmental and market performance. Nevertheless, it serves as a reminder that the environment can be integrated into business practices in ways that reduce risk and contribute to shareholder value in the long run.

Executives at Georgia-Pacific remain deeply skeptical about their ability to increase profits by differentiating any of their products along environmental lines. In their building products businesses, they do not think their customers are willing to pay more for environmentally preferable wood products, even if such products can be unambiguously defined. These executives are singularly unenthusiastic about the attempts of the Forest Stewardship Council (FSC), an independent body attempting to set up certification schemes so that customers can identify "sustainably produced" timber. In their view, building contractors, who account for most of the demand, buy solely on price; even in the smaller retail market, willingness to pay is low and consumer confusion widespread, causing Home Depot, among others, to quit stocking FSC-certified timber despite initial enthusiasm for the idea.[59]

Use of the environment as a mechanism for finding cost savings in the forest products industry requires creativity and thought. Some straightforward cost savings may be available due to inefficient operations in the past. Susan Moore observed in 1998: "There is low hanging fruit to be found in most corporations when managers concentrate for the first time on environmental matters, and we found some—but then once you pick it it's gone, you have to do something else."[60]

Beyond the picking of low-hanging fruit, Georgia-Pacific's cost saving initiatives are intimately related to risk management. By undertaking some voluntary environmental investments, the company reduces regulatory and business interruption risk, enabling it to reduce its overall expected costs. This portfolio approach is especially well suited to the management of timberlands. The geographic dispersion

of the company's lands gives rise to opportunities to reduce overall costs by investing in some highly valuable, but relatively inexpensive, public goods at particular locations.

For example, the 1993 deal with the Interior Department to protect habitat for the red-cockaded woodpecker appears on the surface to be a risk management device, but it encompasses opportunities to create more private value as well. The woodpecker, which inhabits southern coniferous forests, has been listed as an endangered species. Under a memorandum of agreement with the U.S. Fish and Wildlife Service, Georgia-Pacific agreed to withdraw from its harvest schedules roughly fifty tracts of about 500 acres each that contained colonies of woodpeckers. Since then, another fifty colonies have been identified on Georgia-Pacific land, bringing the total affected acreage to 55,000 acres.[61] Although Georgia-Pacific bears the risk that the discovery of additional colonies will further curtail harvests on its lands, the entire acreage affected so far is only about 1 percent of the company's southern pine holdings. In return, according to Executive Vice President Rasor, "Not only do we reduce the chance that we will lose our ability to harvest on the other 99% of our acreage, but we may even be able to unlock more harvestable volumes" on those lands.[62] In other words, the timberlands can be managed as a portfolio, with some dedicated to wildlife habitat and others devoted to intensive timber production. The result may be more habitat protection, and more total timber output, than would be possible if each tract were managed under the same constraints.

In a similar development, Georgia-Pacific and The Nature Conservancy agreed in 1994 to manage jointly 21,000 acres of company timberland in the lower Roanoke River valley of North Carolina. Of this, about a third was placed off-limits to harvesting of any kind, and the company agreed to use exclusively helicopter logging on the rest.[63] Like the agreement about the woodpecker, this deal to protect what The Nature Conservancy calls one of the "last great places" is intended to bolster the company's reputation for environmental probity and hence give it more flexibility in managing other lands.[64] More generally, the company, like other large firms in the forest products industry, is now committed to sustainable forestry, which requires more conservative management than short-run maximization of cash flow would dictate. This commitment stems in part from concern that more rapid timber harvesting would create unacceptable risks of regulation and loss of company control over

harvests. And the company has called attention to its forest management practices in a series of national television ads.[65]

In this context, the American Forest and Paper Association (AF&PA) undertook its Sustainable Forestry Initiative (discussed in chapter 3) to offset the competitive disadvantage that might arise from this approach to the management of business risk. The large firms in the industry, conscious of their individual reputations and that of the industry as a whole, want to bring about a situation in which all forest products companies have to bear similar costs for environmental management. The difficulty is that many of the competitors in the business are based outside the industrial world; thus they are beyond the reach both of the AF&PA and of the kinds of public scrutiny that have driven the large AF&PA companies to reevaluate their environmental policies in the first place.

Georgia-Pacific has been aggressive about establishing informal relationships with government agencies and environmental groups to obtain more information about the perspectives of those organizations' leaders and thus about the likely direction of their policies. For example, Correll served on the President's Council on Sustainable Development, a blue-ribbon panel from government, business, and environmental groups that met regularly from 1993 to 1996 to set a long-term agenda for government environmental policies. Georgia-Pacific's collaborations with The Nature Conservancy are another example of this sort of behavior.

Management of environmental information. At the same time, Georgia-Pacific's executives pride themselves on being discriminating in their approach to opportunities to spend more money on the environment, conscious of the option values that waiting for the resolution of regulatory questions can create. Georgia-Pacific uses the Stern Stewart accounting paradigm called "Economic Value Added," which focuses attention on the goal of delivering returns on invested capital above the capital's opportunity cost. This system, like more traditional cost accounting systems, creates incentives for managers to defer capital investments if they do not deliver a measurable payoff.

The company's attitudes toward changes in bleaching processes at pulp mills provide a useful example. The EPA's "cluster rules" for pulp and paper mills, under development from 1991, were not finalized until 1997. During this period, several of Georgia-Pacific's competitors aggressively installed chlorine-free bleaching processes and oxygen

delignification systems, in advance of regulatory requirements to do so. They did so because they wished to address local public relations problems at specific mills on small rivers (as in the case of Champion's mill in Canton), because their forecasts of future regulatory requirements made early installation seem sensible, or because their company cultures favored technological solutions (as may be the case with Weyerhaeuser Company). Georgia-Pacific waited to learn the final rules before investing significant capital in bleach plant changes. In this particular case, they saw little advantage in getting ahead of the regulatory curve, given the considerable uncertainty about the evolution of the government policies. Capital that is invested to comply with regulations that later change or are not passed at all, so that the capital delivers no return, is called "throwaway money" by Georgia-Pacific managers.

Georgia-Pacific has not made large investments in new environmental cost accounting systems. Capital expenditures for environmental reasons are tracked, but the contributions of various products' environmental impacts to overall operating costs are not routinely disaggregated in a way that would allow managers to consider these costs in day-to-day decision making.

On the other hand, the company's focus on shareholder value has led it to try to determine the value delivered to shareholders by the company's environmental activities. If the environmental staff office has a budget of $12 million, for example, it is expected to be able to demonstrate that it contributes $12 million in pretax profits to the company. Some of the accounting in this arena is relatively straightforward. For example, audits and consultations with plant managers that are conducted by in-house environmental professionals can be costed according to the fees charged by outside consultants for similar work. But Georgia-Pacific's environmental staffers are also expected to assess the contribution they make to shareholder value through such activities as lobbying. For example, in 1997 proposed legislation in Maine would have required Georgia-Pacific's mill in that state to install about $110 million worth of capital equipment to convert bleach lines to totally chlorine free (TCF) processes. An alternative legislative proposal that could be satisfied with a much less expensive switch to elemental chlorine free (ECF) processes seemed to Georgia-Pacific managers to deliver comparable environmental benefits at substantially lower cost. Managers from Georgia-Pacific's Maine mill and its headquarters environmental affairs office together developed and implemented a plan to

provide technical and economic information to legislators in support of the ECF bill. These efforts, according to the firm's own appraisals, were critical in bringing about the passage of that legislation. Under Georgia-Pacific's accounting procedures, the resultant cost savings to the firm were attributed in part to the environmental headquarters staff and in part to the staff at the mill.

Organizational and institutional change. At the strategic level, changes in prices arising from resource scarcity have already had a profound effect on Georgia-Pacific's operations, and will continue to do so. The southern pine plywood industry, which Georgia-Pacific played a key role in creating, would not have arisen but for the depletion of large Douglas fir logs in the Pacific Northwest. More recently, Georgia-Pacific, like the rest of the industry, has learned to make panels out of wood scraps, sawdust, and glue. These new processes allow firms to replace natural capital, in the form of logs large enough to peel for plywood, with human-made capital in the form of particleboard and oriented strandboard plants and technological know-how.

In 1997, Georgia-Pacific spun off its timberlands operations into an entity with its own common stock and its own accounts. Georgia-Pacific now consists of two groups: the Georgia-Pacific Corporation (manufacturing) and The Timber Company (lands and timber). This move is intended to allow the capital markets to value each group on its own financial merits. Transactions of raw materials between the groups will be at arm's length. The reorganization is not a complete spin-off: creditors of one company could look to the assets of the other in case of financial distress, and the company did not have to write up the value of the timberlands for tax purposes when the reorganization occurred. But Georgia-Pacific management is publicly committed not to move rents from timberlands into the manufacturing part of the business. As it promised its shareholders, "The earnings and cash flows of The Timber Company will be reinvested solely in that business or returned to holders of The Timber Company stock in the form of dividends or share repurchases, regardless of the cash needs of the manufacturing business."[66] In explaining the rationale for this reorganization, Georgia-Pacific executives wrote, "Integrated companies compound the problem [of overcapacity in pulp and paper manufacturing] by using cash flows from timberlands to finance manufacturing investments that do not earn their cost of capital. . . . This will no longer be an option at

Georgia-Pacific."[67] The reorganization should also improve the environmental performance of the timberlands operations by alleviating the internal administrative pressure for short-term cash flow.

The global context. In its approach to environmental problems, Georgia-Pacific, like the other companies studied in this chapter and elsewhere in this book, has made enormous progress in recent decades. The business rationale for its environmental policies is firmly rooted in risk management: "We have realized that our property rights are contingent on social acceptance of our exercise of them," said Executive Vice President John Rasor in 1997. "Our destiny is being argued at the polls, in legislatures, in the regulatory arena. We need to assure ourselves a seat at the table in those discussions."[68] Nevertheless, like the rest of its industry and like industry more generally, Georgia-Pacific is not out of the woods. The firm faces considerable challenges in designing a strategy for managing global climate change, and in formulating a workable response to international competition.

Like other American and European forest products firms, Georgia-Pacific could see its economics fundamentally altered if an international accord on global climate change goes into effect and if that accord contains provisions not only for taxing carbon dioxide sources but also for subsidizing carbon dioxide "sinks." An acre of growing forest removes between 0.4 and 3 tons of carbon from the air each year and sequesters this carbon in trunks and branches. (By contrast, U.S. emissions of carbon dioxide are about five tons of carbon per person per year.) If international or national regulations created an accounting system by which companies were charged for each ton of emissions and compensated for each ton of carbon sequestered, the boost to forest products companies' income could be significant.[69]

Georgia-Pacific executives tend to be pessimistic about the chances that any international global climate change convention will enable them to capture for shareholders the values they are creating by sequestering carbon. One reason for the industry's limited ability to influence international debates of this type is that while the industry is global, its firms are not. Firms are based in North America, Europe, or the tropics. They cannot bring a unified position to the debate on climate change, or to other debates on biodiversity or international trade that also affect their interests.

The problem for the European and American firms is even more

acute because the fragmented nature of the industry makes it impossible to prevent tropical competitors from engaging in the old-fashioned cut-and-run forestry that lowers short-run private cost while raising longer-term social costs and depressing the profits of more tightly regulated competitors. Cut-and-run forestry may be optimal from the perspective of the nation conducting it or (even more likely) for the national elite that is making the decisions. Firms already facing tighter regulatory controls have difficulty affecting their more impatient competitors' behavior, either through national regulatory structures or through industry codes of conduct. If national-level forest practice regulations were to converge, large developed-country firms like Georgia-Pacific would likely see higher short-run profits as well as increased regulatory and economic stability in the long term.

INFORMATION REVISITED

In these cases, we have seen that information systems for environmental management can supplement traditional managerial accounts, providing more reliable and more comprehensive information on environmental activities than was previously available. We have also seen that formal management information systems are ideally complemented by informal processes that yield qualitative information about social concerns and expectations. Information that improves managers' understanding of the environmental impacts of alternative investments, production processes, and products can be useful for a number of purposes.

For example, life-cycle analyses like those conducted by Monsanto give managers a deeper understanding of the total environmental and private cost burdens of any particular product. The idea behind the analysis of life-cycle impacts is that companies ought to understand the environmental effects of their products in the broadest possible context. Rather than focusing only on production externalities at the manufacturing plant and on the environmental characteristics of the product as it leaves the shipping dock, companies should understand the environmental impacts of the raw materials they use, the impacts of their products in use, and the final impacts when the products are discarded. This would allow managers to identify opportunities to deliver value to customers while accommodating demands for improved environmental performance and providing superior returns to shareholders.

Information that allows the comparison of various products or investments need not be financial. Life-cycle analysis, for example, is often an engineering-based exercise conducted without reference to economics or accounting: its practitioners do not try to assess the private or social costs of the various material and energy flows. It is natural, however, to consider moving beyond engineering calculations to analyze the effect of environmental change on the cost structure of the firm.

For this reason, many firms are investing in an improved understanding of the private costs and benefits of their environmental activities. Beyond the direct costs of environmental management for a given product (e.g., waste disposal) and the indirect costs (e.g., the maintenance of an environmental staff office), managers are concerned with contingent costs (e.g., the contingent liabilities that would arise in case of an accidental spill or environmental release) and intangible costs (e.g., loss of reputation and public goodwill).[70]

Again, Monsanto has been a pioneer in this arena. But Chevron and Georgia-Pacific, like many other firms not discussed in this chapter, are also experimenting with ways of incorporating more of these costs into capital investment and product development decisions in a systematic way. Georgia-Pacific's attempt to quantify the value for shareholders created by its environmental staff office is an example of this systematic approach to environmental investment. Chevron's quantitative risk assessment tools, discussed in this chapter and in chapter 6, apply similar methods to pursue similar objectives.

The reason for this activity is straightforward: as environmental costs rise, investments in information to track them and allocate them to particular products or processes become more attractive. The costs of improving information management are falling anyway for technological reasons, and in the case of the environment the benefits of the improvements are rising at the same time.

Information of this sort can be useful in identifying regulatory risks and market opportunities, and hence in product development and the selection of product attributes. We saw this, for example, in the case on Ciba Specialty Chemicals and low-salt textile dyes, discussed in chapter 2. More generally, strategy formulation can be improved if managers are knowledgeable about the relative environmental burdens of their own and competing products.

Better information about the environment can also be useful in communicating with customers and others outside the firm. In marketing, for

example, it may be necessary to establish that a particular product is in fact environmentally preferable to another. In government relations, a company will benefit if it can show that the environmental strategies it has chosen are creating social value; it may also be able to use environmental information defensively to discourage governments from pursuing strategies that might prove detrimental to the firm.

On the other hand, most firms have been cautious about a development that might seem a logical extension of these practices: social cost accounting. One might imagine combining elements of the approaches just discussed—the inclusion of effects across a product's life cycle, and the comprehensive inclusion of all costs—to arrive at a social cost accounting system in which each material or energy flow associated with a product's life cycle was analyzed from a social cost point of view. In practice, however, such systems are rare. There are several possible reasons for their failure to arise. First, this sort of analysis would entail significant out-of-pocket costs: even life-cycle analyses are too expensive for most firms to undertake comprehensively, and social cost analysis would require additional resources. Second, if a firm undertakes exercises in social cost accounting, especially if it does so comprehensively, it might increase the liability it would face in any later litigation, for the reasons discussed in chapter 6. Third, life-cycle analyses and improved assessment of private costs already deliver the information of the greatest immediate managerial relevance. The marginal benefits of additional investment in social cost accounting are relatively small.

In practice, then, firms have conducted life-cycle analyses on a limited number of their products, using engineering data rather than combining data on engineering and costs; and they have attempted to become more analytical and systematic about the private benefits to the firm of investments in environmentally preferable products or processes. But attempts to combine these two types of information into a single system are much rarer.

Besides developing formal systems for managing environmental information, all of the companies discussed in the case histories have invested in informal information about social expectations and political concerns. This informal, qualitative information provides a context for the data collected using more formal systems. For example, Monsanto has been trying to understand European opinion leaders' opposition to agricultural biotechnology through a series of informal dialogues.[71] Chevron tracks public opinion about its own performance

and that of the oil industry as a whole.[72] And Georgia-Pacific's joint ventures with The Nature Conservancy and its participation in the President's Council on Sustainable Development foster informal channels of communication between the company's executives and opinion leaders in government and the environmental groups.

Within the firm, too, informal practices for information gathering can be extremely effective. To choose an example from outside the environmental arena, one of the striking aspects of Jack Welch's widely admired leadership of General Electric is his heavy use of informal information channels.[73] By reaching several layers deep into the corporate hierarchy, senior managers can obtain information that would otherwise escape them. Economist Kenneth Boulding is supposed to have said that a hierarchy is an arrangement of wastebaskets designed to prevent information from reaching the executive.[74] Informal information-gathering missions can send strong signals about the importance of the particular issue under discussion, and may have broader therapeutic effects on bureaucracy and organizational rigidity as well.

INCENTIVE DESIGN REVISITED

Large, decentralized companies like those studied in this chapter initially responded to intensified environmental concern by creating staff offices to track the environmental performance of the firms' operating units. Now their challenge is to structure incentives in their decentralized systems so that line managers integrate environmental considerations into their business decision making in an ongoing way. Middle managers, traditionally evaluated according to the short-run profit and cost performance of the units under their direct control, may otherwise behave in ways at odds both with senior executives' environmental objectives and with the environmental expectations of younger employees. The challenge is to move the environment from a specialized function managed by a staff office to one that is internalized in line managers' daily decisions.[75]

Earlier in this chapter I discussed three systems of incentives, which could be categorized as economic, hierarchical, and cultural. The firms in the case histories used all three in trying to influence the environmental behavior of their managers.

The principal way in which environmental concerns have traditionally been managed is through negotiated agreements between managers

and their superiors. Managers are supposed to achieve a particular level of environmental performance, expressed in terms of effort (e.g., managers might be required to conduct environmental training programs for their workers), results (e.g., managers might be required to reduce actual pollutant loadings, by some specified amount), or both. This kind of system is discussed in connection with Chevron in this chapter and in chapter 6.

Incentive systems of this sort can be tied to executive compensation systems tightly, loosely, or not at all. Environmental performance can be used as the basis of as much or as little of a manager's bonus as is desired. In practice, environmental performance accounts for very little of the compensation of most line managers, since it is at best only one of several criteria for bonus payments.

Other mechanisms for integrating environmental concerns into the financial incentives facing managers can easily be imagined. Transfer prices, used in internal firm accounts when goods and services are sold by one business unit to another within the firm, could be altered to reflect the cost to the firm of various activities. Firms might manage environmental risk by requiring line managers to pay experience-weighted premiums to a central account. In practice, however, such innovations are rare, because it is still very difficult to evaluate the costs or benefits to the firm that particular environmental activities create. Decisions about the appropriate transfer prices, or about the appropriate premium value for in-house insurance, would be controversial within the organization; because the prices could be attacked as arbitrary, they could undermine internal confidence in the environmental management system more generally. As information improves, mechanisms of this sort are likely to become more widespread, but for now their disadvantages to most firms appear to outweigh their merits.

More generally, there is considerable controversy about the degree to which financial incentives ought to be used to get managers to devote more time and effort to environmental matters. Recall from chapter 4 that executives at Dow explicitly decided not to provide cash awards for environmental design innovations because they thought such payments would stifle teamwork and send a message that innovation is not part of employees' regular jobs.[76]

On the other hand, ties between environmental performance and the promotions process are both more prevalent and potentially much more important. If environmental performance is systematically

appraised as part of the process of evaluating managers for promotion, this is bound to affect managerial behavior significantly. The economic consequences of failure to achieve promotion, and the consequences for status within the organization, are far more substantial than those of missing some fraction of one's annual bonus. Further, integrating environmental performance into the promotions process is easier than integrating it into a transfer pricing system or a system for calculating bonuses because the promotions process is already known to make extensive use of intangible and nonquantifiable considerations. From an internal marketing perspective, it is far easier to incorporate environmental considerations into a system that is already known to rely heavily on executive judgment.

When Pete Correll took the top job at Georgia-Pacific and then imposed temporary shutdowns of several mills to avoid regulatory noncompliance, he sent a very strong message to line managers about the new place of environmental matters on the list of priorities. He tore up the implicit bargain that plant managers had established with his predecessors and replaced it with a new one. In the process he must have deeply humiliated the managers. Their bonus payments were affected in the short run, since with their mills shut down they could not meet their production or profit targets. But Correll's primary target seems to have been the corporate culture, and the main incentive effect on the line managers was not on their bonuses but on their reputation and status within the firm.

Economic incentives play larger roles when the costs and benefits of particular kinds of managerial behavior are relatively well understood, but where they are subject to continuous small changes on the margin. This sounds like a narrow set of circumstances, but it actually describes a great deal of business practice outside the environmental arena, where there is a good understanding of how the company's profits react to changes in various prices, but the prices themselves are subject to considerable flux. Under these circumstances, entrusting a manager with profit responsibility and tying compensation to the business's performance makes a great deal of sense. In other cases, more common when environmental issues are important, far less may be known about the costs and benefits to the firm of various kinds of managerial activity. In this case, the kind of negotiated agreements seen in Chevron and other firms, complemented and buttressed by cultural incentives and the promotions process, seem more likely to be sensible.

ENVIRONMENTAL INSTITUTIONS REVISITED

We have seen that many of the corporate initiatives discussed in this book can be considered institutional innovations—attempts to change the basic rules under which society addresses environmental problems, including those about the roles of business and government and about the nature of private property rights. We have already noted that product takeback schemes realign property rights among firms and their customers in the electronics business. To cite another example, the companies involved in the Responsible Care program are writing regulations, a task usually performed by government agencies. Although opportunities for a company to bring about institutional change unilaterally are relatively rare, all companies contribute to the evolution of economic institutions over time, and the ability of any company to create and capture environmental value depends on the institutions within which it is operating.

For example, the passage of the Montreal Protocol and its successor treaties, discussed in chapter 3, represents an important institutional innovation. Environmental policy has historically been the province of national governments, and institutional mechanisms to manage global public goods have been lacking. The ability of diplomats and firms to develop a workable institution for managing a phaseout of CFC production provides grounds for optimism about the possibility that new institutions will allow the solution of other global environmental issues. As we saw in chapter 3, the treaties created opportunities for DuPont and other firms to create and capture substantial amounts of value in ways that would otherwise have been impossible. New institutional arrangements at the international level may require changes in a company's internal systems for collecting and managing information and for aligning corporate and managerial incentives. In this respect, the international institutions are no different from any institution in the domestic arena.

As another example of the effect of institutions on companies' opportunities to create value and on the way they are managed, consider the system of tradable pollution permits created by the Clean Air Act Amendments of 1990. This system does not directly affect any of the three companies discussed at length in this chapter, since it encompasses only coal-burning electric utility plants, but its implications are of considerable importance.

Because all coal contains some sulfur, and because coal-fired power plants burn coal in massive quantities, those plants are among the largest sources of sulfur dioxide, a precursor to acid rain. Under the 1990 amendments to the Clean Air Act, coal-fired utility plants in the United States are issued permits that allow them to emit a certain quantity of sulfur dioxide. The companies' initial allocations are based on their historical emissions levels, but they are allowed to trade permits among themselves. Because firms' costs for reducing pollution may be quite different, depending on the kind of coal they currently burn and their location relative to other coal sources, the ability to trade lowers overall compliance costs. Firms for which cleanup costs are low can "overcomply" and sell permits; those for which pollution control is more expensive can buy permits.[77]

The tradability of the permits leads to a more efficient solution than could occur through conventional command-and-control regulation, since the utilities know more about their costs of pollution abatement than the regulators can. This efficiency yields significant savings, estimated to exceed a billion dollars per year.[78] The institutional innovation frees up information about the true costs of pollution abatement and creates incentives for the utilities to seek efficient solutions.[79]

Within the firms, too, incentive systems can change along with external institutions. Prior to the 1990 act, utilities regarded their environmental performance as a constraint rather than as part of their objective. Their goal was to minimize the private cost of producing electricity, subject to the constraint (among others) that sulfur dioxide emissions not exceed the permitted level. They had no incentive, external or internal, to reduce emissions below that level. Under the tradable permit scheme, by contrast, reduction of environmental impact becomes part of the objective of the firm. Sulfur dioxide becomes another variable cost, a component of the total cost that the firm seeks to minimize; the cost per ton is given by the market price of the allowances. Hence utility managers can now use the price mechanism to guide this aspect of their environmental performance rather than relying on blunter instruments. Tradable permits thus affect both cost accounting and management information systems, as well as the systems of incentives within the firm.

Tradable permits are not a panacea for society's environmental problems. They will equalize marginal costs across sources of pollution, but this is desirable only if the marginal benefits of pollution control

are equal across sources as well. Thus they will not make sense for pollutants with acute local effects, since for those pollutants the exact location of the sources would matter a great deal. In the case of sulfur dioxide, the environmental damage of a ton emitted in Ohio is probably not much different from that of a ton emitted in Alabama, because the pollutants are carried for long distances before returning to the earth. This suggests that tradable permits make especially good sense for global pollutants like chlorofluorocarbons (CFCs) and carbon dioxide; in fact, when writing regulations to implement the Montreal Protocol, the EPA incorporated a system of tradable production permits for CFCs.

This history of tradable permits for sulfur dioxide is important because it will affect the efforts of environmentalists and diplomats to create international institutions that will reduce global emissions of carbon dioxide and hence slow global climate change. American diplomats have argued that permits for carbon dioxide should be tradable across international boundaries, because this would substantially lower the cost of achieving any given level of carbon dioxide reduction. For example, accomplishing the cutbacks dictated by the signed but not yet ratified Kyoto Protocol might cost $125 per ton of carbon if permits were not tradable internationally, but only $14 to $23 per ton if emissions reductions were tradable around the world.[80] Whether the attempts to create new institutions to manage carbon dioxide succeed or fail, and whether any such institutions incorporate tradable permit systems, will have profound implications for corporate managers everywhere.

All of the developments discussed here—the Responsible Care initiative, the Montreal Protocol, tradable permits for sulfur dioxide—represented improvements in efficiency over the institutions they complemented or supplanted. And all of these developments, too, were opposed by people or groups who were prospering under the previous institutional setup and stood to suffer losses if the institutions changed. Similar opposition will confront any future institutional innovations as well. For example, international tradability of carbon permits is opposed both by Greenpeace and by opponents of carbon dioxide controls.[81]

Douglass North, who won the Nobel Prize for his analysis of economic institutions, is pessimistic about the ability of efficient institutions to supplant older, less efficient ones, exactly because of the ability of some groups or organizations to block institutional change,

even if such change would be broadly beneficial:

> Institutions, together with the standard constraints of economic theory, determine the opportunities in a society. Organizations are created to take advantage of those opportunities, and, as the organizations evolve, they alter the institutions. The resultant path of institutional change is shaped by (1) the lock-in that comes from the symbiotic relationship between institutions and the organizations that have evolved as a consequence of the incentive structure provided by those institutions and (2) the feedback process by which human beings perceive and react to changes in the opportunity set.[82]

In other words, organizations persist because of their ability to capture value within a given institutional setting, whether or not they create it; and they try to impede institutional change if that change would reduce their own wealth and power, even if it would increase overall social well-being.

On the other side of this debate, Nobel economist Gary Becker has set forth some reasons to expect that over the long run, on average, more efficient institutional arrangements will prevail.[83] Becker argues that government interventions that increase efficiency and social well-being are more likely, on average, to persist than those that do not: "Political policies that raise efficiency are more likely to be adopted than policies that lower efficiency." The reason is not that government officials in Becker's model consciously maximize social well-being; on the contrary, they are interested in maintaining power, and in helping the social groups that help them. They are driven toward more efficient policies because these policies enable them to deliver more wealth to their favorites at a lower cost in opposition from the people who are hurt by the policies. According to Becker, "Competition among pressure groups favors efficient methods of taxation," and by extension efficient methods of environmental public good provision.

Although this may seem an overly optimistic formulation, there is no doubt that environmental behavior is more efficient now than it was a century ago. The near-complete absence of government regulation was clearly inefficient, but that era is now over. Further, where environmental regulatory structures have been shown to be grossly inefficient (the Superfund law is a prominent example), considerable pressure exists to change the institutions to increase their efficiency. The move toward more efficient government policies for environmental regulation

will not occur automatically, but there is no reason to think that it will stop.

One reason to think that environmental institutions are likely to become more efficient is that they are becoming more transparent. Over the past thirty years, enormous progress has been made on environmental problems, as discussed in the opening paragraphs of chapter 1. But the costs of this progress were hidden from consumers and taxpayers, and this cannot be expected to continue. In the United States, for example, water pollution control plants (i.e., sewage treatment plants) were funded nationally. No one community directly raised the money for its own sewage treatment; instead, the funds were bundled into the national tax bill and then doled out to states and municipalities, so the costs were hidden from local taxpayers. Now, areas that failed to take advantage of the federal program must fund sewage treatment plants with readily visible increases in local water fees.[84]

More generally, environmental costs have been hidden from citizens and taxpayers by the way the government regulations have been structured. The costs were "imposed" on "big polluters" with the idea that these entities had the deep pockets, and also the moral responsibility, to cope with the pollution. Of course the lunch was not really free: companies passed some of the costs on to customers, and their shareholders paid for the rest. But again, the costs of environmental quality were hidden from the public.

At this stage of the environmental movement, however, transparency is increasing. Companies are pointing out that the costs of environmental quality do not stop with them. Further, largely because of the business community's success in managing its pollution loadings, more and more of the environmental insults come from households: policies to address them cannot be hidden from taxpayers so easily. Further, the innovation of tradable pollution permits makes control costs easier to see than under traditional regulatory schemes; environmental taxes are even easier to discern. Transparency may mean that not all environmental expenditures will grow as rapidly as environmentalists would like them to. Confronted directly with the costs, taxpayers may decide that some environmental benefits are just not worth the money. The more important effect of transparency, however, is to accelerate the convergence of private and social costs. Whether acting as taxpayers or as consumers, people make better decisions when they know the costs of the goods and services they are buying.

Institutional arrangements that equalize private and social costs offer several advantages to well-managed firms. In the long run, they will reduce regulatory risk, and enable the firms to compete on the basis of characteristics other than their ability to lobby government, obtain superior information about the likely direction of future government policy, and so on. Even if a well-managed firm is very good at these activities, it should want its competitive advantage to rest on a more secure foundation. In the long run, particularly for firms with long-lived assets and with corporate reputations to protect, the opportunities of regulatory instability are surpassed by the rewards possible in a stable regulatory environment.

In the long run, the factors that are likely to make the biggest difference in enabling firms to contribute to the solution of environmental problems while delivering value to their shareholders are old ones: the price mechanism, and the evolution of environmental expectations as societies prosper. Consider the price mechanism first. We have seen that rising prices for old-growth timber created opportunities for Georgia-Pacific to make money by converting smaller, faster-growing, and less valuable southern pine into products once made from giant trees in the Pacific Northwest. Similarly, Monsanto is betting that increases in the price of agricultural land will drive up the value of the science-based agricultural services in which the company is investing so heavily. As we have seen repeatedly in this book, changes in the prices of environmental services and assets create opportunities as well as risks for well-run firms. The price changes alter the value of information, so that investments in information that did not previously pay for themselves now make sense. And they may require changes in the incentive systems through which companies influence their managers' behavior. Long-term price trends that relate to environmental goods are no more or less important than other long-term price trends: that is, they are absolutely critical in the formulation of sensible strategies.

The same can be said for long-term trends in environmental values, even if these are not translated into market prices in any direct or obvious way. Expectations about companies' and governments' environmental performance are changing as incomes increase and as scientific information about environmental conditions becomes cheaper and more widely available. Like the long-term trends in prices, trends in environmental values and expectations create considerable opportunity as well as significant risk.

The Future of Environmental Management

THE BASIC logic of environmental management, as it emerges from the preceding chapters, leads to the conclusion that the environment can be analyzed as a business problem, using the tools and concepts that smart managers would instinctively bring to bear on other business problems. The analysis in this book does not show that every firm can immediately increase its value by trying to improve its environmental performance. But well-managed firms can see, and seize, more such opportunities than their competitors.

Social concern about the environment is not going away. On the contrary, the underlying conditions that made the environment relevant to business in the first place are intensifying. Technological advances enable us to detect substances in the environment at lower and lower levels. New scientific evidence, however controversial, raises concerns about the long-term environmental consequences of economic activity. Social expectations about protection from environmental problems continue to rise. Underlying all of these conditions, rising incomes generate greater demand for environmental quality.

Governments, responding to these trends, will continue to play significant roles in creating both problems and opportunities for firms, and political and regulatory risks will continue to complicate firms' environmental decision making. Government, acting not necessarily as a direct participant in markets, but as a regulator, tax collector, and provider of subsidies, will continue to provide the ultimate impetus for

much of what firms do in the environmental arena. And this, in turn, means that managers must consider not just current government behavior but the likely evolution of government behavior over the lives of the assets that the firm dedicates to environmentally significant lines of business. It also means that executives need to design regulatory and market strategies jointly to manage regulatory risk and preserve or seize opportunities to create value.[1]

The same point applies more generally to other actors besides government: environmental organizations, community groups, and other parties with an interest in firms' behavior. Managers need to map out the likely evolution of those actors' expectations and actions, and design strategies for managing relationships with them for both the short term and the long run.[2]

As always, timing matters. Given the uncertainties about the speed with which environmental institutions, policies, and prices change, firms are likely to be ahead of or behind the curve at least some of the time. Some firms will suffer financially because they cling to old ways of doing business. Other firms will suffer because they introduce environmentally friendly products before the market and the regulators are ready for them. Business historians and management consultants like to talk about buggy-whip manufacturers; the implication is that one should avoid at all costs being the modern-day equivalent, obsolete at a stroke because a better way of doing things emerged. But most of the early automobile companies went just as bankrupt as any buggy-whip manufacturer ever did, and the carmakers did so more quickly and without ever turning a profit.

This point about the timing of product introductions applies to the timing of developing environmental management systems more generally. A firm may go from spending the bare minimum on the environment to spending more than the managers later deem necessary before settling into a more balanced approach. But this oscillation is not as unfortunate as it looks. If a firm never overshoots, it may be moving too slowly.

In this respect, thinking about the environment within the firm appears to be following the same three stages as thinking about quality. First we thought any expenditure was too much. Then we thought no expenditure was too much. With quality, we then arrived at a more nuanced view: that increased quality can confer intangible benefits to the firm that a superficial analysis would miss, but that the desirable

level of quality depends on the economic circumstances of the particular firm.[3] It is reasonable to think we will reach a similar conclusion about the environment.

Environment and quality share other characteristics as well. Both are hard to measure within conventional accounting frameworks. Both are closely related to company culture, and influence the degree to which people associated with the business—especially employees—will identify themselves with it and take pride in that identification. And although both seem difficult to capture within traditional models of business behavior, there is a strong business case to be made for the investment of significant management attention in ensuring that the environment, like quality, is considered rigorously and taken seriously within the firm.

Information—about the scientific aspects of environmental problems, about regulatory and social expectations, about customers' environmental needs and desires—can help companies design environmental policies that are financially sensible and appropriately timed. At a minimum, individual managers ought to obtain information on environmental developments from a broad range of sources. They should draw on their own trade associations and the mainstream press, but also on conversations with, or visits to the Web sites of, the activist groups and regulatory agencies that seek to define the environmental agenda. At the same time, managers need to cultivate an organizational environment in which their colleagues and employees take new information seriously, recognize and reward analytic thinking, and search continuously for better ways of accomplishing company objectives.

EIGHT MISTAKES

The evidence demonstrates that there is no one-size-fits-all environmental policy. Rather, the right policy depends on the circumstances facing the firm. Any cookie-cutter approach to the environment will be misleading and unhelpful. There are, however, some courses of action that are always mistakes. Many business problems involving the environment have been partly or even entirely self-imposed. Avoiding the following eight traps will not guarantee success, but failure to sidestep any one of them can doom an otherwise well-designed approach to environmental management.

Mistake 1. Pessimism.   Most executives owe their success to optimism and opportunism, so it is striking to hear how passive and pessimistic they can sound when talking about environmental pressure. In most arenas, successful managers search for opportunity in adversity, treating complex new problems as chances to separate their firms from competitors that are less well managed. Business problems stemming from the environment demand no less.

Mistake 2. Improper framing of questions.   Businesspeople have long thought about environmental issues as a problem of social responsibility. Environmentalists and regulators have encouraged this kind of thinking, perhaps because of their own ideology, perhaps because they fear that economic reasoning will not give them the answer they want. But managers can tap more potential for creativity and problem solving if they view environmental issues like other business problems. Managers should make environmental investments for the reasons they make other investments: because they expect the investments to deliver positive returns or to reduce risks in ways that benefit the firm.

Mistake 3. Wishful thinking.   It is perfectly reasonable for an oil company manager to believe that if the scientific evidence of global climate change is convincing, the solutions are likely to cost the company money. It is also intellectually defensible for him or her to believe that the scientific evidence of global climate change is not convincing. But a good manager should not believe the second of these things because he or she believes the first; the company's economic stake in climate change should not affect the manager's reading of the science. "It will cost a lot of money if the problem is real, so I think it is not real" is not a responsible argument, and managers who think in this way cannot serve their shareholders effectively.

If they confuse what *is* with what is *desirable*, managers put themselves in double peril. They may fail to respond to problems that do have a solid scientific basis. At the same time, they may overreact to trivial or nonexistent problems, and tacitly encourage empire building by government agencies or their own internal staff offices. They may even make both of these mistakes simultaneously, overspending on environment while failing to seize the opportunities that arise from scientifically well-grounded problems.

Because the scientific consensus about environmental damages has a direct effect on consumer preferences and the direction of regulatory initiatives, managers need to be familiar with the science that underlies environmental concerns affecting their industry. If scientists state that an issue is not particularly significant from a scientific standpoint, managers should still keep track of that issue for risk management purposes, but they will know not to base a strategy of value creation on a response to it.

Mistake 4. Faulty analysis. In considering their environmental policies, managers need to be careful in defining the "baselines" against which they measure the proposed changes. In determining whether some new practice adds value, one needs to answer the question "Compared with what?" Suppose company A is thinking of introducing a new product that may compete with one of its existing lines. The scenario of "we introduce the new product," analyzed against a baseline of the status quo, may seem unappealing. If the default option is not the status quo but instead "company B introduces the new product," the arithmetic is more likely to favor company A's product introduction. It is natural for managers to use the status quo as the baseline even if change is inevitable, but if the baseline is the most likely future scenario, then the calculation may look quite different.[4]

Mistake 5. Insufficient information. Although any environmental decision entails at least some uncertainty or imprecision about costs, benefits, and risks, an adequate base of information is still critical.

As regulatory and social pressure intensifies over time, the value of environmental information rises. Since the costs of information technology are falling, the net value of environmental information rises even faster. Information collection and management policies may become obsolete soon after they are established. This implies a need for periodic reassessments of the firm's investments in environmental information to make sure that they are adequate. "Information" here means more than just formal accounting and measurement systems for cash flow, pollution loadings, and energy consumption, although these are important. It means more, too, than information about the scientific underpinnings of environmental concern, although this is critical as well. It also encompasses informal soundings of political and consumer opinion that affect the institutional climate in which the firm operates. And it encompasses

new ways of processing and analyzing information so that it can point the way to improvements in business practice.

Information is an investment. The acquisition of information, like any educational process, entails short-run out-of-pocket costs. New information may also increase short-term business risk, and it may be psychologically uncomfortable, perhaps extremely so. But investment in information is necessary in order to avoid even larger cash outlays, risk, and discomfort in the future. When deciding whether to invest in more information about a particular decision, managers need to weigh carefully the costs of failing to do so.

Mistake 6. Thinking win-win, or thinking win-lose.   Managers need to know what kind of game they're playing. The traditional view of environmental management has been that the games are zero-sum, so that if anyone wins, someone has to lose. This is how environmental questions have traditionally been framed: if the company wins, the environment (or the environmentalists) lose, and vice versa. This view became prevalent in part because it fit with widespread perceptions that environmental problems are political or moral issues. Elections are win-lose by definition and by design. And so are crusades.

More recently, it has become fashionable to talk about "win-win" strategies, not just in the environmental arena but in business more generally. As we have seen, it is sometimes possible for companies to deliver more value to their shareholders and more environmental value to society, and managers who examine the environment closely as an economic and business problem are more likely to find such opportunities than those who do not. Delivering more value simply means becoming more efficient. Increases in efficiency can transform a zero-sum (and hence inevitably win-lose) game into a positive-sum game that can be win-win if the gains are shared. Proponents of the idea that it may be possible to increase efficiency and transform win-lose games into potential win-win games have been quite influential.[5]

Whether a game is win-win or win-lose depends on three things. Technology, broadly defined, determines whether there is some way to increase the efficiency with which goods and services are produced, and hence to break out of the zero-sum box. The formal rules of the game matter too: if there is no mechanism by which the gains can be shared, there is less reason for the players to abandon their zero-sum practices. And the informal relationships and codes of behavior among the players

matter as well: unless there is some way for the players to commit themselves to the new rules and obtain the trust of the other players, we will
stay in the zero-sum box. In the short run, managers may have no choice
but to accept the terms on which the politicians and environmentalists
want to play the game. But in the long run, as more efficiency gains are
discovered and as the players have time to develop more mutually beneficial rules, win-win situations may become more common.

Mistake 7. Thinking all or nothing.   Managers may borrow the
tendency to think in all-or-nothing terms from politicians and some
environmentalists. But the old Texas adage "There's nothing in the middle of the road but yellow stripes and dead armadillos" applies to politics, not to business.[6] Any manager who runs his or her business
according to that philosophy will not last very long.

Fairness matters, and people will walk away from a deal that would
leave them better off if the structure of the deal violates their sense of
equity. We saw in several of the examples in this book that a willingness
to share the gains from progress is what enables the progress to occur in
the first place. Alberta-Pacific, for example, goes out of its way to facilitate forest access for the communities and land users in the neighbor-
hood of its mill. Despite fears that concessions would only lead to
demands for further concessions, Alberta-Pacific is proving that compromise need not be a sign of weakness.

*Mistake 8. Regarding government and environmentalists exclu-
sively as adversaries.*   Environmental management requires a role for
government; the only question is what kind of role it will play. The
objective of well-managed companies in government relations should
be stability and predictability, not avoidance of regulation. Well-run
firms benefit if regulatory agencies are well run and credible. Crash
programs in "regulatory relief" that trigger political backlash and
increase uncertainty about the rules of the game do not serve firms'
interests.

As we have seen, alliances with regulators can make sense for
some firms. The same is true for alliances with environmental groups.
British Petroleum's collaboration with the Environmental Defense
Fund is aimed at helping the company understand how systems of
tradable permits can work to reduce costs of carbon dioxide reduction
and is also yielding public relations benefits for the firm. Meanwhile,

land conservation organizations like The Nature Conservancy have implemented dozens of joint projects with forest products firms and other corporate landowners in which the companies cede some decision rights over certain pieces of land in return for positive publicity and a reduced risk of business interruption on other lands. Such alliances, like alliances with regulators, are not for everyone, but it makes no sense to dismiss them out of hand.

SEVEN QUESTIONS TO ASK
ABOUT A FIRM'S ENVIRONMENTAL POLICY

When analyzing firms' environmental policies, managers should consider the following seven questions. None of these questions can be answered definitively, but asking them can reveal weaknesses in analysis that could lead to missed opportunities, unnecessary trouble, or both.

Since environmental problems can be seen as business problems, the relevant questions to ask about an environmental management decision are the same as those one should ask about other business questions. None of the questions contains the word "environment"; all are of value in analyzing any complicated business problem.

Question 1. What are the basic economics of the situation? Attempts to capture environmental value succeed or fail depending on the fundamental economics of the business. Managers who consider carefully their market positions and their strategic assets—technology, access to resources, reputation, and so on—can accurately determine the scope of their opportunities. Thus they can seize the real opportunities and avoid wasting cash and time on red herrings. A firm's stance with respect to the environment, like any other aspect of strategy, should be formulated and implemented with a realistic view of industry economics and firm capabilities.

Environmental policies must be integrated with other aspects of strategy, and in particular with related functional areas within the firm. Whether the aim is strategic advantage, cost reduction, improved risk management, or some combination of these, environmental policies that are integrally tied to the firm's overall strategy, like those of Patagonia and Monsanto, are more likely to be successful. Efforts not integrated in this manner are more likely to fail.

Rather than focusing exclusively on its own operations as sources of possible advantage, a firm needs to consider the entire value system of which its activities are a part. Consideration of the firm's own economics is not enough in the environmental arena, just as it is insufficient in strategic thinking more generally. Changes in the regulatory climate or in customers' expectations anywhere in a firm's value system may give rise to opportunities for the firm to create and capture additional value. Increased consumer awareness of an environmental problem may bring about some willingness to pay for a product that contributes to its solution, and hence an opportunity for product differentiation. Tighter environmental regulation of a customer's operations creates opportunities as well.

Question 2. What are the politics?   Politicians care about the distributional consequences of business activities. Managers must consider them too. To identify potential partners and adversaries, managers trying to effect some business change should identify the other actors who may be helped or hurt.

When designing their approaches to environmental management, managers need to consider their appraisals of the scientific and economic aspects of a particular problem, as well as the problem's public relations and political aspects. In the long run, satisfaction of two sets of criteria is necessary: the approach must be compatible with scientific and economic reality, and also with political perception and public opinion.

A corollary: political strategy is too important to leave to the full-timers on the government affairs staff, in the trade associations, and in lobbying firms. It is difficult for staffers in the government affairs office to maintain the understanding of the firm's business strategy that is essential to the design of complementary strategies in the political arena. Trade associations, which need to accommodate the views of all members, may be unable to vigorously promote the interests of any one member, and may be forced instead to take weak positions based on a consensus among competing subgroups.[7] Lobbyists, even if hired directly by the firm, may not have the same interests as their employers at corporate headquarters: they profit from regulatory uncertainty and conflict in ways that the firm as a whole does not.[8]

Question 3. What are the long-term objectives?   We have seen that firms can have a variety of long-term goals in mind for their environmental strategies. The strategies can be aimed at the creation of

shareholder value, at the management of risk, or both. Some environmental strategies are motivated by ethical considerations, although even these strategies commonly need to be justified within and outside of the firm in terms of value creation or risk management.

In some cases, strategies that serve one of these objectives serve one or both of the others as well. Recall, for example, Alberta-Pacific's forestry practices, which were intended both to reduce short-term business risk and to contribute to shareholder value over the long term. In other instances, however, the objectives will be in conflict. Explicit thinking about the trade-offs is not just desirable but essential. To develop a realistic assessment of the benefits of any particular approach to environmental problems, managers need to understand the relative importance of the firm's objectives.

Like all management activities that involve the company's reputation, environmental management is best approached as a matter of long-term investment. There is no short-term or risk-free way to acquire a reputation as a reliable source of environmental information. Such a reputation, once acquired, cannot be used directly for short-term political or commercial advantage, or it will disappear. But if protected and maintained, the reputation may help the firm in its recruiting and employee relations, and in its relationships with government regulators and environmental groups. Given these benefits, a case can be made for firms taking a more active role in providing information about environmental science and economics, despite the fact that this information is a public good.

Question 4. What are the short-term implications? Jack Welch of General Electric says, "Anybody can manage short. Anybody can manage long. Balancing those two things is what management is."[9] Many of the firms studied in this book have been able to transform short-term advantages into long-term strengths. Alberta-Pacific, for example, is able to use its access to low-cost natural resources to fund investments in environmental quality that increase the chance that it will retain that access. Monsanto used its profits from its patented Roundup herbicide to fund research into Roundup Ready plants that increased the value of the Roundup patent; it then used the biotechnological expertise fostered by this research to develop other even more innovative products. This suggests that companies in strong positions can manage for the long term and weather the short-term conse-

quences of a systematic environmental approach, while companies unable or unwilling to weather the short-term consequences cannot expect to benefit in the long run. It suggests, in other words, that environmental pressure helps strong firms and hurts those that are already weak.

Question 5. What are the real costs of the firm's policy? It is usually not difficult to calculate the direct costs of a particular approach to environmental problems. Flue-gas desulfurization equipment, insurance against environmental impairment liability, and advertisements calling attention to the company's environmental record are goods and services purchased in markets at known prices. It makes sense to track these costs to make sure that the company is not paying more than necessary to carry out its policies.

Other costs of corporate environmental practices, although more difficult to measure, also need to be considered. Like most other investments, investments in environmental quality can constrain the investor's future flexibility. Further, the opportunity costs of managers' time need to be considered explicitly, if not quantitatively, in order to arrive at sensible assessments of an environmental policy's total costs.

Question 6. What exactly is being purchased when the company spends money? When a firm spends money on the environment, it can increase environmental quality, shareholder value, both, or neither. The firm's managers should know very clearly what they intend to get for their money before making the investment.

Benefits can arise in the form of increased expected value or reduced risk. Within the risk category, one of the principal benefits of many environmental investments is the retention of the managers' flexibility to manage their operations as they see fit; this was the main objective, for example, of Georgia-Pacific's environmental policies, and of the Chemical Manufacturers Association's Responsible Care program.

The benefits of environmental policies should be scrutinized and weighed carefully against the costs. A simple relationship does not exist between the amount of money society spends on a problem and the environmental benefits that are purchased with that money, as our experience with Superfund shows. Similarly, there is not necessarily a straightforward connection between the money a firm spends and the amount of benefit it is procuring. An increase in expenditure does not

guarantee any reduction in pollution, and a reduction in pollution does not automatically bring about reductions in public concern or in private business risk. For this reason, managers need to be realistic about the benefits that a given approach will produce for the firm.

On the other hand, it is important not to overlook benefits just because they are difficult to quantify, or because it is hard to draw irrefutable causal links between some aspect of the company's behavior and some desirable outcome. The goodwill of customers, a reputation for environmental probity among government officials and other opinion leaders, and the managerial flexibility that these assets create can be hard to value quantitatively. The effect on these assets of any particular environmental investment may be still harder to discern. But the assets are no less real, and the benefits of the investments no less important, for the difficulties we face in integrating them into traditional measurement systems.

Question 7. Is there a better say to do this? This is the basic managerial question. There is no formula for creativity. A better way of doing things may emerge from introspection, from conversations with managers at other firms, from discussions with customers, suppliers, regulators, or environmental groups—even from books! Ideas about improvements need to be subjected to the same rigorous analytic scrutiny as the status quo. Not every idea is going to prove to be a good one, but it makes sense to keep looking.

Because a continuous search for improvements will, over the long term, yield more and better ideas than would otherwise be available to managers, it is important to create an organizational culture that values this approach. It is for this reason that investments in new information, and in better ways of analyzing information, are so important: improvements in management practice arise from new facts, or from new ways of looking at the facts already available. A company that identifies and rewards curiosity about the way the world works can build a durable advantage over its competitors.

FINAL WORDS

Managers benefit from systematic, realistic consideration of their environmental choices in the context of their overall business strategy, in view of economic fundamentals, government behavior, and social expectations over the entire value chain and across time. A systematic approach to the environment will not show that it pays every company to be "green," but it is likely to reveal more possibilities for reconciling environmental and shareholder value objectives than may be evident to competitors. Creative but realistic management, building on the firm's strengths and on its understanding of society's environmental demands, can play an important role in the realization of those possibilities.

Social responsibility is often invoked in discussions about business and the environment. I have been more concerned in this book with a manager's responsibilities to shareholders and to his or her own intellectual integrity. While disagreement about the definition of social responsibility is inevitable, responsibility to shareholders and intellectual responsibility impel managers toward positions in the middle of the environmental debate.

To behave responsibly, by definition, is to behave as though one's actions had consequences. This may seem trivial—of course actions have consequences—but the two dominant voices in the environmental debate have been opposed to this commonsense view. On one hand, die-hard Malthusians assert that environmental disaster is inevitable, and that resource scarcity and environmental degradation will bring about social collapse. On the other hand, their cornucopian adversaries assert that serious environmental problems are inconceivable, that scarcity is a myth, that the Malthusians are at best dupes and at worst malevolent troublemakers. These two groups have more in common than they would like to admit: both hold ideas of the world that are fully deterministic. They can't both be right, but it could be that they are both wrong. If we are honest with ourselves, we have to admit that we do not know the precise consequences of our actions. Both the Malthusians and the cornucopians offer counsels of despair: they want us to believe that human agency doesn't matter. These counsels ought to be rejected. The responsible place is in the middle of the road.

Basic Approaches to Environmental Management

THE FOUR figures in this appendix show the relationships among the approaches to environmental management discussed in chapters 2 through 5. In each figure, a firm starts out (at time 0) with a certain amount of revenues, a certain amount of costs, and a certain amount of profits. Each figure is a plot of the possible revenues and costs of the firm. The firm's initial position is shown with a circle.

If the firm's revenues and costs change by the same amount, its profits will stay the same. On the figure, the firm will move along the "iso-profit line" running northeast to southwest through its original point. Other iso-profit lines run parallel to the current one. Iso-profit lines farther to the northwest are better from the firm's standpoint, since in that region the firm earns higher revenues and incurs lower costs. Iso-profit lines to the southeast are worse.

Now suppose that the firm needs to incur extra costs to address some environmental problem or to improve its environmental performance. At least initially, this cost shock does not affect revenues, so the firm at time 1 has moved due east on the figure—to a lower iso-profit line (see Figure 1).

To regain its original profitability, or to achieve an even higher level of profits, the firm must move back to the north, the west, or the northwest. The approaches discussed in chapters 2 through 5 discuss ways in which this might be done.

Chapter 2 discusses product differentiation, which enables the

firm to capture additional revenue that offsets the environmental cost increase. Firms following this approach hope to move north on the map (see Figure 2). Chapter 3 discusses another way to move to the north: by increasing rivals' costs and thus making a price increase possible.

Chapter 4, by contrast, discusses the possibility of a move straight back to the west, by finding cost savings that offset the cost increases imposed by environmental pressure (see Figure 3). And chapter 5 discusses the possibility that a firm may be able to move north and west simultaneously, achieving both cost reductions and revenue increases by redefining the markets in which it competes (see Figure 4).

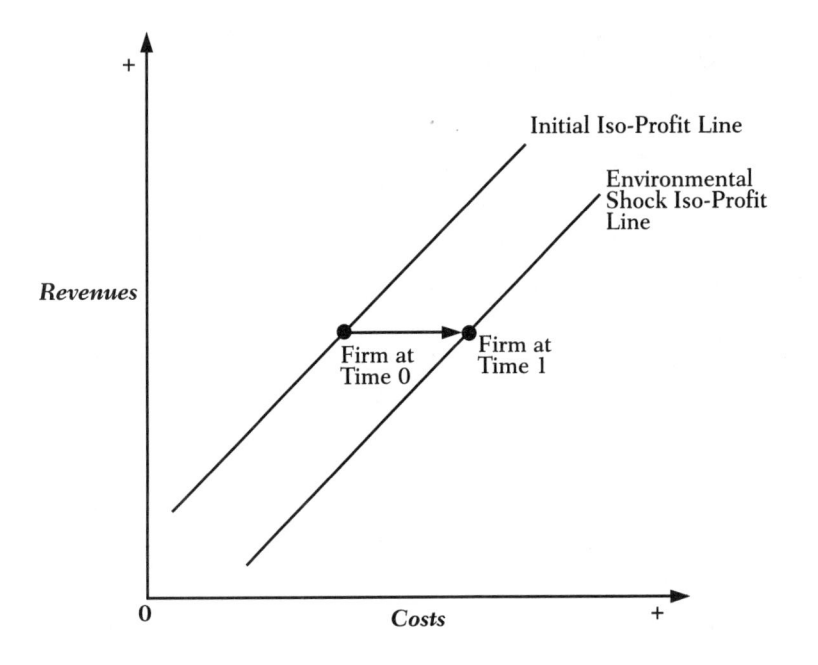

Figure 1. The Problem: Environmental Cost Shock

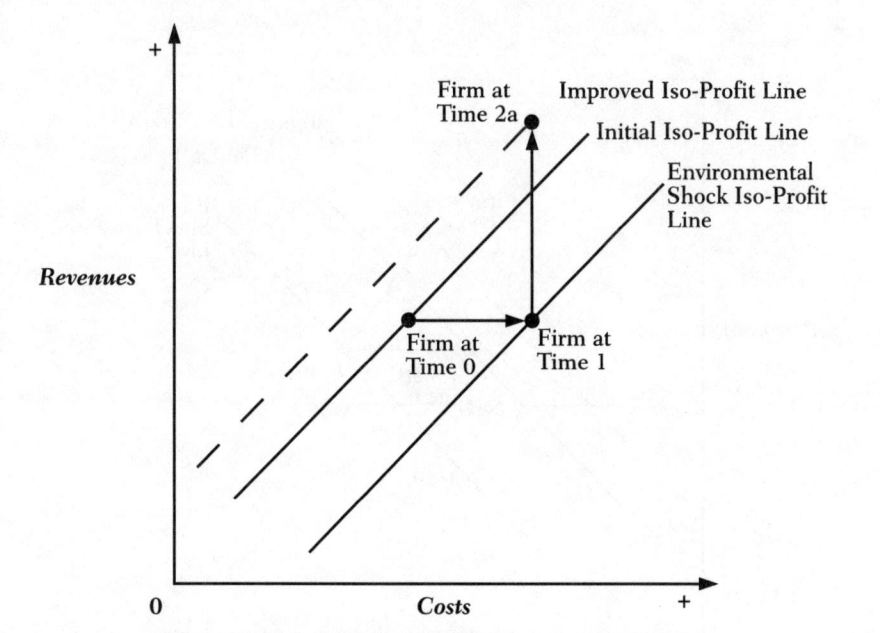

Figure 2. Solution "a": Increase Revenues.

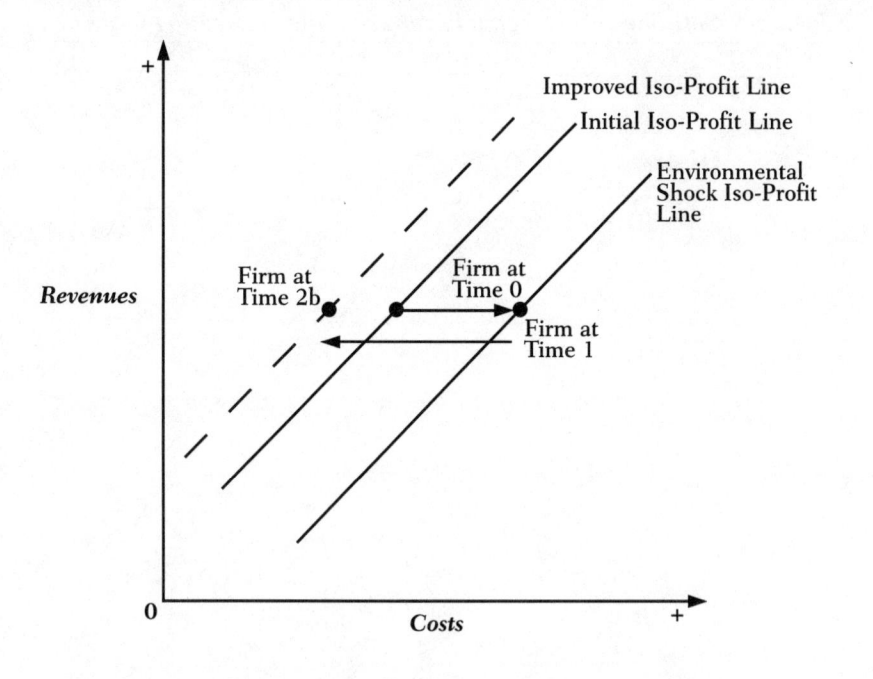

Figure 3. Solution "b": Decrease Costs

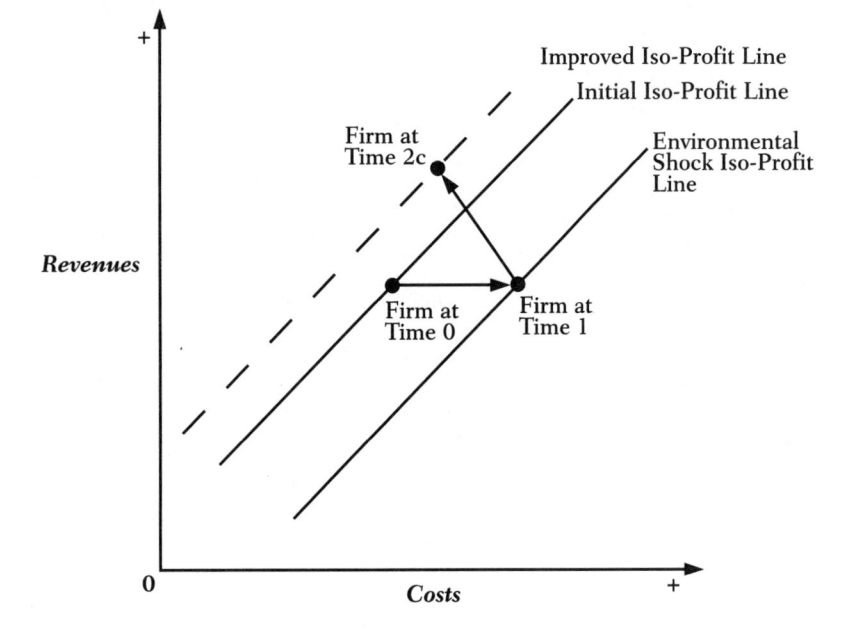

Figure 4. Solution "c": Increase Revenues while Decreasing Costs

Notes

Preface

1. Al Gore, *Earth in the Balance* (Boston: Houghton Mifflin, 1992), 269.

2. See, for example, Michael E. Porter and Claas van der Linde, "Toward a New Conception of the Environment-Competitiveness Relationship," *Journal of Economic Perspectives* 9, no. 4 (fall 1995): 97–118; Karen Palmer, Wallace E. Oates, and Paul R. Portney, "Tightening Environmental Standards: The Benefit-Cost or the No-Cost Paradigm?" *Journal of Economic Perspectives* 9, no. 4 (fall 1995): 119–132.

3. The use of case-based research methods to study business problems has its roots in business history and in the study of general management. See, for example, Alfred D. Chandler, Jr., *Strategy and Structure* (Cambridge: MIT Press, 1962); and Joseph L. Bower, *Managing the Resource Allocation Process: A Study of Corporate Planning and Investment* (Boston: Harvard Business School Division of Research, 1970). More recently, case-based approaches have proven useful in economics and strategy as well; for an example and a discussion of some of the methodological questions, see Pankaj Ghemawat, *Games Businesses Play* (Cambridge: MIT Press, 1997). See also Gary King, Robert O. Keohane, and Sidney Verba, *Designing Social Inquiry: Scientific Inference in Qualitative Research* (Princeton, N.J.: Princeton University Press, 1994).

Chapter 1

1. U.S. Bureau of the Census, *Statistical Abstract of the United States: 1996*, 116th ed. (Washington, D.C., 1996), 234, 443.

2. Al Gore, *Earth in the Balance* (Boston: Houghton Mifflin, 1992), 109; Robert V. Percival, Alan S. Miller, Christopher H. Schroeder, and James P. Leape, *Environmental Regulation: Law, Science, and Policy*, 2d ed. (Boston: Little, Brown, 1996), 875.

3. Environment Agency, Government of Japan, *Quality of the Environment in Japan 1993* [Tokyo, 1993], 8.

4. Organization for Economic Cooperation and Development, *OECD Environmental Performance Reviews: Germany* (Paris: OECD, 1993), 71.

5. Chlorofluorocarbons and stratospheric ozone are discussed from a business perspective in chapter 3 of this book. The standard diplomatic history is Richard Elliot Benedick, *Ozone Diplomacy: New Directions in Safeguarding the Planet,* enlarged ed. (Cambridge: Harvard University Press, 1998).

6. For an overview of environmental public policy in the United States, an excellent introduction is Paul Portney, ed., *Public Policies for Environmental Protection* (Washington, D.C.: Resources for the Future, 1990). See also Daniel J. Fiorino, *Making Environmental Policy* (Berkeley: University of California Press, 1995).

7. This point is articulated forcefully by Susan J. Colby, Tony Kingsley, and Bradley W. Whitehead, "The Real Green Issue," *McKinsey Quarterly* (1995): 132–43.

8. An excellent short introduction to the basic microeconomics of business strategy is "Primer: Economic Concepts for Strategy" in David Besanko, David Dranove, and Mark Shanley, *Economics of Strategy* (New York: Wiley, 1996), 1–37.

9. It is to take this fact into account that many firms are adopting the notion of "Economic Value Added," which considers the opportunity cost of the capital deployed, as a complement to other measures of financial performance. The acronym EVA® is registered by consultants Stern Stewart & Co.

10. Under perfect competition, "every relevant good is traded in a market at publicly known prices and all agents act as price takers." Andreu Mas-Colell, Michael D. Whinston, and Jerry R. Green, *Microeconomic Theory* (New York: Oxford University Press, 1995), 307.

11. The term "social cost" is widely used both in economics and in general discourse. In economics, it has a precise meaning: "The social cost of a given output is defined as the sum of money which is just adequate when paid as compensation to restore to their original utility levels all who lose as a result of the production of the output"; David Pearce, ed., *The MIT Dictionary of Modern Economics,* 4th ed. (Cambridge: MIT Press, 1992). "All who lose as a result of the production of the output" would include those who voluntarily supply inputs to its production, and are compensated through wages or other payments, and also those, for example, who are affected by pollution from the production process, who ordinarily are not compensated. The classic analysis of these problems from an economic standpoint is Ronald Coase, "The Problem of Social Cost," *Journal of Law and Economics* 3 (1960): 1–44. In general discourse, "social cost" is often not well defined. This book uses it only in the economic sense.

12. Suppose, for example, that a used-car salesman and his customer both know all the relevant facts about the quality of the salesman's various cars. Then striking a bargain—or determining that there is no bargain to be struck—is a straightforward procedure. Now suppose, instead, that the salesman knows which of his cars are "lemons," that the customer knows that the salesman has this information, and that the customer himself cannot tell the lemons from the good cars. In this second situation, striking a bargain is enormously complicated: the customer suspects that the salesman may have an incentive to lie about the cars' quality; the salesman, even if he is telling the truth, may find it hard to convince the customer of his veracity; and so on.

13. See, for example, Pearce, *MIT Dictionary of Modern Economics.* Like "social cost," the term "public good" appears frequently in political discussions, usually without any clear definition. This book uses it only in the economic sense defined here.

14. This vocabulary is adopted from Douglass North; see, for example, *Institutions, Institutional Change and Economic Performance* (Cambridge: Cambridge University Press, 1990).

15. North's definition implies that institutions are *basic* rules: those that involve the general structure of property rights, the scope and limits of state activity, and so on. He sees these basic rules, whether formal or informal, as resistant to change, and as generally (though not immutably) creating constraints on economic behavior. In modern society there exist many formal rules that are sufficiently flexible that they do not seem to fall within the spirit of North's definition of "institutions." For example, suppose a governmental authority amended a regulation that specified a maximum discharge of some water pollutant, so that the permissible level fell by 10 percent. This would be a change in a formal rule, but it would not constitute "institutional change" as defined here. That term is reserved for changes in the basic structure of regulatory architecture, such as a change from command-and-control regulation to marketable permits, or transfer of authority of compliance monitoring from a government agency to a self-policing private body.

16. David P. Baron, *Business and Its Environment,* 2d ed. (Upper Saddle River, N.J.: Prentice Hall, 1996).

17. Michael E. Porter, *Competitive Advantage* (New York: Free Press, 1985), 33–34.

18. The arguments for this normative conclusion are discussed in chapter 6.

19. Several other motives for corporate behavior in the environmental arena can be seen as means to some combination of these ends. For example, regulatory compliance does not appear in this list of possible objectives. This is not because regulatory pressure on environmental performance is unimportant—regulation is an extremely potent force in changing companies' behavior with respect to the environment—but because complying with regulations is ordinarily a means to value creation, risk reduction, or protection of reputation, not an end in itself. To cite another example, companies may be motivated in designing their environmental policies by the desire to create or maintain goodwill among some group of internal or external actors: employees, regulators, residents of communities where the firm does business, and so on. This goodwill is desirable, though, because it creates value for firms directly or enables them more effectively to manage risk. Similarly, firms may be motivated in the environmental arena by the desire to maintain or create flexibility and option values, which again can be reduced (in theory, although in practice the valuation can be difficult) to value creation, risk reduction, or both.

20. Robert H. Hayes, Steven C. Wheelwright, and Kim B. Clark, *Dynamic Manufacturing* (New York: Free Press, 1988), 30.

Chapter 2

1. Some marketers use "process differentiation" to refer to the sale of products manufactured in alternative (and putatively preferable) ways, reserving "product differentiation" to refer only to the sale of products whose characteristics in use are different. In this taxonomy, the sale of low-emission gasoline would be an example of product differentiation, but the sale of "green" electricity (produced from renewable energy sources, but indistinguishable in use from the electricity produced at coal-fired boilers or nuclear reactors) would be an example of process differentiation. This chapter, following common usage, employs the term "product differentiation" to encompass marketing strategies in both of these categories.

2. For some firms, the provision of this additional environmental quality can actually lower the producing firm's private costs; see Michael E. Porter and Claas van der Linde, "Toward a New Conception of the Environment-Competitiveness Relationship," *Journal of Economic Perspectives* 9, no. 4 (fall 1995): 97–118. This chapter

focuses on the case in which the provision of environmental quality adds to the selling firm's costs. For a discussion of the idea that improved environmental performance can result in cost savings, see chapter 4.

From the standpoint of microeconomic theory, product differentiation is simply the creation of a new market, protected by barriers to entry or to mobility, in which an individual producer faces finite elasticity of demand. See Richard E. Caves and Michael Porter, "From Entry Barriers to Mobility Barriers: Conjectural Decisions and Contrived Deterrence to New Competition," *Quarterly Journal of Economics* 91, no. 2 (1977): 241–262; Richard E. Caves and Peter J. Williamson, "What Is Product Differentiation, Really?" *Journal of Industrial Economics* 34 (1985): 113–132. The economic literature on product differentiation focuses on identifying the conditions that will lead to lesser or greater differentiation, and on the social welfare consequences of differentiation and advertising; for a survey, see Jean Tirole, *The Theory of Industrial Organization* (Cambridge: MIT Press, 1988), chap. 7.

3. Philip Kotler's widely used basic marketing textbook, *Marketing Management,* 9th ed. (Upper Saddle River, N.J.: Prentice Hall, 1997), includes a list of seven criteria that managers should use to analyze potential "differentiators" of their products: "Important: The difference delivers a highly valued benefit to a sufficient number of buyers. Distinctive: The difference either isn't offered by others or is offered in a more distinctive way by the company. Superior: The difference is superior to other ways of obtaining the same benefit. Communicable: The difference is communicable and visible to buyers. Preemptive: The difference cannot be copied easily by competitors. Affordable: The buyer can afford to pay for the difference. Profitable: The company will find it profitable to introduce the difference" (pp. 294–295). Of these seven criteria, the first, third, and sixth relate directly to willingness to pay; the fourth to credible information; the second and fifth to protection from imitation. The seventh follows from the first six.

4. Ciba Specialty Chemicals, *Global Offering of Registered Shares* (Basel, 1997); Ciba Specialty Chemicals, *Financial Review 1997* (Basel); Ciba Specialty Chemicals, *Business Review 1997* (Basel); and Ciba Specialty Chemicals, *Financial Review 1998* (Basel).

5. For example, if the probability of a particular reactive group fixing to the fiber is 0.6, then 60 percent = $1 - 0.4$ of a monoreactive dye will fix, while $1 - 0.4^2 = 84$ percent of a bireactive dye will fix.

6. Ciba-Geigy Limited, *Cibacron LS Reactive Dyes for Dyeing Cellulosic Fibres by the Exhaust Method* (Basel, 1995); Ciba-Geigy Limited, *Summary Report 1995* (Basel), 20.

7. Monsanto Company, *Roundup into the Twenty-first Century* (St. Louis, 1995). Glyphosate is N-(phosphonomethyl)-glycine.

8. Monsanto Company, *Roundup: From Prairie to Pompeii* (St. Louis, 1991).

9. Monsanto Company, *1996 Annual Report to Shareholders* (St. Louis), 11A–11B; U.S. Bureau of the Census, *Statistical Abstract of the United States,* 116th ed. (Washington, D.C., 1996), 676.

10. Monsanto Company, *1992 Annual Report* (St. Louis).

11. Monsanto Company, *Roundup into the Twenty-first Century.*

12. Union of Concerned Scientists, *Case Study: Roundup Ready Soybeans,* http://www.ucsusa.org/agriculture/soybeans.html, accessed 5 May 1998. I am indebted to an anonymous referee at the *California Management Review* for emphasizing to me the degree of controversy concerning agricultural biotechnology.

13. See, for example, Peggy Duxbury and Forest Reinhardt, "Reading Energy," Case 9-

794-102 (Boston: Harvard Business School), reprinted in *Business Management and the Natural Environment: Cases and Text* (Cincinnati: South-Western, 1996).

14. Haig Simonian, "Business and the Environment: Plastic Fashion," *Financial Times* 12 April 1995, 16.

15. David Clark Scott, "Sartorially Correct '90s Camper or Hiker Wears Soda Bottles," *Christian Science Monitor,* 20 January 1995, 8.

16. "Patagonia's Environmental Marketing—A Boomer Paradigm? Barry Lenson Interviews Mike Harrelson of Patagonia," *Boomer Report,* 15 April 1994, 4.

17. Andrea Adelson, "Earning It: Casual, Worker-Friendly, and a Moneymaker, Too," *New York Times,* 30 June 1996, 3–8.

18. Edward Welles, "Lost in Patagonia," *Inc.,* August 1992, 44.

19. Yvon Chouinard and Michael S. Brown, "Going Organic: Converting Patagonia's Cotton Product Line," *Journal of Industrial Ecology* 1, no. 1 (spring 1997): 117–130.

20. Staci Bonner, "Patagonia: A Green Endeavor," *Apparel Industry Magazine,* February 1997, 46.

21. Chouinard and Brown, "Going Organic," 117–130.

22. Patagonia, Inc., *Patagonia Fall 1997* [mail-order catalog], 62.

23. National Research Council, Committee on Reducing Porpoise Mortality from Tuna Fishing, *Dolphins and the Tuna Industry* (Washington, D.C.: National Academy Press, 1992), 34–37, 52–71.

24. National Research Council, *Dolphins and the Tuna Industry,* 52–90; U.S. International Trade Commission, *Tuna: Current Issues Affecting the US Industry,* USITC publication 2547 (August 1992), 3-1 through 3-22, and 5-2 through 5-4.

25. See Richard H. K. Vietor and Forest Reinhardt, "StarKist (A)," Case 9-794-128 (Boston: Harvard Business School, 1994), reprinted in *Business Management and the Natural Environment* (Cincinnati: South-Western, 1996).

26. H. J. Heinz internal file notes, February 1990, cited in Vietor and Reinhardt, "StarKist (A)," 12. At the time, the retail price of branded tuna (StarKist, Bumble Bee, or Chicken of the Sea) ranged from 70 to 75 cents per can.

27. Philip Shabecoff, "Big Tuna Canners Act to Slow Down Dolphin Killings," *New York Times,* 13 April 1990, A-1.

28. Quoted in Vietor and Reinhardt, "StarKist (B)," Case 9-794-139 (Boston: Harvard Business School, 1994), 3.

29. See Vietor and Reinhardt, "StarKist (B);" Philippe Charat, interview, Boston, April 1994.

30. Unpublished data from the Interamerican Tropical Tuna Commission (IATTC), cited, inter alia, in Brad Warren, "The Downside of Dolphin-Safe," *Audubon,* November–December 1993, 20–22, and Mexico Secretaría de Pesca, "Mexico's Commitment to Dolphin Protection" (Mexico City, 1994).

31. David Phillips, "Breakthrough for Dolphins: How We Did It," and Sam La Budde, "Notes from the Field," *Earth Island Journal,* summer 1990, 26–28.

32. White House Press Office, "Clinton Statement on Dolphin Conservation Act," 19 August 1997.

33. The distinction between private consumption goods and public goods is similar to the distinction between "tangible, personal benefits" and "intangible, societal benefits" drawn by V. Kasturi Rangan, Sohel Karim, and Sheryl K. Sandberg in "Do

Better at Doing Good," *Harvard Business Review* 74, no. 3 (May–June 1996): 42–54.

34. Mancur Olson explicitly excludes "philanthropic and religious organizations" from his classic study of collective action, arguing that they "are not necessarily expected to serve only the interests of their members; such organizations have other purposes that are considered more important, however much their members 'need' to belong, or are improved or helped by belonging. . . . this study will focus on organizations with a significant economic aspect." Olson, *The Logic of Collective Action* (Cambridge: Harvard University Press, 1965), 6 n. 6.

35. The team responsible for this analysis included executives from DDB Needham, the Ad Council, the Environmental Federation of America (a consortium of environmental organizations), and GTE Service Corporation. See V. Kasturi Rangan and Jayne D. Kramer, "The Advertising Council Earth Share Campaign: Strategy, Execution, and Final Campaign," Case 9-593-062 (Boston: Harvard Business School, 1992).

36. For a summary, see, for example, W. Kip Viscusi, John M. Vernon, and Joseph E. Harrington Jr., *Economics of Regulation and Antitrust,* 2nd ed. (Cambridge: MIT Press, 1995), 676–678.

37. Data on the income elasticity of the demand for environmental quality are surprisingly sparse. One study found voluntary contributions to American environmental groups like Ducks Unlimited, the Environmental Defense Fund, Greenpeace, and the Sierra Club to be significantly and negatively correlated with the unemployment rate, a finding broadly supportive of the idea that environmental goods behave like luxuries; see Jerrell Richer, "Green Giving: An Analysis of Contributions to Major U.S. Environmental Groups," discussion paper 95-39, Resources for the Future, Washington, D.C., 1995.

38. David Besanko, David Dranove, and Mark Shanley, *The Economics of Strategy* (New York: Wiley, 1996), 465–471; see also Pankaj Ghemawat, *Commitment: The Dynamic of Strategy* (New York: Free Press, 1991), chap. 4.

39. The question of the prevalence of opportunities for vertical differentiation relates closely to the famous debate about the prevalence of private cost savings within the firm that can be discovered with the help of pressure to improve environmental performance. As mentioned in earlier notes, this chapter concentrates on the case in which vertical differentiation is not possible because the provision of environmental quality adds to the selling firm's costs.

40. Psychologists and experimental economists have studied how people's perceptions of the motives and intentions of others affect their own behavior toward them. For an overview, see Matthew Rabin, "Psychology and Economics," *Journal of Economic Literature* 36, no. 1 (1998): 11–46, esp. 16–24.

41. An anonymous reviewer at the *California Management Review* pointed out that, owing to halo effects of this sort, a possible "avenue to shareholder wealth is to sacrifice profitability on a single green product in order to benefit the firm's image and capitalize on that image elsewhere." In other words, it might be sensible for executives in multiproduct firms to use some of their products to enhance the firm's overall reputation among environmentally conscious customers, in effect subsidizing the firm's other products.

42. For an articulation of this view, see, for example, Environmental Defense Fund, "Is It Real or Is It Greenwashing?" (New York, 1993) (http://web.edf.org/pubs/brochures/greenwashing, accessed 18 November 1997).

43. See Patricia Markovich and Forest Reinhardt, "Metsä-Serla: Environmental Labels in the European Forest Products Markets," Case 9-795-148 (Boston: Harvard

Business School, 1995); Jackie Prince Roberts and Forest Reinhardt, "Aracruz Celulose S.A.," Case 9-794-049 (Boston: Harvard Business School, 1993), reprinted in Forest Reinhardt and Richard H. K. Vietor, *Business Management and the Natural Environment: Cases and Text* (Cincinnati: South-Western, 1996).

44. See David Vogel, *Trading Up: Consumer and Environmental Regulation in a Global Economy* (Cambridge: Harvard University Press, 1995), chap. 4. As noted above, the act was later amended to allow "no-mortality" tuna to obtain the label.

45. I am grateful to an anonymous reviewer at the *California Management Review* for emphasizing this point.

46. See, for example, Janet Shaner, Mary Shelman, and Ray Goldberg, "Loblaw Companies Limited," Case 9-590-051 (Boston: Harvard Business School, 1989), 9–10.

47. See Jaclyn Fierman, "The Big Muddle in Green Marketing," *Fortune*, 3 June 1991, 91ff.; Alex Pham, "Mobil in FTC Pact to Drop Claims of Plastic Degradability," *Washington Post*, 28 July 1992, C-1; Dan Wascoe Jr., "FTC Issues Guidelines to Prevent Misleading Environmental Claims," *Minneapolis Star Tribune*, 28 July 1992, 1-D.

48. See, for example, John Tierney, "Recycling Is Garbage," *New York Times Magazine*, 30 June 1996. For rebuttals to Tierney, see "Too Good to Throw Away" (New York: Natural Resources Defense Council, 1997); and Richard Denison and John Ruston, "Anti-Recycling Myths" (Washington, D.C.: Environmental Defense Fund, 1996) (http://www.igc.org/nrdc/nrdcpro/recyc/recyinx.html and http://edf.org/pubs/reports/armythfin.html, respectively, accesed 22 September 1997 and 26 November 1997).

49. See David A. Aaker, *Managing Brand Equity* (New York: Free Press, 1991), chap. 1.

50. This idea is central to Patagonia executives' own understanding of their initiatives: "Our experience reinforced for us that successful implementation of environmental improvements requires an integrated approach across the entire organization." Yvon Chouinard and Michael S. Brown, "Going Organic: Converting Patagonia's Cotton Product Line," *Journal of Industrial Ecology* 1, no. 1 (spring 1997): 117–130, quotation on 127.

Chapter 3

1. See Mancur Olson, *The Logic of Collective Action* (Cambridge: Harvard University Press, 1965), 22–36.

2. Stuart Diamond, "The Bhopal Disaster: How It Happened," *New York Times*, 28 January 1985), A-1.

3. In addition to the Chemical Manufacturers Association documents cited below, see Jeffrey Rayport and George Lodge, "Responsible Care," Case 9-391-135 (Boston: Harvard Business School, 1991), and Stephan Schmidheiny, *Changing Course* (Cambridge: MIT Press, 1992), 221–224.

4. Chemical Manufacturers Association, "The Year in Review 1995–1996: Responsible Care® Progress Report" (Arlington, Va.), iv.

5. Between 1988, when Responsible Care was initiated, and 1994, U.S. chemical firms reduced their yearly total releases of toxic materials by 49 percent. Other U.S. industries accomplished significant reductions during this period, but the chemical industry's declines were steeper than those of the American industry as a whole. See U.S. EPA *1995 Toxic Release Inventory Public Data Release Report*, ch. 5, http://www.epa.gov.opptintr/tri/pdr95/chap5a.pdf, accessed 27 April 1999. In

1992, CMA members averaged 3.15 injuries and incidents of work-related illness per 100 employees; the overall average for U.S. manufacturing was 12.5. In 1994, CMA's rate fell to 2.85. See CMA, "10 Elements of Responsible Care®" (Washington, D.C.: 1995), 23–24.

6. CMA, "Product Stewardship Code of Management Practices" (Arlington, Va., 1992).

7. Susan J. Ainsworth and Ann M. Thayer, "Chemical Manufacturers Welcome Challenges of Product Stewardship," *Chemical and Engineering News,* 17 October 1994, 10ff.

8. Ibid.

9. CMA, "The Year in Review 1995–96", 16; CMA, "Responsible Care® in Action: 1993–94 Progress Report" (Washington, D.C.), 31.

10. CMA, "The Year in Review 1995–1996," 5, 12.

11. Jennifer Nash and John Ehrenfeld, "Code Green: Business Adopts Voluntary Environmental Standards," *Environment* 38, no.1 (January–February 1996): 16ff.

12. CMA, "The Year in Review 1995–1996," iii.

13. See David Vogel, *Trading Up: Consumer and Environmental Regulation in a Global Economy* (Cambridge: Harvard University Press, 1995), chap. 7.

14. American Forest & Paper Association, "Sustainable Forestry for Tomorrow's World: Second Annual Report on the American Forest & Paper Association's Sustainable Forestry Initiative" (Washington, D.C.: AF&PA, 1997), 4.

15. See American Forest & Paper Association, "Sustainable Forestry: Principles and Implementation Guidelines" (Washington, D.C.: AF&PA, December 1995), 3.

16. See ibid., 5–8.

17. American Forest & Paper Association, "Sustainable Forestry for Tomorrow's World: Second Annual Report," 22.

18. American Forest & Paper Association, "Executive Summary: Sustainable Forestry for Tomorrow's World: Second Annual Report on the American Forest & Paper Association's Sustainable Forestry Initiative" (Washington, D.C.: AF&PA, 1997), 4.

19. Julie Jack, American Forest & Paper Association, Washington, D.C.; telephone interview with research associate Jennifer Burns, 29 September 1998.

20. Jack Swanner, T&S Hardwoods, Sylva, North Carolina; telephone interview with research associate Jennifer Burns, 29 September 1998.

21. American Forest & Paper Association, "Sustainable Forestry for Tomorrow's World: First Annual Report on the American Forest & Paper Association's Sustainable Forestry Initiative" (Washington, D.C.: AF&PA, 1996), 1–2; American Forest & Paper Association, "Sustainable Forestry for Tomorrow's World: Second Annual Report," i–ii.

22. Robin Bulman, "Conservationists Question Sustainable Forestry Effort but Industry Says the Program Is Moving in the Right Direction," *Journal of Commerce,* 24 October 1996.

23. Alfred D. Chandler Jr., *The Visible Hand: The Managerial Revolution in American Business* (Cambridge: The Belknap Press of Harvard University Press, 1977), 320–331. See also Thomas K. McCraw, *Prophets of Regulation* (Cambridge: Belknap Press of Harvard University Press, 1984), chap. 2.

24. Anthony Downs, *An Economic Theory of Democracy* (New York: Harper and Row, 1957).

25. George Stigler, "The Theory of Economic Regulation," *Bell Journal of Economics and Management Science* 2 (1971): 3–21; Sam Peltzman, "Toward a More General Theory of Regulation," *Journal of Law and Economics* 19 (1976): 211–240. For an early application of these methods to environmental regulation, see Michael T. Maloney and Robert E. McCormick, "A Positive Theory of Environmental Quality Regulation," *Journal of Law and Economics* 25 (1982): 99–123. See also David P. Baron, *Business and its Environment*, 2d ed. (Upper Saddle River, N. J.: Prentice Hall, 1996).

26. Anne O. Krueger, "The Political Economy of the Rent-Seeking Society," *American Economic Review* 64 (1974): 291–303.

27. Bruce Yandle, "Bootleggers and Baptists: The Education of a Regulatory Economist," *Regulation* 7 (May–June 1983): 12–16: "Bootleggers, you will remember, support Sunday closing laws that shut down all the local bars and liquor stores. Baptists support the same laws and lobby vigorously for them. Both parties gain, while the regulators are content because the law is easy to administer" (13).

28. See Steven C. Salop and David T. Scheffman, "Raising Rivals' Costs," *American Economic Review Papers and Proceedings* 73 (1983): 267–271. See also Robert A. Leone, *Who Profits: Winners, Losers, and Government Regulation* (New York: Basic Books, 1986); Scott Barrett, "Strategy and the Environment," *Columbia Journal of World Business* 27, no. 3, 4 (fall/winter 1992): 202–208; Sharon Oster, *Modern Competitive Analysis*, 2d ed. (New York: Oxford University Press, 1994).

29. For additional background information, see Forest Reinhardt and Richard H. K. Vietor, "DuPont Freon® Products Division (A)," Case 9-389-111 (Boston: Harvard Business School, 1989), reprinted in *Business Management and the Natural Environment: Cases and Text* (Cincinnati: South-Western, 1996).

30. Ibid., 10, 29–30.

31. U.S. Environmental Protection Agency, "Regulatory Impact Analysis: Protection of Stratospheric Ozone" (Washington D.C.: December 1987).

32. Reinhardt and Vietor, "DuPont Freon® Products Division (A)," 13.

33. U.S. Environmental Protection Agency, "Regulatory Impact Analysis."

34. Putnam, Hayes, and Bartlett, Inc., "Report to the Alliance for Responsible CFC Policy" (Washington, D.C.: 1987).

35. Reinhardt and Vietor, "DuPont Freon® Products Division (A)," 8.

36. Richard Elliott Benedick, *Ozone Diplomacy: New Directions in Safeguarding the Planet,* enlarged ed. (Cambridge: Harvard University Press, 1998), 231–232.

37. Julie Edelson Halpert, "Freon Smugglers Find Big Market," *New York Times,* 30 April 1995.

38. David Rotman, Michael Roberts, and Kara Sissell, "Dawn of the Post-CFC Era; Ice-Cold Markets Spell Trouble," *Chemical Week,* 17 January 1996, 18ff.

39. Some North American forest products firms have followed exactly this course: one of these businesses, Alberta-Pacific Forest Industries, is discussed in chapter 6. Other possible objectives for these tactics—in particular, the improved management of business risk—are far more likely to be attainable.

40. The pioneering works in this field are Downs, *An Economic Theory of Democracy;* and Olson, *The Logic of Collective Action.* James Q. Wilson, "The Politics of Regulation," in *The Politics of Regulation,* ed. James Q. Wilson (New York: Basic Books, 1980), emphasizes the importance of the distribution of costs and benefits.

41. See Allan R. Gold, "Helping Boston Harbor: A Big Job Begins at Last," *New York Times,* 2 April 1989; Fox Butterfield, "Fight on Cleanup of Harbor Goes On," *New York Times,* 3 February 1990.

42. The EPA's regulatory impact analysis, cited earlier, concluded that the domestic costs of the Montreal Protocol would amount to about $27 billion, but that the benefits would be close to $6.5 trillion, for a benefit-cost ratio of about 239 to 1. To achieve this benefit estimate, which substantially exceeded the entire American GDP in 1987, the EPA valued each statistical life saved at $3 million, in keeping with the opportunity costs of saving statistical lives in other environmental regulatory programs. Many of these statistical averted deaths would occur far in the future—the EPA considered all Americans who would be expected to be born before 2076—and so, according to conventional benefit-cost analysis methodologies, ought to be discounted. But the EPA assumed that GDP per capita (and hence the current value of a life saved) would rise at nearly the same rate as the discount rate used to convert current values in the future to present values. This methodological sleight of hand was not necessary to achieve an impressively favorable benefit-cost ratio. Even without these projected increases in values of lives, the benefits of the protocol might exceed the $27 billion in costs by a factor of twenty or so.

43. See Gary Becker, "A Theory of Competition among Pressure Groups for Political Influence," *Quarterly Journal of Economics* 98 (1983): 371–400.

44. See, for example, John Elkington, "Towards the Sustainable Corporation: Win-Win-Win Business Strategies for Sustainable Development," *California Management Review* 36, no.2 (winter 1994): 90–100: "Business is now developing new 'win-win-win' strategies in this area to simultaneously benefit the company, its customers, and the environment."

45. See Paul R. Portney, "Air Pollution Policy," in *Public Policies for Environmental Protection*, ed. Paul P. Portney (Washington, D.C.: Resources for the Future, 1990).

46. See Matthew Wald, "ARCO Offers New Gasoline to Cut Up to 15 Percent of Old Cars' Pollution," *New York Times*, 16 August 1989, A-1; Gerald Parkinson, "Making and Promoting Clean Fuels," *Chemical Engineering* 100, no. 8 (August 1993): 63; Richard E. Cohen, *Washington at Work: Back Rooms and Clean Air* (New York: Macmillan, 1992), 137.

47. Mark Ivey, "Fuel Wars: Big Oil Is Running Scared," *Business Week*, 4 June 1990, 132.

48. John Holusha, "All About Reformulated Gasolines: As Pressure Grows, Refiners Develop Cleaner Fuels," *New York Times*, 8 July 1990, 3–5; "ARCO's New EC-Premium Gas Introduced," *San Diego Union-Tribune*, 7 September 1990, E-1. For more detail on the immediate aftermath of ARCO's decision, see the case study by Scott Schaefer and Jeremy Bulow, "Cleaner Fuels for Competitive Advantage: ARCO and EC-1" (Stanford: Stanford University Graduate School of Business, 1993).

49. Wald, "ARCO Offers New Gasoline," A-1.

50. John Holusha, "Talking Business with Cook of Atlantic Richfield; Oil Industry's Environment Role," *New York Times*, 3 April 1990, D-2.

51. Public Law 101-549 (101st Cong. 2d. sess., 15 November 1990); 104 Stat. 2399-2712. See also California Air Resources Board, "Cleaner Burning Gasoline Fact Sheet 3" (Sacramento, February 1996).

52. California Air Resources Board, "Cleaner Burning Gasoline Fact Sheet 3."

53. Jane Kay, "Chemical Threat to State's Water Wells," *San Francisco Examiner*, 10 August 1997, A-1.

54. James P. Sweeney and Ken Leiser, "Fuming over Gas Prices," *San Diego Union-Tribune*, 26 April 1996, A-1; Patrick Lee, "Q&A; So, What Is Fueling Gas Hikes?; ARCO Executive Says It's Competition, Supplies," *Los Angeles Times*, 27 April 1996, D-1.

55. Kay, "Chemical Threat to State's Water Wells," A-1; see also California Environmental Protection Agency, "MTBE (Methyl Tertiary Butyl Ether) Briefing Paper" (Sacramento, September 1997).

56. Nancy Rivera Brooks, "Fuel Additive Subtracted; Tosco to Test Gasoline That Omits MTBE," *Los Angeles Times*, 16 April 1998.

57. Gerry Karey, "Proposed Changes to California RFG Rules Split Oil Companies," *The International Petrochemical Report*, 30 April 1998, 2.

58. Dave O'Reilly, "Statement before the House Commerce Committee Health and the Environment Subcommittee," 22 April 1998; Alex Barnum, "Oil Giants Face Lawsuit; Group Says Gas Additive Taints Water," *San Francisco Chronicle*, 6 August 1998.

59. Alan Krauss, "Arco Develops Cleaner Gasoline, Anticipating New Rules in State," *Investor's Daily*, 12 July 1991, 7, quoting Philip Dodge of Dillon Read & Co.

Chapter 4

1. The 3M and Dow programs are described in Stephan Schmidheiny, *Changing Course: A Global Business Perspective on Development and the Environment* (Cambridge: MIT Press, 1992), 189–193, 265–270; and in Livio DeSimone and Frank Popoff, *Eco-efficiency: The Business Link to Sustainable Development* (Cambridge: MIT Press, 1997).

2. Michael E. Porter and Claas van der Linde, "Green and Competitive: Ending the Stalemate," *Harvard Business Review* 73, no.5 (September–October 1995): 120–134, quotation on 125. See also Porter and van der Linde, "Toward a New Conception of the Environment-Competitiveness Relationship," *Journal of Economic Perspectives* 9, no. 4 (fall 1995): 97–118.

3. See Philip Crosby, *Quality Is Free: The Art of Making Quality Certain* (New York: McGraw-Hill, 1979); Peter Senge, *The Fifth Discipline: The Art and Practice of the Learning Organization* (New York: Currency Doubleday, paperback edition 1994).

4. See Adam B. Jaffe, Steven R. Peterson, Paul R. Portney, and Robert N. Stavins, "Environmental Regulation and the Competitiveness of U.S. Manufacturing: What Does the Evidence Tell Us?" *Journal of Economic Literature* 33 (March 1995): 132–163; see also Karen Palmer, Wallace E. Oates, and Paul R. Portney, "Tightening Environmental Standards: The Benefit-Cost or the No-Cost Paradigm?" *Journal of Economic Perspectives* 9, no. 4 (fall 1995): 119–132.

5. The ten-dollar bill metaphor is ubiquitous, cited inter alia by Palmer and coauthors, Jaffe et al., and Porter and van der Linde (in the *Journal of Economic Perspectives* and the *Harvard Business Review*). Marc Epstein argues that "win-win" opportunities for cost reduction are far from exhausted because "most companies are just beginning their analyses of pollution-prevention opportunities" and "they have not yet fully investigated the areas where the redesign of products and processes can lead to significant reductions in environmental costs." Epstein, *Measuring Corporate Environmental Performance* (Chicago: Irwin, 1996), 248.

6. See Michael E. Porter, "America's Green Strategy," *Scientific American*, April 1991, 168.

7. See, for example, Al Gore, *Earth in the Balance* (Boston: Houghton Mifflin, 1992), 342.

8. See Palmer, Oates, and Portney, "Tightening Environmental Standard," 119–132; see also James Boyd, "Searching for the Profit in Pollution Prevention: Case Studies in

the Corporate Evaluation of Environmental Opportunities," Resources for the Future, Discussion Paper 98-30 (Washington: Resources for the Future, 1998).

9. Brian Alexander, "Luxury Hotels Save Money by Being Kind to the Environment," *San Francisco Examiner*, 2 October 1994, T-14.

10. David M. Stipanuk and Jack D. Ninemeier, "The Future of the U.S. Lodging Industry and the Environment," *Cornell Hotel and Restaurant Administration Quarterly* 37, no. 6 (December 1996): 74ff.

11. HVS Eco Services, Case Study: "Holiday Inn, Palo Alto–Stanford, California" (Mineola, N.Y.: n.d.); HVS Eco Services, Case Study: "Norfolk Waterside Marriott, Norfolk, Virginia" (Mineola, N.Y.: n.d.); HVS Eco Services, Case Study: "Shutters on the Beach, Santa Monica, California" (Mineola, N.Y.: n.d.).

12. Tedd Saunders and Loretta McGovern, *The Bottom Line of Green is Black: Strategies for Creating Profitable and Environmentally Sound Businesses* (San Francisco: HarperSanFrancisco, 1993), 70; Molly Arost Staub, "Hotels Look to Save Bucks While Saving the Environment," *South Florida Business Journal* 16, no. 35 (19 April 1996): 3B.

13. HVS Eco Services, Case Study: "Little Dix Bay, Virgin Gorda, British Virgin Islands" (Mineola, N.Y.: n.d.); HVS Eco Services, Case Study: "Howard Johnson, Whippany, New Jersey" (Minoeola, N.Y.: n.d.).

14. Saunders and McGovern, *The Bottom Line of Green Is Black*, 70–71.

15. HVS Eco Services, Case Study: "The York Hotel, San Francisco" (Mineola, N.Y.: n.d.).

16. Keith L. Alexander, "Green Movement Sprouts at Hotels," *USA Today*, 6 June 1995, 5–E.

17. Heather Gooch, "Environment Takes Center Stage at Some Properties," *Hotel and Motel Management* 212, no. 17, 6 October 1997: 63.

18. David Churchill, "Saving Money in a Classy Environment," *FT Energy World*, 6 (January–February 1998): 38–41.

19. Alexander, "Luxury Hotels Save Money," T–14.

20. Schmidheiny, *Changing Course*, 265–266.

21. Ibid., 266–267.

22. Mark H. Dorfman, Warren R. Muir, and Catherine G. Miller, *Environmental Dividends: Cutting More Chemical Wastes* (New York: INFORM, 1992), 150–153; discussed in Porter and van der Linde, "Green and Competitive," 125–126; and Porter and van der Linde, "Toward a New Conception of the Environment-Competitiveness Relationship," 103.

23. DeSimone and Popoff, *Eco-efficiency*, 216.

24. Kenneth Nelson, "Finding and Implementing Projects That Reduce Waste," in *Industrial Ecology and Global Change*, ed. Robert Socolow, Clinton Andrews, Frans Berkhout, and Valerie Thomas (Cambridge: Cambridge University Press, 1994).

25. DeSimone and Popoff, *Eco-efficiency*, 214.

26. Joseph A. Avila and Bradley W. Whitehead, "What Is Environmental Strategy?" [interview with Frank Popoff, Dow Chemical CEO and chairman, and David T. Buzzelli, Dow Chemical vice president of the environment, health, and safety], *McKinsey Quarterly* 4 (1993): 53–68.

27. DeSimone and Popoff, *Eco-efficiency*, 33.

28. "Dow to Spend $1 Billion on Environment," *Chemical Marketing Reporter* 249, no. 10 (29 April 1996): 5.

29. Schmidheiny, *Changing Course*, 266–267.

30. John H. Sheridan, "Attacking Wastes and Saving Money . . . Some of the Time," *Industry Week* 241, no. 4 (17 February 1992): 43–46.

31. Dow Chemical, "1996 Environment, Health & Safety Report" (Midland, Mich.); Dow Chemical, "1997 Progress Report on Environment, Health and Safety Goals for 2005" (Midland, Mich.).

32. Michael Porter, *Competitive Strategy* (New York: Free Press, 1980), 10.

33. Krista McQuade and Benjamin Gomes-Casseres, "Xerox and Fuji Xerox," Case 9-391-156 (Boston: Harvard Business School, 1991), 8–10, 18–19.

34. Xerox Corporation, "Environment, Health and Safety 1996 Progress Report" (Webster, N.Y.), 3.

35. Xerox Corporation, "Environment, Health and Safety Progress Report 1995" (Webster, N.Y.), 13–14; Xerox Corporation, "Environment, Health and Safety 1996 Progress Report," 12–15.

36. Xerox Corporation, "Environment, Health and Safety 1996 Progress Report," 7.

37. Xerox Corporation, "Environment, Health and Safety Progress Report 1995," 14.

38. Xerox Corporation, "Environment, Health and Safety 1996 Progress Report," 17.

39. Quoted in Fiona Murray and Richard Vietor, "Xerox: Design for the Environment," Case 9-794-022 (Boston: Harvard Business School, 1993), 6, reprinted in Forest Reinhardt and Richard H. K. Vietor, *Business Management and the Natural Environment: Cases and Text* (Cincinnati: South-Western, 1996).

40. Quoted in Murray and Vietor, "Xerox: Design for the Environment," 9, 18, 13.

41. Dr. Rainer Kaufel, Ciba Specialty Chemicals, interview, Basel, Switzerland, 1 September 1997.

42. Further discussion of risk and uncertainty appears in chapter 6; incentive systems are discussed in chapter 7.

43. See, for example, Stuart Hart and Gautam Ahuja, "Does it Pay to be Green? An Empirical Examination of the Relationship Between Emission Reduction and Firm Performance," *Business Strategy and the Environment* 5 (1996): 30–37.

44. Stanley J. Feldman, Peter A. Soyka, and Paul Ameer, "Does Improving a Firm's Environmental Management System and Environmental Performance Result in a Higher Stock Price?" (Fairfax, Va.: ICF Kaiser International, 1996).

45. Stephan Schmidheiny and Federico J.L. Zorraquin, *Financing Change: The Financial Community, Eco-Efficiency, and Sustainable Development* (Cambridge: MIT Press, 1996), 84–89.

46. See, for example, John Rothchild, "Why I Invest with Sinners," *Fortune*, 13 May 1996, 197.

47. McDonald's Corporation and Environmental Defense Fund Waste Reduction Task Force, *Final Report* (April 1991). Public documents produced by McDonald's and by the Task Force did not include any data on the cost impacts of the waste reduction measures, although the waste reduction data appear to imply that the firm did realize some savings.

48. "McDonald's Corporation," in W. Earl Sasser, Kim B. Clark, David A. Garvin, Margaret B. W. Graham, Ramchandran Jaikumar, and David H. Maister, *Cases in Operations Management: Analysis and Action* (Homewood, Ill.: Richard Irwin, 1982).

49. See Theodore Panayotou and Clifford Zinnes, "Free-Lunch Economics for Industrial Ecologists," in *Industrial Ecology and Global Change*, ed. Robert Socolow, Clinton

Andrews, Frans Berkhout, and Valerie Thomas (Cambridge: Cambridge University Press, 1994), 383–397.

50. Edward Prewitt and Richard H. K. Vietor, "Allied-Signal: Managing the Hazardous Waste Liability Risk," Case 9-793-044 (Boston: Harvard Business School, 1992), reprinted in Forest Reinhardt and Richard H. K. Vietor, *Business Management and the Natural Environment: Cases and Text* (Cincinnati: South-Western, 1996).

51. See Panayotou and Zinnes, "Free-Lunch Economics for Industrial Ecologists," 383–397, for a formal treatment of this question. See also the Porter and van der Linde pieces cited in note 2.

52. Incentive design is discussed in more detail in chapter 7.

53. See, for example, Peter J. Kolesar, "Vision, Values, Milestones: Paul O'Neill Starts Total Quality at Alcoa," *California Management Review* 35, no. 3 (spring 1933): 133–165.

54. Nelson, "Finding and Implementing Projects That Reduce Waste," 379.

55. Jeffrey Rayport and George Lodge, "Responsible Care," Case 9-391-135 (Boston: Harvard Business School, 1991), 17.

Chapter 5

1. See, for example, John Elkington, "Towards the Sustainable Corporation: Win-Win-Win Business Strategies for Sustainable Development," *California Management Review* 36, no. 2 (winter 1994): 90–100.

2. Fiona Murray and Richard H. K. Vietor, "Xerox: Design for the Environment," Case 9-794-022 (Boston: Harvard Business School, 1993), 7–9; reprinted in Forest Reinhardt and Vietor, *Business Management and the Natural Environment: Cases and Text* (Cincinnati: South-Western, 1996).

3. Xerox Corporation, "Asset Recycling at Xerox, in Enviroene Technical/Research & Development Information Pollution Prevention Case Studies," compiled by U.S. EPA (http://es.epa.gov/techinfo/case/comm/asset-d.html, accessed 16 April 1998).

4. Xerox Corporation, "Environment, Health and Safety 1996 Progress Report" (Webster, N.Y.), 20.

5. Xerox Corporation, "Environment, Health and Safety Progress Report 1995" (Webster, N.Y.), 11.

6. Murray and Vietor, "Xerox: Design for the Environment," 12.

7. Xerox Corporation, "Environment, Health and Safety Progress Report 1995," 10.

8. Ibid., 8.

9. Ibid., 9–10.

10. Xerox Corporation, "1996 Annual Report." In 1995, Xerox took a $1.65 billion loss on its discontinued financial services operations, so its consolidated after-tax loss that year was $470 million.

11. Murray and Vietor, "Xerox: Design for the Environment," 15.

12. For overviews of the regulation of natural monopoly, see Stephen Breyer, *Regulation and Its Reform* (Cambridge: Harvard University Press, 1982); W. Kip Viscusi, John M. Vernon, and Joseph E. Harrington Jr., *Economics of Regulation and Antitrust*, 2d ed. (Cambridge: MIT Press, 1995).

13. Robert E. Taylor, *Ahead of the Curve: Shaping New Solutions to Environmental Problems* (New York: Environmental Defense Fund, 1990), 84–97; David Roe,

Dynamos and Virgins (New York: Random House, 1984), 157–196. Roe's book is a personal and highly readable account of early demand-side management initiatives from the perspective of an attorney at the Environmental Defense Fund.

14. Joseph Eto, *The Past, Present, and Future of U.S. Utility Demand-Side Management Programs* (Berkeley: Lawrence Berkeley National Laboratory, December 1966).

15. Timothy J. Brennan, Karen L. Palmer, Raymond J. Kopp, Alan J. Krupnick, Vito Stagliano, and Dallas Burtraw, *A Shock to the System: Restructuring America's Electricity Industry* (Washington, D.C.: Resources for the Future, 1996), 37–59, 122–124; Eto, *The Past, Present, and Future of U.S. Utility Demand-Side Management Programs;* "NEES [New England Electric System] Proposes Five-Year, $250-Million Plan to Wed Efficiency and Competition," *Energy Services and Telecom Report,* 31 July 1997, 3.

16. "Regulators Kill All Georgia DSM Programs That Fail Rate Impact Test," *Electric Utility Week's Demand-Side Report,* 17 August 1995; "Connecticut tells United Illuminating to Drop Most DSM Programs by July," *Northeast Power Report,* 11 April 1997, 2.

17. U.S. Energy Information Administration, "U.S. Electric Utility Demand-Side Management 1996," DOE/EIA-0589(96) (Washington D.C., December 1977).

18. See George Loewenstein and Drazen Prelec, "Anomalies in Intertemporal Choice: Evidence and an Interpretation," in *Choice over Time,* ed. George Loewenstein and Jon Elster (New York: Russell Sage Foundation, 1992); Jerry A. Hausman, "Individual Discount Rates and the Purchase and Utilization of Energy-Using Durables," *Bell Journal of Economics* 10, no. 1 (1979): 33–54; Dermot Gately, "Individual Discount Rates and the Purchase and Utilization of Energy-Using Durables: Comment," *Bell Journal of Economics* 11 (1980): 373–374.

19. Amory B. Lovins and L. Hunter Lovins, "Least-Cost Climatic Stabilization," *Annual Review of Energy and the Environment* 16 (1991): 433–531.

20. Eto, *The Past, Present, and Future of U.S. Utility Demand-Side Management Programs,* 11; U.S. Bureau of the Census, *Statistical Abstract of the United States: 1996,* 116th ed. (Washington, D.C., 1996).

21. Forest Reinhardt, "Acid Rain: The Southern Company (A)," Case 9-792-060 (Boston: Harvard Business School, 1992); reprinted in Forest Reinhardt and Richard H. K. Vietor, *Business Management and the Natural Environment: Cases and Text* (Cincinnati: South-Western, 1996).

22. Ron Stodghill II, "So Shall Monsanto Reap?" *Business Week,* 1 April 1996, 66.

23. Monsanto Company, "Biotechnology: Solutions for Tomorrow's World" (St. Louis, 1996).

24. Monsanto Company, *1997 Annual Report* (St. Louis); Monsanto Company, *1997 Report on Sustainable Development Including Environmental, Safety and Health Performance* (St. Louis, 1998).

25. "Plant Biotech: Transgenic Crops Head to Market," *Chemical Week,* 27 September 1995, 25; "EU Approves Four Biotech Crops," *Chemical Week,* 25 March 1998, 8; Andrew Wood and Peter Fairlie, "Biotech Crops Flourish," *Chemical Week,* 4–11 February 1998, 27.

26. Monsanto Company, "Yieldgard™ Technical Guide" (St. Louis, 1996); Joan Magretta, "Growth through Global Sustainability: An Interview with Monsanto's CEO, Robert B. Shapiro," *Harvard Business Review* 75, no. 1 (January-February 1997): 78–88; Monsanto Company, "Biotechnology"; Monsanto Company, *1997 Annual Report;* Monsanto Company, *1997 Report on Sustainable Development.*

27. Barnaby J. Feder, "Out of the Lab, a Revolution on the Farm," *New York Times,* 3 March 1996, 3-3.

28. Robert Steyer, "Farmers Go to Seed to Halt Pests; Genetically Engineered Corn Will Battle European Borer," *St. Louis Post-Dispatch*, 7 October 1996, 12.

29. Repps Hudson, "Resistant Plants Are Threatened; Environmental Groups Plan Suits Against EPA," *St. Louis Post-Dispatch*, 18 September 1997, 1-C.

30. Feder, "Out of the Lab," 3-3.

31. Robert Steyer, "Farmers Are Warming to Altered Seed," *St. Louis Post-Dispatch*, 29 March 1998, G-1.

32. Monsanto Company, "Sustainability in Action: POSILAC® Bovine Somatotropin Improves Dairy Efficiency" (St. Louis: n.d.).

33. "FDA Approves Monsanto's Milk Producing Hormone," *Chemical Marketing Reporter*, 15 November 1993, 3.

34. Robert Steyer, "Will Monsanto's BST Send Flood of Milk into Supermarkets?" *St. Louis Post-Dispatch*, 6 December 1993, 12; Barnaby J. Feder, "Business Technology; Wider Use of Cow Drug Is Reported," *New York Times*, 1 February 1995, D-4; Steven H. Lee, "Dairymen's Dilemma; Milk Producers Weighing Risks of Hormone Use," *Dallas Morning News*, 17 February 1994, 1-D; Robert Steyer, "Monsanto Offers Discounts Again on BST," *St. Louis Post-Dispatch*, 16 March 1995, 8-C; Peter Fritsch and Scott Kilman, "Growth Hormone Sales Go Sour for Monsanto," *Capital Times* [Madison, Wisconsin], 17 August 1996, 3-C.

35. Stodghill, "So Shall Monsanto Reap?" 66; Robert Steyer, "BST Continues to Lose Money for Monsanto; Sales Fall Short of Expectation," *St. Louis Post-Dispatch*, 11 February 1996, 1-E.

36. "BST Moratorium until the End of the Century," *Agra Europe*, 16 December 1994, E-8.

37. Monsanto Company, *1997 Report on Sustainable Development*; "EU Approves Four Biotech Crops," *Chemical Week*, 25 March 1998, 8.

38. Repps Hudson, "Resistant Plants Threatened; Environmental Groups Plan Suits against EPA," *St. Louis Post-Dispatch*, 18 September 1997, 1-C.

39. "Scientists Question EPA's Resistance Management Strategy for Transgenic Bt Crops," *Pesticide and Toxic Chemical News*, 21 January 1998.

40. "Union of Concerned Scientists Urges EPA to Adopt New Bt Resistance Management Plans," *Pesticide and Toxic Chemical News*, 4 February 1998.

41. Feder, "Out of the Lab," 3-3.

42. Quoted in Linda Grant, "Monsanto's Bet: There's Gold in Going Green," *Fortune*, 14 April 1997, 116–118.

43. Livio D. DeSimone and Frank Popoff, *Eco-efficiency: The Business Link to Sustainable Development* (Cambridge: MIT Press, 1997), 48.

44. Ibid., 47–48.

45. Magretta, "Growth through Global Sustainability," 83; italics in original.

46. Daniel B. Luten, "The Limits-to-Growth Controversy," in *Sourcebook on the Environment*, ed. K. A. Hammond, G. Macinko, and W. Fairchild (Chicago: University of Chicago Press, 1978), reprinted in *Progress against Growth: Daniel B. Luten on the American Landscape*, ed. Thomas Vale (New York: Guilford Press, 1986).

47. Audi AG, "Striking a Balance: Environmental Protection at Audi" (Ingolstadt, Germany: Audi AG, 1996).

48. Robert Solow, "The Economics of Resources or the Resources of Economics," *American Economic Review* 64, no. 2 (May 1974): 1–14; Solow, *An Almost Practical Step toward Sustainability* (Washington, D.C.: Resources for the Future, 1992).

49. See Douglass C. North, *Institutions, Institutional Change and Economic Performance* (Cambridge: Cambridge University Press, 1990), especially chap. 5.

Chapter 6

1. See, for example, Richard Brealey and Stewart Myers, *Principles of Corporate Finance*, 5th ed. (New York: McGraw-Hill, 1996), 143–146.

2. U.S. Environmental Protection Agency Science Advisory Board, "Reducing Risk: Setting Priorities and Strategies for Environmental Protection," September 1990, quoted in Rao V. Kolluru, "Risk Assessment and Management," in *Environmental Strategies Handbook: A Guide to Effective Policies and Practices,* ed. Rao V. Kolluru (New York: McGraw-Hill, 1994), 331.

3. See, for example, Lloyd W. Landreth, "How the Government Prosecutes Environmental Crime," *Public Utilities Fortnightly* 130, no. 4 (15 August 1992): 21ff.; Judah Best, Lance Cole, and David Darland, "Complying with Sentencing Guidelines," *National Law Journal,* 8 June 1992, 19ff.; Gary E. Marchant, "Environmental Legal Liabilities: Prevention and Control," in *Environmental Strategies Handbook: A Guide to Effective Policies and Practices,* ed. Rao V. Kolluru (New York: McGraw-Hill, 1994).

4. John S. Hammond III, Ralph L. Keeney, and Howard Raiffa, *Smart Choices: A Practical Guide to Making Better Decisions* (Boston: Harvard Business School Press, 1998).

5. Some analysts characterize this difference as one between a "well-specified probability" of loss and an "ambiguous probability," or, more concisely, as one between "risk" and "ambiguity." See, for example, Paul K. Freeman and Howard Kunreuther, *Managing Environmental Risk through Insurance* (Boston: Kluwer, 1997), 40–42. In this vocabulary, a probability can be well specified but have a high variance, or can have a low (subjective) variance but at the same time be ambiguous. Insurance industry practitioners also distinguish between risk and ambiguity: see, for example, Cornelia Wetzel-Binder and Jürg Spühler, "The Risk of Change—A Challenge for Underwriters of Liability Insurance" (Zurich: Swiss Reinsurance Company, 1995).

6. See Knight, *Risk, Uncertainty, and Profit* (1921; reprint Chicago: University of Chicago Press, 1971), 233; Milton Friedman and Leonard J. Savage, "The Utility of Choices Involving Risk," *Journal of Political Economy* 56 (1948): 279–304.

7. This taxonomy is related closely to those discussed by experts on financial risk management. For example, Robert Merton and Zvi Bodie, in their textbook *Finance* (Upper Saddle River, N.J.: Prentice Hall, 1998, 223–227), discuss four basic risk management approaches: risk avoidance, loss prevention and control, risk retention, and risk transfer. Risk avoidance means eliminating exposure to the risk by ceasing the activity associated with it (in the oil spill case, this might mean getting out of the oil shipping business altogether; but even that drastic course might not eliminate the oil company's risk if other companies' ships continue to transport its crude oil). Loss prevention and control encompasses both reducing probabilities and reducing contingent impacts. Risk retention means bearing risk internally. And risk transfer is analogous to the third factor: reducing the amount of damage for which the firm is responsible. Merton and Bodie point out that in general this can be done through hedging, insurance, or diversification; environmental risk is most commonly transferred through insurance, since hedging instruments tend not to exist.

8. For a comprehensive overview of the historical development of government risk management practices, see David A. Moss, "Public Risk Management and the Private Sector: An Exploratory Essay," working paper 98–073, Harvard Business School, Boston, 1998.

9. The first of these problems is called adverse selection; the second, moral hazard. Both cause difficulties for risk management, whether in the governmental arena or in firms. The difference between the two is memorably summarized by Paul Milgrom and John Roberts in an example involving the drivers of Volvo cars. Volvos have a reputation as cars constructed so as to provide unusually high levels of traffic safety for their owners. In a 1990 study in the Washington, D.C., area, Volvos were overrepresented among cars that ran stop signs. Was this because drivers who knew themselves to be accident-prone bought Volvos to protect themselves against their own poor driving (a selection argument)? Or did the cars' tanklike qualities encourage drivers, once they had purchased a Volvo, to behave more recklessly (moral hazard)? See *Economics, Organization and Management* (Englewood Cliffs, N.J.: Prentice Hall, 1992), 169.

10. See David Fite and Paul Pfleiderer, "Should Firms Use Derivatives to Manage Risk?" in *Risk Management: Problems and Solutions,* ed. William H. Beaver and George Parker (New York: McGraw-Hill, 1995), 139–169. See also Kenneth A. Froot, David S. Scharfstein, and Jeremy C. Stein, "Risk Management: Coordinating Corporate Investment and Financing Policies," *Journal of Finance* 48, no. 5 (December 1993): 1629–1658; and Froot, Scharfstein, and Stein, "A Framework for Risk Management," *Harvard Business Review* 72, no. 6 (November–December 1994); 91–102.

11. Darryl Hebert, environmental manager, Alberta-Pacific forestry operations, interview, 19 November 1993.

12. Alberta-Pacific's mill is capable of making totally chlorine free (TCF) pulp, using neither chlorine gas nor chlorine dioxide, but the costs would be higher and the pulp would not be as bright. Alberta-Pacific planned to concentrate on making ECF pulp. As of 1998, it had not produced any TCF pulp because demand was insufficient to allow the firm to recapture the additional variable costs of producing it. Mac Palmiere, Alberta-Pacific, personal communication, 6 September 1998.

13. Ibid.

14. Carol Fries, environmental manager, Alberta-Pacific mill operations, interview, 19 November 1993.

15. Doug Sklar, Alberta-Pacific forestry operations, interview, 19 November 1993.

16. Darryl Hebert, environmental manager, Alberta-Pacific forestry operations, interview, 19 November 1993.

17. Bart Johnson, "PCs Use Report to Back Al-Pac Pact," *Edmonton Sun,* 20 May 1998, 16; "Alberta Government Loan Repaid" and "CFI Withdraws from Joint Venture," *Forest Landscape* [a newsletter published by Alberta-Pacific Forest Industries Inc.], 1–2.

18. Forest Reinhardt, "Alberta-Pacific Forest Industries Inc.," Case 9-794-099 (Boston: Harvard Business School, 1994), 17–18, reprinted in Forest Reinhardt and Richard H. K. Vietor, *Business Management and the Natural Environment: Cases and Text* (Cincinnati: South-Western, 1996).

19. Gerry Fenner, vice president, Alberta-Pacific Forest Industries, interview, 19 November 1993.

20. See, for example, Linda Sandler, "Knightly Warren Buffett Trips Up 'Rescued' Champion Investors," *Wall Street Journal,* 15 December 1989, C1.

21. Champion's return on book equity from continuing operations over the eighteen-year period from 1978 to 1996 was 6.3 percent. It was, further, quite cyclical: 17 percent in the inflationary year of 1979, 14 percent at the peak of the next business cycle in 1987 and 1988, and 23 percent in 1995, an excellent year throughout the industry; but less than 3 percent in six other years.

22. Champion International Corporation, *Fact Book 1996* (Stamford, Conn.).

23. Richard A. Bartlett, *Troubled Waters: Champion International and the Pigeon River Controversy* (Knoxville: University of Tennessee Press, 1995), 44.

24. Jaakko Pöyry Oy, *Complementary Scientific Review of the Proposed Alberta-Pacific Pulp Mill Project Environmental Impact Assessment: Main Report* (Helsinki, [consultant report published by firm]: Jaakko Pöyry Oy, 1990); U.S. Bureau of the Census, *Statistical Abstract of the United States: 1996*, 116th ed. (Washington, D.C., 1996).

25. "Hail to Champion: Champion International Corp. is *Papermaker's* 'Company of the Year,'" *American Papermaker*, June 1995, 23–25.

26. "Champion Finds Solutions to Environmental Problems," *American Papermaker*, June 1995, 30–31.

27. Richard Diforio, senior vice president, Champion International Corporation, personal communication, 30 November 1998.

28. The "cluster rule" was so called because the EPA, in a departure from historic practice, wrote standards for air and water pollution simultaneously. The idea was to avoid imposing water pollution requirements that would worsen air pollution problems, and vice versa; the EPA also hoped to increase the overall cost-effectiveness of the regulations by considering the regulated mill as a whole. This sort of approach had been discouraged by the way EPA's enabling statutes were written, with one focused on air, another on water, and so forth. See 63 *Federal Register* 18501–18751, 15 April 1998, available at http://www.epa.gov/ostwater/pulppaper/pulppaper.html, accessed 30 September 1998.

29. Richard Diforio, personal communication, 10 August 1998.

30. Richard Diforio, personal communication, July 1998.

31. Associated Press, "Another Suit Filed against Champion," *Chattanooga Free Press*, 25 September 1997, C2; "Federal Judge Sends Champion Suit to State Court," *Knoxville News Sentinel*, 24 February 1998, A3.

32. Richard Diforio, personal communication, 10 August 1998.

33. See Exxon Corporation, *1991 Annual Report* (Irving, Tex.), F9; John Duffield, "Nonmarket Valuation and the Courts: The Case of the *Exxon Valdez*," *Contemporary Economic Policy* 15 (October 1997): 98–110.

34. Exxon Corporation, *1996 Annual Report* (Irving, Tex.), F16.

35. Chevron Corporation, "Policy 530," *Chevron Policy Manual* [internal document: San Francisco, 1989].

36. Chevron's internal audit program is discussed in more detail in chapter 7.

37. Chevron Corporation, "Protecting People and the Environment: Implementing Our Policy 530" [internal document: San Francisco, 1992].

38. Advertising copy provided by Chevron Corporation, San Francisco, January 1998.

39. R. J. Hunt, Chevron Chemical Company, interview, San Ramon, California, 26 March 1998.

40. See Monica Mandelli, Jennifer L. Burns, and Forest Reinhardt, "Environmental Risk Management at Chevron Corporation," Case 9-799-062 (Boston: Harvard Business School, 1999).

41. Susan Stendebach, U.S. Environmental Protection Agency, interview with research associate J. P. Gownder, September 1998.

42. See International Cooperative for Environmental Leadership, "The International Cooperative for Ozone Layer Protection (ICOLP) 1990 to 1995: A New Sprit of Industry and Government Cooperation," at http://www.icel.org/heritage.htm, accessed 15 June 1998. ICOLP's founder members included AT&T, Boeing, Digital Equipment Corporation, Ford, General Electric, Honeywell, Motorola, Nortel, and Texas Instruments.

43. Xerox Corporation, *Environment, Health, and Safety Requirements for Suppliers (EH&S1001)* (Webster, N.Y., 1997).

44. June Andersen and Hsia Choong, "The Development of an Industry Standard Supply-Base Environmental Practices Questionnaire" (paper presented at Institute of Electrical and Electronics Engineers, Inc., Technical Activities Board, International Symposium on Electronics and the Environment, San Francisco, May 1997).

45. "Procuring environmentally responsible material: Meeting HP's commitment to the environment," [Palo Alto:] Hewlett-Packard Company, 1995; Hsia Choong, Hewlett-Packard Company, personal communication, 31 August 1998.

46. "HP has found that to achieve environmental goals, there must be cooperation and open dialogue between parties. Effective relations are based on mutual trust and long-term commitments. Joint problem-solving and goal-setting between HP and the suppliers are much more effective in improving environmental outcomes than mandates or other approaches are." Susan Resetar, Frank Camm, and Jeffrey Drezner, *Environmental Management in Design: Lessons from Volvo and Hewlett-Packard for the Department of Defense* (Santa Monica, Calif.: RAND, 1998), 140.

47. William H. Rodgers, *Environmental Law* (St. Paul, Minn.: West Publishing, 1994), 657.

48. Gary E. Marchant, "Environmental Legal Liabilities: Prevention and Control," in *Environmental Strategies Handbook: A Guide to Effective Policies and Practices,* ed. Rao V. Kolluru (New York: McGraw-Hill, 1994).

49. For a comprehensive analysis of the prevalence of command-and-control regulation, see Nathaniel O. Keohane, Richard L. Revesz, and Robert N. Stavins, "The Choice of Regulatory Instruments in Environmental Policy," *Harvard Environmental Law Review* 22 (1998): 313–367.

50. For an accessible introduction, see Charles W. Smithson, Clifford W. Smith Jr., and D. Sykes Clifford, *Managing Financial Risk: A Guide to Derivative Products, Financial Engineering, and Value Maximization* (Burr Ridge, Ill.: Irwin Professional Publishing, 1995).

51. A useful treatment of this issue is H. Landis Gabel and Bernard Sinclair Desgagné, "Corporate Responses to Environmental Concerns," in *Principles of Environmental and Resource Economics,* ed. Henk Folmer, H. Landis Gabel, and Hans Opschoor, (Cheltenham, UK: Edward Elgar, 1995), 347–362.

52. The decision is discussed in Loyti Cheng and Katrin N. Rouner, "The Fleet Factors Decision: Implications for Lender Liability," *Journal of Environmental Law and Practice* (September–October 1993); 56–64.

53. Marchant, "Environmental Legal Liabilities," 310.

54. Frank Friedman, "Is This Job Worth It?" *Environmental Forum* 8, no. 3 (May–June 1991), 23, quoted in Jackie Prince Roberts, Richard H. K. Vietor, and Forest Reinhardt, "Note on Contingent Environmental Liabilities," Case 9-794-098 (Boston: Harvard Business School, 1994); reprinted in Reinhardt and Vietor, *Business Management and the Natural Environment: Cases and Text* (Cincinnati: South-Western, 1996.

55. U.S. Department of Justice, "Factors and Decisions on Criminal Prosecutions for Environmental Violations in the Context of Significant Voluntary Compliance or Disclosure Efforts by the Violator," Washington, D.C.: 1 July 1991, quoted in Lloyd W. Landreth, "How the Government Prosecutes Environmental Crime," *Public Utilities Fortnightly*, 15 August 1992, 21ff.

56. Irvin B. Nathan and Michael B. Gerrard, "In-House Probes Reveal Liabilities," *National Law Journal*, 14 October 1996, C1ff.

57. "Statement of Paul G. Wallach, Esq., Senior Partner, Hale and Dorr, LLP, on behalf of the National Association of Manufacturers (NAM) and the Corporate Environmental Enforcement Counsel (CEEC), before the Committee on Environment and Public Works, United States Senate, 30 October 1997" [Washington, D.C.: Hale and Dorr]; Paul Wallach, personal communication, 20 March 1998.

Chapter 7

1. These categories are discussed by Kenneth Boulding, who identified three incentive mechanisms that he asserted were qualitatively different from one another. They are threat, exchange, and the "integrative system," which "involves such things as status, identity, love, hate, benevolence, malevolence, legitimacy." Kenneth Boulding, "Economic Libertarianism," in *Beyond Economics: Essays on Society, Religion and Ethics* (Ann Arbor: University of Michigan Press, 1968), 43–54.

2. See Douglass North, *Structure and Change in Economic History* (New York: Norton, 1981), 45–58; North, *Institutions, Institutional Change and Economic Performance* (Cambridge: Cambridge University Press, 1990).

3. See, for example, Monsanto Company, *1997 Annual Report* (St. Louis), 11; Monsanto Company, *1997 Report on Sustainable Development Including Environmental, Safety and Health Performance* (St. Louis).

4. DDT is dichlorodiphenyltrichloroethane. For the early history of Monsanto, see Dan J. Forrestal, *Faith, Hope and $5,000: The Story of Monsanto* (New York: Simon and Schuster, 1977).

5. 2,4,5-T is 2,4,5-trichlorophenoxyacetic acid. See U.S. Environmental Protection Agency Office of Pesticide Programs, "List of Pesticides Banned and Severely Restricted in the U.S.," (http://www.epa.gov/oppfead1/international/piclist.htm, accessed 3 August 1998).

6. Rachel Carson, *Silent Spring* (1962; reprint, with introduction by Al Gore, Boston: Houghton Mifflin, 1994); Forrestal, *Faith, Hope and $5,000*.

7. See Robert V. Percival, Alan S. Miller, Christopher H. Schroeder, and James P. Leape, *Environmental Regulation: Law, Science, and Policy*, 2d ed. (Boston: Little, Brown, 1996), 647ff. The substances were not explicitly listed in the legislation; an already existing EPA list of "extremely hazardous substances" was incorporated by reference in the statute.

8. See "Goals, Measurement, and Accountability: Monsanto," in *Beyond Compliance: A New Industry View of the Environment*, ed. Bruce Smart (Washington, D.C.: World Resources Institute, 1992); and Nicholas Reding, "Finding People to Make It Happen: Monsanto," in the same volume.

9. Monsanto Company, *Environmental Annual Review July 1991* (St. Louis), 3.

10. Monsanto Company, *1992 Corporate Data Book* (St. Louis), 23.

11. "The Corporate Elite: Chief Executives of the Business Week 1000," *Business Week* (special issue), 1990; Forrestal, *Faith, Hope and $5,000*.

12. Monsanto Company, *1996 Annual Report to Shareowners* (St. Louis), 5.

13. Joan Magretta, "Growth through Global Sustainability: An Interview with Monsanto's CEO, Robert B. Shapiro," *Harvard Business Review* 75, no. 1 (January–February 1997), 78–88, quotation on 80–81. In *An Essay on the Principle of Population*, first published in 1798, Thomas Robert Malthus postulated that human populations tend to grow geometrically, while food production tends to grow arithmetically; Malthus reasoned that this disparity would lead inevitably to severe food shortages and hence to "misery and vice," (Norton Critical Edition, ed. Philip Appleman [New York: Norton, 1976], 20). Widely thought discredited among economists, Malthus has heavily influenced the thinking of biologists and other scientists concerned with environmental questions. See Daniel B. Luten, "The Limits-to-Growth Controversy," *Sourcebook on the Environment,* in e.d. K. A. Hammond, G. Macinko, and W. Fairchild (Chicago: University of Chicago Press, 1978), reprinted in *Progress against Growth: Daniel B. Luten on the American Landscape,* ed. Thomas R. Vale (New York: Guilford Press, 1986).

14. In Monsanto's 1994 annual report, issued about the time of Shapiro's accession, he appears in a photograph with Mahoney; both wear suits. In the 1995 annual report, Shapiro wears a tie but no jacket. In 1996, he wears a plaid shirt.

15. Monsanto Company, *1997 Report on Sustainable Development*, 4–5.

16. Ibid., 5.

17. Ibid., 19.

18. "Splicing Drugs and Agriculture," *Chemical Week*, 29 October 1997, 33ff.

19. See, for example, "American Home Products, Monsanto Agree to Combine," *Wall Street Journal*, 2 June 1998; Ron Winslow and Scott Kilman, "Merger Is Experiment in Splicing Together Two Chief Executives," *Wall Street Journal*, 2 June 1998; Clive Cookson and Nikki Tait, "From Corn to Cancer," *Financial Times*, 2 June 1998, 17.

20. Thomas M. Burton and Elyse Tanouye, "Another Drug Industry Megamerger Goes Bust: Clash of Cultures Kills Monsanto, AHP Marriage," *Wall Street Journal*, 14 October 1998.

21. Clive Cookson and Nikki Tait, "Monsanto Dismisses Charles' Attack on Genetic Engineering," *Financial Times*, 9 June 1998, 20 (Britain's Prince Charles is among the critics of biotechnology).

22. Youssef M. Ibrahim, "Genetic Soybeans Alarm Europeans," *New York Times*, 7 November 1996, D1.

23. Alison Maitland, "Genetic Feast or Famine: Designer Crops, from Maize to Soyabeans, Are Spreading with Phenomenal Speed – Except in Europe," *Financial Times*, 9 January 1998, 15; "Manipulating the Genetic Debate [Leader]," *Financial Times*, 9 June 1998, 19.

24. Steve Farrar and Margarette Driscoll, "Is It Safe?" *London Sunday Times*, 14 February 1999.

25. Union of Concerned Scientists, "Biotechnology FAQs" (http://www.ucsusa.org/agriculture/gen.faqs.html, accessed 13 October 1998).

26. Monsanto Company, *1997 Report on Sustainable Development*, 19.

27. Ibid., 20–21.

28. Monsanto Company, *1995 Annual Report* (St. Louis), 22.

29. Gerald T. White, *Formative Years in the Far West: A History of Standard Oil Company of California and Predecessors through 1919* (New York: Appleton-Century-Crofts, 1962), chap. 1.

30. See Ibid.; Harold J. Haynes, *Standard Oil Company of California: 100 Years Helping to Create the Future* (New York: Newcomen Society in North America, 1980).

31. See Daniel Yergin, *The Prize: The Epic Quest for Oil, Money, and Power* (New York: Simon and Schuster, 1991), 738–742; William H. Miller, "Chevron Bridges the Gulf," *Industry Week*, 12 May 1986, 65.

32. Haynes, *Standard Oil Company of California*.

33. See Richard H. K. Vietor, *Energy Policy in America since 1945* (Cambridge: Cambridge University Press, 1984), 229; Samuel P. Hays, *Beauty, Health, and Permanence: Environmental Politics in the United States, 1955–1985* (Cambridge: Cambridge University Press, 1987), 52.

34. Chevron Corporation, *1997 Annual Report* (San Francisco, 1998), 1.

35. Chevron Corporation, *1997 Annual Report*, inside front cover.

36. Chevron Corporation, *Chevron Policy Manual, Policy 530* [internal company document: San Francisco, 1989].

37. Chevron Corporation, *Protecting People and the Environment: Implementing Our Policy 530* [internal company document: San Francisco, 1992].

38. Chevron Corporation, *1997 Annual Report*, 23.

39. "Engaging the Organization: Chevron," in *Beyond Compliance: A New Industry View of the Environment*, ed. Bruce Smart (Washington, D.C.: World Resources Institute, 1992), 101–105.

40. John Quelch, "Chevron Corporation: Corporate Image Advertising," Case 9-591-005 (Boston: Harvard Business School, 1991), 2.

41. Quoted in ibid.

42. Advertising copy provided by Chevron Corporation, San Francisco, January 1998.

43. "Beyond Corporate Walls: Chevron," in *Beyond Compliance: A New Industry View of the Environment*, ed. Bruce Smart (Washington, D.C.: World Resources Institute, 1992), 163–166.

44. James N. Sullivan, "Five Things I've Always Wanted to Tell a Room Full of Crisis Management Professionals," American Petroleum Institute Crisis Seminar, San Francisco, 11 September 1996, available at http://www.chevron.com/newsvs/index.html, accessed 26 April 1999. The study to which Sullivan refers is Charles J. Fombrun, *Reputation: Realizing Value from the Corporate Image* (Boston: Harvard Business School Press, 1996); the "value of reputation" in this study is just the market value of the firm's equity minus the book value of the equity.

45. John Browne, "Climate Change: The New Agenda, A Presentation to Stanford University, California," 19 May 1997 (London: British Petroleum Company, May 1997).

46. John Browne, "Climate Change: the policy options, A presentation at the Berlin Parliament," Germany, 30 September 1997 (London: The British Petroleum Company, September 1997).

47. BP's emissions in 1990 were about 40 million tons, and BP planned to lower this annual figure to 36 million tons. In the absence of this initiative, a BP spokesman asserted that 2010 emissions would be 58 million tons, so (depending on the baseline chosen) the cuts could be seen as larger than 10 percent. See Alan Cowell, "British Petroleum Planning 'Firm' Cuts in Emissions," *New York Times*, 19 September 1998; Martha M. Hamilton, "British Petroleum Sets Goal of 10% Cut in 'Greenhouse' Gases," *Washington Post*, 18 September 1998. The planned cuts applied only to carbon dioxide emitted during BP's own operations, not to carbon dioxide emitted when its products were burned in customers' vehicles; product-related emissions were several times as great as the process emissions.

48. Lee R. Raymond, "Energy—key to growth and better environment for Asia-Pacific Nations," Remarks at World Petroleum Congress, Beijing, People's Republic of China, 13 October 1997, available at http://www.exxon.com/exxoncorp/main_frame_1.html, accessed 26 April 1999.

49. Mark Keller, personal communication, 7 August 1998.

50. For the early history of Georgia-Pacific see Owen R. Cheatham and Robert B. Pamplin, *The Georgia-Pacific Story* (New York: Newcomen Society in North America, 1966); T. Marshall Hahn Jr., *Georgia-Pacific Corporation: "The Growth Company"* (New York: Newcomen Society of the United States, 1990).

51. John R. Ross, *Maverick: The Story of Georgia-Pacific Corporation* (Portland, Oreg.: Georgia-Pacific, 1980), 233ff.

52. Hahn, *Georgia-Pacific Corporation.*

53. Forest Reinhardt, "Champion International Corporation: Timber, Trade, and the Northern Spotted Owl," Case 9-792-017 (Boston: Harvard Business School, 1991), reprinted in Forest Reinhardt and Richard H. K. Vietor, *Business Management and the Natural Environment: Cases and Text* (Cincinnati: South-Western, 1996).

54. Jackie Prince Roberts, Richard H. K. Vietor, and Forest Reinhardt, "Note on Contingent Environmental Liabilities," Case number 9-794-098 (Boston: Harvard Business School, 1994), reprinted in Reinhardt and Vietor, *Business Management and the Natural Environment: Cases and Text* (Cincinnati: South-Western, 1996); Susan Harte, "$3.2 Million Judgment against G-P over Alleged Dioxin Release Thrown Out," *Atlanta Journal and Constitution*, 20 October 1995, 3F; "Business in Brief: Georgia-Pacific Dioxin Verdict Reversed," *Atlanta Journal and Constitution*, 14 December 1996, 03H.

55. Ross, *Maverick*, 286.

56. Kelly Ferguson, "Georgia-Pacific: Deals, Debt, and Redirection," *Pulp and Paper* 68, no. 3 (March 1994), 34.

57. Jim Bostic, interview, Atlanta, 19 November 1997.

58. John Rasor, interview, Atlanta, 19 November 1997.

59. John Rasor and Donald Glass, interview, Atlanta, 19 November 1997.

60. Susan Moore, interview, Atlanta, 29 May 1998.

61. Georgia-Pacific Corporation, *Forests for the Future: Georgia-Pacific's Commitment to Sustainable Forestry* (Atlanta, 1995), 14.

62. John Rasor, interview, Atlanta, 19 November 1997.

63. Chris Burritt, "One-of-a-Kind Deal: Unique Environmental Pact with Georgia-Pacific Will Protect One of the Nation's 'Last Great Places,'" *Atlanta Constitution*, 18 December 1994, M4.

64. Kevin G. Salwen, "Environmentalists, Southern Firms Learn a New Trick: Getting Along," *Wall Street Journal (Southeast Journal)*, 23 November 1994, S1.

65. Ferguson, "Georgia-Pacific," 34.

66. Georgia-Pacific Corporation, *1997 Annual Report* (Atlanta, 1998), 13.

67. Ibid., 6.

68. John Rasor, interview, Atlanta, 19 November 1997.

69. The 0.4 to 3 tons per acre figure is converted from Intergovernmental Panel on Climate Change, *Climate Change 1995: Economic and Social Dimensions of Climate Change* (Cambridge: Cambridge University Press, 1996), 247. In 1998 Janet Yellen

of the President's Council of Economic Advisers cited figures of fourteen to twenty-three dollars per ton of carbon as the approximate cost, with international trading of emissions rights, of reaching the targets set out in the Kyoto Protocol negotiated in December 1997. Given these numbers, the gross carbon sequestration services performed annually by Georgia-Pacific's 5.5 million acres of timberlands are worth somewhere between $30 and $400 million. This number indicates the magnitude of the issue for the companies; its range indicates the difficulty of assessing the actual values and constructing a working system for the accounting. The need to take into account the net effects of timber harvesting further complicates the accounting problems.

70. This taxonomy was developed by Earl Beaver, a chemical engineer and environmental manager at Monsanto Company. Beaver, interview, 6 August 1996; personal communication, 14 August 1998.

71. Monsanto Company, *1997 Report on Sustainable Development,* 20–21.

72. Quelch, "Chevron Corporation."

73. See, for example, John A. Byrne, "Jack: A Close-Up Look at How America's #1 Manager Runs GE," *Business Week,* 8 June 1998, 90ff.

74. Cited in H. Edward Wrapp, "Good Managers Don't Make Policy Decisions," *Harvard Business Review* 62, no. 4 (July–August 1984), 8ff.

75. For additional discussion of these questions, see Forest Reinhardt, "Ciba Specialty Chemicals," Case 9-799-086 (Boston: Harvard Business School, 1999).

76. Kenneth Nelson, "Finding and Implementing Projects That Reduce Waste," in *Industrial Ecology and Global Change,* ed. Robert Socolow, Clinton Andrews, Frans Berkhout, and Valerie Thomas (Cambridge: Cambridge University Press, 1994), 379.

77. For an introduction, see Forest Reinhardt, "Acid Rain: The Southern Company (A) and (B)," Cases 9-792-060 and 9-793-040 (Boston: Harvard Business School, 1992), reprinted in Reinhardt and Richard H.K. Vietor, *Business Management and the Natural Environment: Cases and Text* (Cincinnati: South-Western, 1996). See also Richard Schmalensee, Paul L. Joshow, A. Denny Ellerman, Juan Pablo Montero, and Elizabeth M. Bailey "An Interim Evaluation of Sulfur Dioxide Emissions Trading," *Journal of Economic Perspectives* 12, no. 3 (summer 1998): 53–68. Note that the permit system complements but does not supplant earlier regulations of sulfur dioxide, so that it is not possible for a firm to increase its overall emissions relative to the levels it was emitting before the 1990 amendments were passed.

78. Robert N. Stavins, ed., *Project 88—Round II: Incentives for Action: Designing Market-Based Environmental Strategies,* A Public Policy Study sponsored by Senators Timothy E. Wirth and H. John Heinz (Washington, D.C., 1990), 9.

79. From a political standpoint, this innovation had the additional advantage of spreading the costs of pollution control across a large number of consumers. Because permits were tradable, utilities that installed flue-gas desulfurization systems to reduce their emissions were able to sell surplus permits, offsetting the cost of the scrubbers. Without this cost-sharing feature, it is not clear that the legislation establishing the controls would have passed. See Richard E. Cohen, *Washington at Work: Back Rooms and Clean Air* (New York: Macmillan, 1992).

80. Kimberly O'Neill Packard and Forest Reinhardt, "Global Climate Change (A)," Case 9-798-076, 18 (Boston: Harvard Business School, 1998), citing cost estimates from the Clinton administration. See also Raymond J. Kopp and J. W. Anderson, "Estimating the Costs of Kyoto: How Plausible Are the Clinton Administration's Figures?" *Weathervane* (Washington, D.C.: Resources for the Future, March 1998), at http://www.weathervane.rff.org/features/feature034.html, accessed 9 August 1998.

81. John J. Fialka, "International Emissions Trading Is Key to Kyoto-Pact Compliance, Study Says," *Wall Street Journal*, 3 August 1998.

82. North, *Institutions, Institutional Change and Economic Performance,*7.

83. Gary Becker, "A Theory of Competition among Pressure Groups for Political Influence," *Quarterly Journal of Economics* 98 (1983): 371–400.

84. See chapter 3.

Chapter 8

1. See Forest Reinhardt and Richard H. K. Vietor, "Environmental Management: A Framework for Business Strategy," in *Business Management and the Natural Environment* (Cincinnati: South-Western, 1996). See also Vietor, *Contrived Competition: Regulation and Deregulation in America* (Cambridge: Belknap Press of Harvard University Press, 1994).

2. David Baron offers a comprehensive treatment of what he calls "the nonmarket environment" in *Business and Its Environment*, 2d ed. (Upper Saddle River, N.J.: Prentice Hall, 1996).

3. See David A. Garvin, "What Does 'Product Quality' Really Mean?" *Sloan Management Review* 26, no. 1 (fall 1984): 25–43.

4. See Robert H. Hayes, Steven C. Wheelwright, and Kim B. Clark, *Dynamic Manufacturing* (New York: Free Press, 1988), 74–76. See also John S. Hammond, Ralph L. Keeney, and Howard Raiffa, "The Hidden Traps in Decision Making," *Harvard Business Review* 76, no. 5 (September–October 1998): 47–58.

5. See, for example, Ernst U. von Weizsäcker, Amory B. Lovins, and L. Hunter Lovins, *Factor Four: Doubling Wealth, Halving Resource Use: The New Report to the Club of Rome* (London: Earthscan Publications, 1997).

6. This adage is the title of a book by Texas politician Jim Hightower (New York: HarperCollins, 1997).

7. David B. Yoffie, "The Politics of Business: How an Industry Builds Political Advantage," *Harvard Business Review* 66, no. 3 (May–June 1988): 82–89.

8. See, for example, Joseph Stiglitz, "The Private Uses of Public Interests: Incentives and Institutions," *Journal of Economic Perspectives* 12, no. 2 (spring 1998): 3–22. Stiglitz discusses the demise of improvements to the Superfund law in 1994; he mentions the role of "lobbyists, a small but influential group who, unlike the groups they were lobbying for, had little incentive for a speedy resolution of the issue" (12 n. 14).

9. John A. Byrne, "Jack: A Close-Up Look at How America's #1 Manager Runs GE," *Business Week*, 8 June 1998, 92.

Selected Bibliography

Note: The following list is a selection of the works that were most help-ful to me in developing the ideas presented in this book. The endnotes contain comprehensive information about the sources of facts on particu-lar environmental issues discussed in the book, and those sources are not all listed here.

BOOKS

Baron, David P. *Business and Its Environment.* 2d ed. Upper Saddle River, N.J.: Pren-tice Hall, 1996.

Besanko, David, David Dranove, and Mark Shanley. *Economics of Strategy.* New York: Wiley, 1996.

Brealey, Richard, and Stewart Myers. *Principles of Corporate Finance.* 5th ed. New York: McGraw-Hill, 1996.

Breyer, Stephen. *Regulation and Its Reform.* Cambridge: Harvard University Press, 1982.

Carson, Rachel. *Silent Spring.* Boston: Houghton Mifflin, 1962.

DeSimone, Livio, and Frank Popoff. *Eco-efficiency: The Business Link to Sustainable Development.* Cambridge: MIT Press, 1997.

Downs, Anthony. *An Economic Theory of Democracy.* New York: Harper and Row, 1957.

Epstein, Marc. *Measuring Corporate Environmental Performance.* Chicago: Irwin, 1996.

Folmer, Henk, H. Landis Gabel, and Hans Opschoor, eds. *Principles of Environmental and Resource Economics.* Cheltenham, UK: Edward Elgar, 1995.

Freeman, Paul K., and Howard Kunreuther. *Managing Environmental Risk through Insurance.* Boston: Kluwer Academic Publishers, 1997.

Ghemawat, Pankaj. *Games Businesses Play.* Cambridge: MIT Press, 1997.

Gore, Al. *Earth in the Balance.* Boston: Houghton Mifflin, 1992.

Hammond, John S. III, Ralph L. Keeney, and Howard Raiffa. *Smart Choices: A Practical Guide to Making Better Decisions.* Boston: Harvard Business School Press, 1999.

King, Gary, Robert O. Keohane, and Sidney Verba. *Designing Social Inquiry: Scientific Inference in Qualitative Research.* Princeton, N.J.: Princeton University Press, 1994.

Kolluru, Rao V., ed. *Environmental Strategies Handbook: A Guide to Effective Policies and Practices.* New York: McGraw-Hill, 1994.

Kotler, Philip. *Marketing Management: Analysis, Planning, Implementation, and Control.* 9th ed. Upper Saddle River, N.J.: Prentice Hall, 1997.

Mas-Colell, Andreu, Michael D. Whinston, and Jerry R. Green. *Microeconomic Theory.* New York: Oxford University Press, 1995.

Milgrom, Paul, and John Roberts. *Economics, Organization and Management.* Englewood Cliffs, N.J.: Prentice Hall, 1992.

North, Douglass C. *Institutions, Institutional Change and Economic Performance.* Cambridge: Cambridge University Press, 1990.

Olson, Mancur. *The Logic of Collective Action.* Cambridge: Harvard University Press, 1965.

Pearce, David W., ed. *The MIT Dictionary of Modern Economics.* 4th ed. Cambridge: MIT Press, 1992.

Percival, Robert V., Alan S. Miller, Christopher H. Schroeder, and James P. Leape. *Environmental Regulation: Law, Science, and Policy.* 2d ed. Boston: Little, Brown, 1996.

Porter, Michael E. *Competitive Advantage.* New York: Free Press, 1985.

———. *Competitive Strategy.* New York: Free Press, 1980.

Portney, Paul R., ed. *Public Policies for Environmental Protection.* Washington, D.C.: Resources for the Future, 1990.

Reinhardt, Forest, and Richard H. K. Vietor. *Business Management and the Natural Environment: Cases and Text.* Cincinnati: South-Western, 1996.

Schaltegger, Stefan, with Kaspar Müller and Henriette Hindricksen. *Corporate Environmental Accounting.* Chichester, U.K.: John Wiley, 1996.

Schmidheiny, Stephan. *Changing Course.* Cambridge: MIT Press, 1992.

Smart, Bruce, ed. *Beyond Compliance: A New Industry View of the Environment.* Washington, D.C.: World Resources Institute, 1992.

Socolow, Robert, Clinton Andrews, Frans Berkhout, and Valerie Thomas, eds. *Industrial Ecology and Global Change.* Cambridge: Cambridge University Press, 1994.

Solow, Robert. *An Almost Practical Step toward Sustainability.* Washington, D.C.: Resources for the Future, 1992.

Stavins, Robert N., ed. *Project 88—Round II: Incentives for Action: Designing Market-Based Environmental Strategies.* A Public Policy Study sponsored by Senators Timothy E. Wirth and H. John Heinz. Washington, D.C., 1990.

Tirole, Jean. *The Theory of Industrial Organization.* Cambridge: MIT Press, 1988.

Vale, Thomas, ed. *Progress against Growth: Daniel B. Luten on the American Landscape.* New York: Guilford Press, 1986.

Vietor, Richard H. K. *Contrived Competition: Regulation and Deregulation in America.* Cambridge: Belknap Press of Harvard University Press, 1994.

Vogel, David. *Trading Up: Consumer and Environmental Regulation in a Global Economy.* Cambridge: Harvard University Press, 1995.

von Weizsäcker, Ernst U., Amory B. Lovins, and L. Hunter Lovins. *Factor Four: Doubling Wealth, Halving Resource Use: The New Report to the Club of Rome.* London: Earthscan Publications, 1997.

Wilson, James Q., ed. *The Politics of Regulation.* New York: Basic Books, 1980.

ARTICLES

Becker, Gary. "A Theory of Competition among Pressure Groups for Political Influence." *Quarterly Journal of Economics* 98 (1983): 371–400.

Coase, Ronald. "The Problem of Social Cost." *Journal of Law and Economics* 3 (1960): 1–44.

Colby, Susan J., Tony Kingsley, and Bradley W. Whitehead. "The Real Green Issue." *McKinsey Quarterly* 2 (1995): 132–143.

Elkington, John. "Towards the Sustainable Corporation: Win-Win-Win Business Strategies for Sustainable Development." *California Management Review* 36, no. 2 (winter 1994): 90–100.

Froot, Kenneth A., David S. Scharfstein, and Jeremy C. Stein. "A Framework for Risk Management." *Harvard Business Review* 72, no. 6 (November–December 1994): 91–102.

Garvin, David A. "What Does 'Product Quality' Really Mean?" *Sloan Management Review* 26, no.1 (fall 1984): 25–43.

Hart, Stuart L. "Beyond Greening: Strategies for a Sustainable World." *Harvard Business Review* 75, no. 1 (January–February 1997): 67–76.

Jaffe, Adam B., Steven R. Peterson, Paul R. Portney, and Robert N. Stavins. "Environmental Regulation and the Competitiveness of U.S. Manufacturing: What Does the Evidence Tell Us?" *Journal of Economic Literature* 33 (1995): 132–163.

Keohane, Nathaniel O., Richard L. Revesz, and Robert N. Stavins. "The Choice of Regulatory Instruments in Environmental Policy." *Harvard Environmental Law Review* 22 (1998): 313–367.

Krueger, Anne O. "The Political Economy of the Rent-Seeking Society." *American Economic Review* 64 (1974): 291–303.

Lovins, Amory B., and L. Hunter Lovins. "Least-Cost Climatic Stabilization." *Annual Review of Energy and the Environment* 16 (1991): 433–531.

Maloney, Michael T., and Robert E. McCormick. "A Positive Theory of Environmental Quality Regulation." *Journal of Law and Economics* 25 (1982): 99–123.

Moss, David A. "Public Risk Management and the Private Sector: An Exploratory Essay." Working paper 98-073, Harvard Business School, Boston, Mass., 1998.

Palmer, Karen, Wallace E. Oates, and Paul R. Portney. "Tightening Environmental Standards: The Benefit-Cost or the No-Cost Paradigm?" *Journal of Economic Perspectives* 9, no. 4 (Fall 1995): 119–132.

Porter, Michael E. "America's Green Strategy." *Scientific American,* April 1991, 168.

Porter, Michael E., and Claas van der Linde. "Green and Competitive: Ending the Stalemate." *Harvard Business Review* 73, no. 5 (September–October 1995): 120–134.

————."Toward a New Conception of the Environment-Competitiveness Relationship." *Journal of Economic Perspectives* 9, no. 4 (fall 1995): 97–118.

Rangan, V. Kasturi, Sohel Karim, and Sheryl K. Sandberg. "Do Better at Doing Good." *Harvard Business Review* 74, no. 3 (May–June 1996): 42–54.

Salop, Steven C., and David T. Scheffman. "Raising Rivals' Costs." *American Economic Review Papers and Proceedings* 73 (1983): 267–271.

Solow, Robert. "The Economics of Resources or the Resources of Economics." *American Economic Review* 64, no. 2 (May 1974): 1–14.

Stigler, George. "The Theory of Economic Regulation." *Bell Journal of Economics and Management Science* 2 (1971): 3–21.

Walley, Noah, and Bradley Whitehead. "It's Not Easy Being Green." Harvard Business Review 72, no.3 (May-June 1994): 46–52.

Yandle, Bruce. "Bootleggers and Baptists: The Education of a Regulatory Economist." *Regulation* 7 (May-June 1983): 12–16.

Yoffie, David B. "The Politics of Business: How an Industry Builds Political Advantage." *Harvard Business Review* 66, no. 3 (May–June 1988): 82–89.

Index

global climate change, 3, 205–207,
219–220, 228, 236
global competition, 2–3
in forest products industry, 208,
219–220
GNN. *See* Great Northern Nekoosa
goodwill, 10, 26, 171, 176, 244, 253n19
Gore, Al, *x*, 261n7, 278
government intervention and
regulation, 239
costs and benefits as factors in,
66–70
costs of, 67–68
and eco-labels, 40–42
factors influencing, 66–70
future of, 233–234
and institutional environment,
226–233
market redefinition strategies
and, 124
in markets, 7–9
in no-cost paradigm, 80
of public goods, 26–27, 45–46, 229
and risk assessment, 134–135
risk management by, 138–140
strategic use of, *xii*, 60–77, 248, 249f
and willingness to pay, 26–27
government subsidies. *See* subsidies
Great Northern Nekoosa (GNN), 209
Green, Jerry R., 252n10, 278
Greenpeace
and biotechnology, 120–121, 193
and internationally tradable carbon
permits, 228
Gulf Corporation, 195

Hahn, Marshall, 209
Hale and Dorr, LLP, 271n57
Hammond, John S. III, 267n4,
276n4, 278
Harrington, Joseph E., Jr., 256n37,
264n12
Hart, Stuart L., 263n43, 279
Harvard Business Review, 188–189, 191
Hausman, Jerry A., 271n18
Hayes, Robert H., 253n20, 276n4
hazardous waste, 88, 142
legislation for, 49, 95, 185–187
and Responsible Care program, 49
Hebert, Darryl, 146, 147–148
herbicides. *See* chemicals, agricultural
Hewlett-Packard, 113, 161–167, 173
Hightower, Jim, 276n6
Hindrichsen, Henriette, 278
H.J. Heinz, 31, 39–40

Hoechst, 192
Hooker Chemical, and Love Canal, 49
horizontal differentiation, 37–38
hotels, 82–84
Howard Johnson, 83
HVS Eco Services, 83–84

IBM, 87, 113, 161–165
ICI, 65
ICOLP. *See* International Cooperative
for Ozone Layer Protection
imitation, barriers against
in environmental differentiation, 18,
28–29, 43–44
in market redefinition strategies,
122–123
incentives, 181–183, 223–225, 271n1
at Chevron, 158, 205
and cost savings
long-term, 100
short-term, 90, 95–96
at Georgia-Pacific, 212
institutions and, 226–228
at Monsanto, 187, 189–190
price-based, 142–143, 171–172
industrial markets, product differentiation in, 19–29
information
provision of, to customers, 18
in consumer markets, 40–43
in industrial markets, 27–28
quality of, 136–137
information flows, 180–181, 220–223,
235, 237
at Chevron, 200–201, 205
and cost savings
long-term, 99–100
short-term, 93–95
at Georgia-Pacific, 216–218
informal, 222–223
and liability, 173–172
and mandatory disclosure, 95,
138, 187
and market redefinition, 125–127
at Monsanto, 190–191
and risk management, 140–141
inputs, and cost savings, 89–91
institutional innovations, 183–184, 226–229
institutions
economic, 7, 125, 129, 192–193, 217,
226, 252n15–253n15
environmental, 179, 183–184,
191–194, 226–231
insurance, in risk management, 135, 138,
142, 157, 163, 172, 176, 243

About the Author

Forest L. Reinhardt is an Associate Professor at the Harvard Business School. He received his Ph.D. in Business Economics from Harvard University. He also holds an MBA from the Harvard Business School, where he was a Baker Scholar, and an A.B., cum laude, from Harvard College.

At Harvard, Reinhardt teaches an elective course for MBA students on Business and the Environment. He also teaches the required MBA course, "Business, Government, and the International Economy," which covers topics in macroeconomics, business-government relations, and international trade and finance.

Reinhardt's current research explores business strategy and internal firm management in the energy, forestry, and agricultural biotechnology industries, with an emphasis on the management of the international operations of firms.